THE BOOK OF
FORTUNE TELLING

THE BOOK OF

FORTUNE TELLING

Agnes M. Miall

CRESCENT BOOKS
New York

Originally published in Great Britain in 1951 by
C. Arthur Pearson Limited as
Complete Fortune Telling

This edition was first published in 1972 by
The Hamlyn Publishing Group Limited

© The Hamlyn Publishing Group Limited 1972

This 1987 edition published by Crescent Books,
distributed by Crown Publishers, Inc.,
225 Park Avenue South, New York, New York 10003

By arrangement with Octopus Books Limited

Printed in Czechoslovakia

ISBN 0-517-64730-3

h g f e d c b a

CONTENTS

DIAGRAMS

FOREWORD

HOWEVER sceptical we may pretend to be, all of us have an open or sneaking belief in fortune-telling. Offer to read people's hands, for example, and not one of them, even though they may protest that it is "all nonsense," will refuse ! So this book, which collects all kinds of fortune-telling under one cover, should find a niche of its own.

How to cast and read a horoscope is fully explained and the section on the luck and meanings of Christian names is reinforced with the meanings of over 1,100 surnames.

Incidentally, a fascinating thing *Book of Fortune Telling* enables you to do is to see how closely one method of fortune-telling tallies with another. Read your hand by the rules given. Cast your horoscope according to your birth date. Delineate your character by your face and features. Make a study of your own temperament by your hand-writing; and so on. You will be surprised to find how nearly the different readings coincide, which in itself tends to prove the truth of fortune telling.

Books of this sort seldom or never have indexes. But because of the way in which one method works in with another, so that you will often want to refer back and forth, an index is very helpful. So we have provided you with one.

AGNES M. MIALL

READING YOUR HAND

PALMISTRY—judging the character and past and future events by the shape of the hands and the lines on the palm—is a very ancient science. Many, many centuries ago wise men first discovered that the lines on the palm are not accidental or caused by the work done by the hands, but are there from the very first hours of a baby's life and all have their definite meaning.

We do not know exactly why the outlines of our lives and characters should be traced beforehand on our palms. The reason for this is still among the many unsolved mysteries of life, and probably one day greater knowledge will provide the reason. But meanwhile we can all learn quite easily to interpret our hands and so discover something of the futures of ourselves and our friends.

There are many advantages in doing so. If you take palmistry merely as a parlour trick, you wil find that to be able and willing to read hands makes you always popular at a party.

Or why not look upon it, as it deserves, as a serious science to be taken seriously? Then you will find it absorbingly interesting, not only a forecasting events but even more in the study of character. It throws new light on people's minds and helps you to understand them better and love them more.

Again, forwarned is forearmed. If you see in your hand or another's some bad mistake that is going to be made, there is time to prevent it occurring. I have known this to happen a number of times.

Don't argue, "But if it's in my hand it's bound to occur and nothing I can do will avoid it." That's quite a mistake—more, it's defeatism. What is written in your hand is not what *must* happen, but what will happen *if you go on as you are doing now.* The line of least resistance, in fact. When you realise where your present trend of life or thought is leading and make a determined effort, it is mostly possible to change the course of events.

The indications in your palm will alter in accordance with this change and the mistake you were going to make will fade out of your hand.

For example, even on the palm of a tiny baby one may see the age at which this child will fall in love. She cannot alter those ages by anything she does. But that is not to say that she *must,* during that year marry a drunkard and be later divorced. The probabilities may be that she will do so, but the only certainty is that she will fall in love—with someone. She can change the probability. There is no fate compelling a woman to marry one particular person if she prefers not to, or to marry at all, however much she may be in love. The same, of course, applies to man.

How We Hold our Hands

If you are setting out to teach yourself palmistry you will need to study this book carefully, to read up the subject elsewhere whenever you get a chance and to examine as many hands as you can for practice. All these things must be done more or less at special suitable times and in special suitable places.

But a very interesting part of the subject remains which you will be able to study almost anywhere you happen to be—as you walk along a street, in a crowded shop while waiting to be served, in buses or trains during a short journey or while lunching at a restaurant. This is the general way on which the hands are held and used, when the subject is not thinking about them at all.

When people know their hands are going to be read, they are apt to arrange them more or less stiffly and tidily. This arrangement will disguise the real pose of the hands, but you can study it at your leisure among the people you rub up against every day of your life and so gain much insight into their general natures, even if there is never an opportunity to read their palms.

This adds a great interest to tedious journeys or waiting times, and you will find that the dullest-looking people become absorbing to you when you begin to observe their management of their hands. Take special notice of the hands when they are empty or not doing anything, as then they are carried in the most natural way.

If you had an idea before starting that everybody did the same things with unoccupied hands, you will be surprised to find how much they differ.

For instance, you can judge the frankness or otherwise of the nature by whether the hands are held open or closed. The open hand shows the open disposition, with little tendancy to conceal things—and also little ability to keep even necessary secrets!—or to prevent them from trickling between those widely held-apart fingers. Hence the term, "open-handed" for a person who is generous and careless with cash.

The close-fisted man, who keeps his hands firmly closed, is as you might expect, secretive, with some untruthful tendencies, or, at any rate, particular secrets which he wishes to conceal. It is difficult to coax money from that tightly-closed hand. In fact, he does not show or give up anything readily, whether it is his feeling, his opinions or his income!

A hand pose between these two, where the fingers are partly closed but the palm is visible, is the best sign, for it shows a trustworthy person who can keep essential secrets and is neither too mean and reserved not too extravagant.

If the hands dangle in a lifeless way, as though their owner had no control over them, you may diagnose an undecided person who will not think for himself and has little concentration. Should the fist be clenched firmly when there seems no special cause, you have a person who is very determined, at any rate, for the moment, and has come to a firm decision.

The fidget, whose hands constantly change their position and their actions, is often strong but undisciplined, full of emotions which he does not know how to control.

Some people, chiefly women, carry their hands clasped in front of them. They are calm, dignified, slow and serene.

Others, chiefly men, walk with hands clasped behind their backs. These are cautious, investigating people, with a fine sense of justice and balance. They won't accept anything until it is proved, so they are well suited for the legal profession.

A common pose of the hands is, the left one hanging at the side of the right at the waistline in front, with the elbow bent up at right angles and the palm upwards, with fingers partly closed over it. The owner of these hands has a sense of his own importance and expects you to defer to him.

Hands swung vigourously in walking belong to an active, restless person with, perhaps, more energy than good judgment.

These are only some of the commonest poses. If you notice others not given here, try to work out for yourself the characteristics indicated, checking them, when you can, by your knowledge of that person's nature or by the signs in his palm if you have a chance to read his hand in detail.

General Points about Hands

Now let us suppose you have an opportunity to study a hand at close quarters, and see what it is like in more detail than when just passing someone in the street or sitting opposite to them in a train. Even if you cannot see the lines on the palm at all, you will find you can learn quite a lot about the owner's temperament (though not about her fate) merely by noticing the size, colour and texture of the hands and the shapes of the fingers and thumb.

This general survey should always be made first of all, although you may have the hand spread out before you for reading in detail. Just as in a drawing you would outline the positions of the main objects before putting in the tiny touches, so when doing palmistry you should study the hands as a whole before rushing at the particular lines which deal with such exciting points as love affairs and money matters!

In this way you will be able to sum up a person far more accurately and the detailed reading which follows is much likelier to be correct. Good palmistry is very largely a matter of judgment. Often tendencies noticed in one part of the hand may seem to be contradicted in another part and must be set one against the other to decide which will conquer. This cannot be done if you quickly "pick out" titbits of information here and there to provide a little sensation!

For instance, you might start by concentrating on a very good headline and announcing from this that the subject was extremely clever and would have great success in life. Whereas, if you have surveyed the whole hand first, you would have noticed by the feel of it that it belonged to a very lazy person, with the brains, but without the industry, to succeed.

The first thing to notice about a hand is its size—in proportion to the size of its owner, of course. Would you call it a large, small or medium hand? It is a curious rule in palmistry that the small hand belongs to the person with large ideas and the big hand to the person with an aptitude for small things or for detail.

Thus the owner of the small hand wants to rule, to be at the head of things, to run large schemes or institutions. He thinks in general terms and cannot be bothered with details, at which the large-handed person excels. The large-handed person, on the contrary, makes an excellent subordinate or worker at very small things, such as miniatures or models, for he has endless patience and those big fingers can do tiny operations very skilfully. He cannot lead, though, for he is apt not to be able to see the wood for the trees!

The person with "stock size" hands—most of us, that is to say—can do some leading and has some skill with details, but does not run to either extreme.

Colour of the Hands.—The amount of colour is due to the richness of the blood and the vigour with which the heart pumps it—in other words, the more vitality, as a rule, the less pale the hands will be. So expect enthusiasm, energy, generosity and sympathy, combined with good health, when the hands are a good pink and still more when they are red. · The whiter the skin the calmer and less energetic the nature will be, with a tendency also to pessimism. A sallow or yellow tint shows a less healthy condition of the liver, giving more or less of what we call the jaundiced outlook on life—a suspicious, irritable person inclined to the blues.

Texture of the Skin.—Notice whether the skin is fine and delicate, smooth to the touch, or of coarser grain and feel. The fine skin belongs to a sensitive and refined nature, which will do everything delicately and with imagination, feel easily hurt and be little able to stand a hard life. A rough, coarse skin shows a temperament to match, vigorous, able to work hard, not inclined to take offence at trifles, often preferring quantity to quality.

Between the two comes the average hand, possessed by a majority of people. It is fairly fine-skinned but firm and elastic. This belongs to the person who is refined without being supersensitive or finicky; who can work hard, but appreciates comfort and harmony; who has ideals combined with commonsense.

The feel of the hand tells you the amount of energy and industry that is present. You can judge this by the hand-shake someone gives you, or by taking the palm between your thumb and forefinger and pressing it quite firmly. If you meet a soft, cushiony feeling that gives no resistance, the hand belongs to a lazy, drifting, easeloving person—though, if the Head Line is good, there may be an active brain in that indolent body.

The ideal palm feels firm, but not hard, when pressed, giving its owner's character the right balance of energy and repose. A definitely hard hand, without elasticity, denotes someone who drives himself incessantly and does not know how to rest. When there is a soft but not yielding surface over underlying hardness, you can deduce a hard worker who insists on plenty of comfort in his off-time.

The Shape of the Hand

This is very important. Indeed, you can always judge the general temperament in this way. There are several recognised shapes, each with its own characteristics. You should teach yourself to identify at a glance the type of hand you are reading.

Here are the various types.

The Square or Useful Hand is broad for its length. The palm is more or less square in shape, the fingers are even in breadth and rather square-ended and the nails are usually of square formation and inclined to be short. *Characteristics:* Honest, practical, orderly, methodical, logical, serious, reliable and obedient to authority. A thoroughly useful person.

The Spatulate or Active Hand is large with a broad palm and with finger-tips which spread or broaden outwards like a chemist's spatula (a spreading or mixing tool). The finger joints are generally large and noticeable. *Characteristics:* Very active and energetic, restless, always "on the go", original, creative, emotional, a bit "cranky" and impulsive. A real pioneer.

The Conic or Artistic Hand is graceful and tapering. The palm narrows towards the wrist, the fingers and thumb taper towards the tips, which are somewhat pointed. The hand is rather soft. *Characteristics:* Artistic in taste but

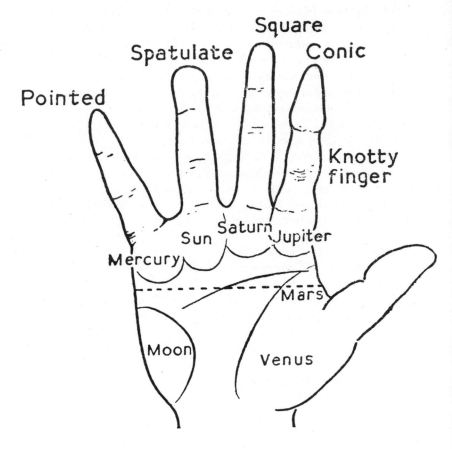

FIG 1.

The fingers and mounts.

seldom able to *be* artists, sympathetic, very emotional, rather lazy, quick-tempered, sensitive, especially to music and colour, warm-hearted, full of moods.

The Psychic or Idealistic Hand is really an exaggeration of the Conic, and is rare. It is a lovely hand, long and slender, with very fine, pointed fingers and thumb. *Characteristics:* Dreamy, unpractical, highly imaginative and idealistic, delicate, sensitive, unbusinesslike, intuitive and refined.

The Knotty or Philosophic Hand is bony and angular with the finger joints prominent and knotted. *Characteristics:* Neat, careful, orderly, thoughtful, argumentative, fond of detail, solitary, seeking after wisdom and knowledge, cautious, indifferent to money. The true scholar type.

The Mixed or Versatile Hand is much commoner than any of the pure types and mingles the characteristics of several. The palm may be square, spatulate or pointed and the fingers are mixed—often the first and fourth rather pointed, the second square and the third slightly spatulate. But almost any other mixtures may be found. *Characteristics:* Some belonging to each of the types represented in the hand. In addition, people with these hands are versatile. Jacks-of-all-trades, talkative and rather changeable. For the main traits, go by the type to which the palm belongs, modifying it according to the fingers.

The various types of finger-tips are also illustrated in Fig. 1, page 18.

Finger Tip Pads. The finger-tips of some hands have noticeable pads or mounts of flesh on them, giving them rather a bumpy appearance. When you see these pads well developed you will know that their owner is a highly nervous and almost super-sensitive person, who easily feels slighted or hurt and is careful of the feelings of others.

The Fingers in General

Measure the *back* of the hand in two divisions, one consisting of the entire length of the second finger, the other the length from knuckle to wrist. Note which is the longer.

The fingers represent the mind, the rest of the hand material things. So if the second finger measurement is the longer, you may take it that the subject is intellectual and a thinker, with the head ruling—especially if the Head Line is stronger than the Heart Line (see Fig II). Finger and hand even give a good balance between mundane and mental matters. If the palm part of the hand is the longer, the subject is practical rather than brainy.

The proportions of second finger and hand often appear reversed when seen from the palm side, but it is the *outside* of the hand measurements one should always go by for these characteristics.

Now notice the relative lengths of the fingers to each other, their thickness and whether they lean towards one another or tend to separate.

Finger Lengths. Normally, the second finger is the longest. When seen from the *palm* side of the hand, the third finger is usually next longest, with the first finger only a trifle shorter. The little finger often does not reach beyond the first joint of the third one.

Below I give a list of the character traits belonging to each finger. A normal finger shows a normal degree of these qualities. Sometimes one finger is extra long, extra thick or seems to stand away or bend forward noticeably. Again, all the other fingers may seem to lean towards the middle one. In these cases you would read an excess of the qualities which belong to the finger thus singled out.

If a finger is unusually short or thin, then its characteristics are weak.

Each finger is named after a planet. It has the same traits and governs the same qualities as that planet. These traits are given below, but for more details consult also the descriptions of the corresponding planets on page 117 in the Astrology Section.

First or Jupiter Finger gives self-confidence, self-respect, reliability, kindness, liking for food, desire for leadership, pride and responsibility. *In excess:* A conceited, over-bearing and too-ambitious nature. *When weak:* Dislike of responsibility.

Second (Middle) or Saturn Finger indicates seriousness, prudence, reserve, love of solitude and of sacred and classical music, economy, aptitude for mathematics. *In excess:* Gloom, great caution, pessimism, meanness in finance. *When weak:* A frivolous nature which cannot take anything seriously.

Third (Ring) or Sun Finger governs cheerfulness, love of art, beauty and praise, sociability, honesty, pride, sensitiveness, quick temper and sympathy. *In excess,* Affection, strong gambling tendency, vanity. *When weak:* Timidity and carelessness about money.

Fourth (Little) or Mercury Finger denotes mental ability, quickness, tact, power of expression in speech, business ability, wit, changeableness, love of excitement, ease in learning languages. *In excess:* A chatterbox, instability, fickleness, dishonesty. *When weak:* Difficulty in expressing ideas, perhaps an impediment of speech, clumsiness.

When summing up the finger tendencies, remember to consider also the mounts belonging to them (see page 29).

The Finger Knots

Notice the finger joints (called knots in palmistry). The larger these are, sticking out and making the finger outlines irregular, (Fig.1), the more cautious and thoughtful is the subject. He insists on thinking things out fully and will not act hastily. He is orderly and a good organiser. Large knots are most often found on hands of the Square or Philosophic type.

When the fingers have smooth outlines with no noticeable knots, their owner is quick, impulsive and flyaway, with generally artistic ideas. Smooth fingers are commonly found on the Conic type of hand.

Generally speaking, even on smooth fingers the knots become more prominent as time goes on and youthful impulse is slowed up by middle-aged caution and a more philosophical outlook.

Other Finger "Tips"

If you are reading a hand, ask its owner to hold it up to the light, quite naturally, not stiffly and neatly arranged. Then you can see what distances there are between the various fingers.

In general, too great a space is not good, as it shows over-independence, a person who will go too much against public opinion and who is extravagent. You know the old saying about money slipping through the fingers—when they are wide apart, we might add.

Nor should the hand when in repose close up so that the fingers are pressed together, for this shows someone who can't bear parting with money and is over-cautious, also a great worrier over the future.

A wide space between the thumb and first finger denotes independence, generosity and dislike of control; between the first and second fingers independence of thought; between the second and third, independence of circumstances, one who can be happy whether it rains or shines, whether she is rich or poor, for instance. When the third and fourth fingers stand well apart there is independence of action. You must not ask these people what they are up to or what time they will come home!

Some fingers are naturally stiff and straight, others flexible, with bending-back tips and even double joints. Stiff, straight fingers belong to rather unbending, narrow, but stricktly honest natures, while those which are flexible or double-jointed show more or less dramatic talent, adaptability and (sometimes) unscrupulousness.

The Thumb

This is very important. In fact, it is often called the signpost of the hand, for it indicates the amount of determination, logic and tact in the character. If you are only able to take a passing glance at a hand before summing up its owner, be sure that the glance includes a look at the thumb. Fortunately, it is one of the most visible parts.

The thumb has this great importance because talent, charm or good opportunities are of small use without the determination and "drive" which can turn them to account. By the thumb you can judge whether this strength of character is present or not.

Within reason, the larger the thumb and the heavier its tip, the better, and it is also an advantage for the thumb to join the hand low down rather than high up, giving a wide space between the base of the first finger and that of the thumb. He who has such a hand has a strong will and ability for leadership, excellent brains, independence and adaptability to people and circumstances.

Small thumbs, especially if set high, show unpractical and rather undecided people. They are usually found on hands where the Heart Line is stronger than the Head Line, indicating a nature with more emotion than judgment.

As with the fingers, a stiff, straight thumb shows someone with firm opinions and rather unbending ideas. The thumb with a backward curve belongs to a more careless and impulsive type, more attractive in many ways but without quite the same unbending sense of honour and responsibility.

Double-jointed thumbs are not uncommon and are like the backward curved ones—but a good deal more so! Ideas and codes are flexible, opinions change quite rapidly, there is dramatic ability and they adapt themselves easily to others.

A clubbed thumb has a short, thick, bulging first joint and a short nail. It indicates a very obstinate person with a violent temper, though probably these characteristics will only show when things go badly. Such a person will cut off her nose to spite her face, especially in matters of love.

A paddle-shaped thumb is broad, with a rather long first joint but, unlike the clubbed thumb, flat and not bulging in thickness. This formation indicates a strong personality, always equal to an emergency, but very likely collapsing from nerve strain when it is over. There is sometimes great possessiveness and even tyranny.

The broader and longer you find the middle joint (called a phalange) of the thumb, the more logical and reasonable its owner will be. When dealing with such a person, give him time to think, and produce good sound arguments for anything you want him to do.

On the other hand, a waisted thumb, caused by the middle joint being thin, belongs to a tactful and coaxing nature, one who himself can be wheedled instead of having to be convinced.

A thumb which in repose tends to hug the side of the hand is that of a person who is economical, nervous and rather narrow-minded.

The Nails and Temperament

Palmistry, as its name indicates, is almost confined to the palm, or the palm side, of the hand. But when reading a hand you will need to turn over its back at least once and that is when you make a careful examination of the nails.

These are chiefly valuable as health indications (in conjunction with the Life and Health Lines) but the shape, size and colour of the nails also give some useful tips as to personality.

When judging nails by their shape you will find that they belong to one or other of five types, each with its own character traits. These five types are:

Long Nails: Sweet-tempered folk, slow to anger, but, once aroused, very unforgiving. They are gentle, sensitive and

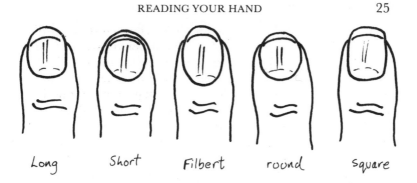

Long   Short   Filbert   round   Square

Examples of nail types

rather unpractical, but, if the nails are large as well as long, such people have strength and can lead. They are easily discouraged by adversity and dislike argument or any kind of struggle.

Short Nails: These belong to practical and often very critical people, fond of argument and good at details, with much courage and sometimes pig-headedness. They love arguing and investigating. If the nail is very short, they are fault-finding and never satisfied.

Filbert Nails: These pretty oval nails go with a nature which is sensitive and intuitive but rather lacking in push, and inclined to have a grievance if life does not go well with her.

Round Nails: are those of ardent and quick-tempered folk, of the "soon up and soon over" type. They never sulk.

Square Nails: The owner of nails with a squarish outline is orderly, straightforward and a lover of discipline. She is inclined to be set in her ideas.

The colour of the nails—or rather, of the flesh under them showing through—indicates the amount of warmth in the nature. White or pale nails are a sign of coldness and calmness; pink nails, of affection and sympathy; red ones, of ardour and passion. A yellow tinge indicates an unsociable and melancholy tendency.

The Nails and Health

The nails are a good general guide to health and they also often indicate a *tendency* towards certain diseases, as given below. Be careful, however, if you see these signs, not to prophesy such an illness for a person *as a certain fact*. It is merely that in times of stress or run-downness any trouble is likely to go to the particular spot indicated by the nail.

In fact, whenever dealing with health matters, whether in connection with the nails, the Health Line (see page 34) or any other part of the hand where illness may be shown, it is wise to *say very much less than you see*. Many people are sensitive to suggestions on this subject and the mind influences the body so powerfully that a foretelling of an illness may be enough to bring it about.

Err on the safe side. Ill-health is one of the most difficult sides of palmistry and you may so easily be mistaken.

Give a mild warning, if you think that will avert trouble, but *never* foretell any serious or incurable illness or operation —still less the date of death.

The nails give the following health indications, if their signs are confirmed by the Health Line.

Curved rather than flat as to surface, nails show respiratory weakness; the throat or asthma if they are short, chest or lungs if long. If they are more or less triangular, which is rare, and also tend to sink into the flesh, paralysis is a possibility in later life.

In general the health is not so robust if the nails are curved or fluted as if they are flat. Curves combined with length and narrowness show a tendency to spinal weakness, while fluting or white spots indicate that the nerves need building up.

The half-moons should be normal in size. Large moons are considered beautiful, but they show over-stimulation and their owner should lead a quiet life without too much strain, violent exercise or excitement. When the moons are so small that they hardly show, or have a blue tinge, the circulation is poor and there is often some degree of anaemia.

Ridges *across* the nails (most often seen on the thumb) show a severe illness, not fully recovered from, during the last few months. Extra care should be advised until the ridge has grown out.

Bitten nails are both a health and a character indication. He who has this ugly trick is nervy to a high degree, and this unreliable nerve condition causes the irritability which also goes with nails of such a kind.

The Palm as a Whole

We have looked at the fingers alone. Now let us consider the palm by itself, in a general way, without reference to any particular line on it.

The palm and the fingers, taken together, are divided into what are known as the three words of palmistry. These correspond in general with the three divisions into body, soul and spirit. Everybody's nature, of course, is made up of body, soul and spirit but in varying proportions; and which is the strongest or weakest of these three the fingers and palm will tell you at a glance.

The fingers represent mind or spirit and if they are longer when measured as described on page 20 or important-looking enough in other ways to overshadow the palm, you will know that your subject has mainly a mental outlook on life. This will be confirmed if the Head Line (page 34) is the most noticeable line in the hand and the thumb is strong.

The palm contains both the other two worlds and you will get each in its proper place if you draw an imaginary line across the palm from about midway between the base of the forefinger and the base of the thumb to midway between the base of the little finger and the wrist. (See the dotted line in Fig. 1)

The upper division so made includes most of the Mounts (see page 18) and at least half of the Head Line and relates to practical and business matters. The lower portion shows the strength of the subject's instincts or appetites—in fact the bodily forces and the amounts of self-indulgence in his nature.

So if the palm is broad across the bases of the fingers and tapers somewhat towards the wrist, you will know your subject is predominantly practical, and business-like, but has his sensual side not too fully developed. While if the lower half of the palm is wider and heavier than the finger end, you may suspect that your subject is more interested in eating, drinking, sex and other bodily sensations than in the mundane affairs of life. This will be especially the case when the hand is soft and the thumb weak, with a coarse skin texture.

Consider if the palm is broad or narrow in proportion to its length. These traits have just the effect you would expect. She of the broad palm is broad-minded, tolerant and Bohemian, while a person with a narrow palm has fixed and rather rigid ideas, little sympathy, but is very upright in a narrow-minded way.

Are there many lines on the palm, breaking it up into a confused network? Or is it comparatively smooth, with only a few lines which stand out more clearly?

The palm crowded with lines belongs to a sensitive, emotional person on whom even small things make a great impression and whose mind and feelings are very energetic; she is nervy and excitable and has difficulty in making up her mind. In spite of her teeming palm, her life is probably no more eventful than that of the person with the few clear lines. But the latter is of a calmer, steadier nature, which takes things quietly and is not impressed except by outstanding events and emotions.

It is best when the palm can be opened and nearly flat. A hollow palm denotes a temperament which will be less popular with others, and so give its owner a harder struggle for the good things of life.

The Seven Mounts

A hollow palm is partly caused by the pads of flesh which go round the palm on the three sides being higher than usual. These pads or mounts are seven in number, corresponding with the seven great planets in astrology and no palm-reading can be complete without taking into account these mounts and the traits and talents they denote. (See Fig. 1.)

High and well-developed mounts show a large dose of the qualities they stand for; if flat and unnoticeable, the subject is rather lacking in such qualities. Often some mounts in a hand are high, some normal and some low, but in other cases there is a prevailing tendency for all of them to be either high, which is the sign of an emotional nature or flat, which shows a certain coldness and lack of enthusiasm.

If any mount seems a little out of place, cuddling up towards another one instead of keeping strictly in its proper place, you must consider that the qualities of these two mounts influence each other and combine in some way.

As an example, suppose the mount under the third finger, giving artistic qualities, seems to mingle with that under the fourth or busines finger, so that they form one big bump between the bases of these two fingers. Then you would not be far out in saying that journalism or dress designing, which is a combination of an art and a trade.

Often all the mounts in a hand seem to be evenly developed, and are neither very high nor noticeably flat. This is a good sign, as such mounts go with a well-balanced character without crankiness or extremes. If not contradicted by anything in the main lines, you can safely predict that such a person is even-tempered, healthy, reasonable and tolerant.

When one mount is noticeably higher than any of the others (allowing for the fact that it is normal for the Mount of Venus, at the base of the thumb, to be particularly large and high) you will find that the characteristics of the specially well-developed mount give you the type to which the subject belongs and two or three of her ruling traits.

For instance, if the Mount of Venus, already mentioned, seems particularly noticeable, you are dealing with a kind, emotional, pleasure-loving woman. Whatever the lines on her hand may be like, you will find that these qualities pervade her personality as a whole. They are linked particularly with the Heart Line, so you should give this line special attention when reading her hand.

The positions and qualities of the seven mounts, and the main lines which specially link up with them, are as follows:

1. *Mount of Jupiter* (under the first finger): Ambition, pride, leadership, religion, compassion. Give particular attention to the Head Line (see page 34).

2. *Mount of Saturn* (under the second finger): Steadiness, prudence, pessimism, industry, wisdom. Study especially the Fate Line, which runs towards this mount.

3. *Mount of the Sun or Apollo* (under the third finger): Cheerfulness, conventionality, honour, enthusiasm, artistry. This mount links up particularly with the Success Line (see page 34), which runs up towards it.

4. *Mount of Mercury* (under the little finger): Versatility, nervous energy, quickness, diplomacy, shrewdness, wit. The twin line of this mount is the Health Line (see page 34),

which runs up the hand towards it.

Apply also to these four mounts the qualities given on page 21 for their corresponding fingers.

5. *Mount of Mars* (between the thumb and the Mount of Jupiter); Courage, energy, drive, resistance, passion. When this mount predominates, the Life Line also (page 34) should receive close attention.

Most palmists consider that there is a second Mount of Mars located on the outside of the hand between the end of the Heart Line and the Mount of the Moon; these two divisions of the Mount are thought to have slightly different qualities.

You will notice, however, that very few hands have two separate pads along the outside of the hand, apart from that of Mercury, under the little finger. Below the Mercury Mount, one pad runs right down to the wrist, and it seems to me more reasonable to call the whole of this the Mount of the Moon, rather than to divide one mount only of the seven into two different parts. This plan, allotting the hand only one Mount of Mars, as described above, is followed in this book, as it has always, in my experience, given accurate hand-reading results.

6. *Mount of the Moon or Luna* (down the outside edge of the hand, between the Heart line and the Wrist): Sympathy, imagination, moodiness, love of travel, intuition. When present—it is rather rare—the Intuition Line (see page 52) should be considered linked to this mount.

7. *Mount of Venus* (the fleshy base of the thumb): kindness, love of pleasure, gaiety, warmth, sex attraction. Pay special attention to the Heart Line in connection with this mount.

Remember that if a strong mount has one of more grilles (see page 59) or confused lines, the *faults* rather than the virtues of the mount are likely to be present.

Mounts in the Two Hands. Before leaving this section of your palmistry reading, remember to examine each mount in both hands, for it may not be the same in each. A mount which is flat on one hand may be much more developed in the other. If so, you must read accordingly. The left hand indicates the character and temperament one was born with and the right what one has made of them, so a high Mount of Jupiter, say, in the left hand and a flat one in the right would indicate innate ambition, power of leading and religion which have not yet been fulfilled in the life. And so on with all the mounts.

Notice also, by gentle pressure, if one mount is soft and the other hard. Hardness and softness here have the same meaning as when the palm is pressed (see page 16). Briefly, a hard mount gives energy in using the qualities it typifies, while a soft one means that there is slackness in employing them.

The Lines on the Hand

Strictly speaking, of course, the word palmistry means the study of the palm and the lines on it. What you have read in the preceding pages about the hand, fingers and nails is not veritably palmistry and actual events, whether of the past, present or future, cannot be told from this science of cheirognomy, as it is properly called.

But we get so much valuable and interesting information about people's characters from the general outlines of the hand that all palmists go by them as well as by the lines, and the word palmistry is used in a general way to cover cheirognomy as well.

Now we come to the more fascinating science of palmistry proper. This is the study of the actual lines of the palm, from which we can learn to deduce a certain amount about people's characters (helped by much more than cheirognomy tells us) and also to read their past lives and look ahead into their future years.

When you start, as we all do, by looking at your hand

lines, there is one question you are sure to ask at once.
"Which hand shall I read?" For even a momentary glance
will be enough to show you that the lines only match in a
very general way (and sometimes not even that) on your two
hands. There are so many points of difference in normal
hands that it becomes important to know whether you
should go by what you see in the right hand or what you see
in the left.

The answer is, "Read both," for each will reveal different
things to you.

Right and Left Hands

Read the left palm for the traits and tendencies that prevail
in your family and which consequently were born in you.

Read the right palm to see what you have done with that
inheritance, whether it has remained much as it was (in
which case the lines on the two hands will vary little),
whether you have left talents and good qualities uculti-
vated or whether you have improved on what you were born
with.

Again, taking the matter from another angle, *the left hand*
shows your inner life—your plans, feelings and secret
wishes. *The right hand* shows what has happened to you in
actual events, wishes that have been realised, plans that
have gone astray, and so on. Usually the past is read best in
the right hand, because the past is an accomplished fact; but
more of the future will show in the left hand, if your
subject is one who wishes and plans ahead, because our
plans are usually a good way in advance of their accomplishment.

All this, of course, applies to the ordinary right-handed
person. If your subject is left-handed, to some extent the
positions will be reversed; but not entirely so, because even
the naturally left-handed person is forced by circumstances
to become more or less right-handed. In such cases you will

not be able to divide up the two palms in such a clean-cut way as is given above, and you should pay equal attention to both until you can discover which takes the lead in this particular instance.

The Three Main Lines

Think of the palm as a map of the life—as it is—and you will at once notice three long lines which might be said to correspond with the main roads on a map. These lines

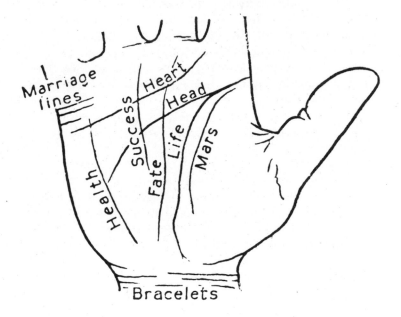

Fig. II.

The main lines of the hand.

vary in length and detail in each hand, but you will easily identify their most usual position from Fig. II on this page.

They are the lines of Life, Head and Heart. Very, very rarely, instead of the two horizonal lines of Head and Heart, there is only one going across the palm. But in practically all hands these three lines stand out even at a casual glance.

The Fate Line, running up the hand towards the middle finger, is almost equally a "main road" on the life's map. But it can be missing and is in a fair number of hands, whereas, with the very rare exception I have just mentioned, the three principal lines are *always* there.

For this reason I will start with these three most important "main roads," going on afterwards to the Fate and other lines which are not quite so essential.

When reading a hand, always give this trio of lines your first and longest attention, and do not foretell anything seen in other parts of the palm if it is contradicted by the indications in the Life, Head and Heart Lines. There influence in the character and life are so strong that what *they* say should be accepted in preference to contradictory portents elsewhere.

If these three lines are all long, clear and well formed, you may know that their owner has a good constitution and abilities, a nice nature and should do at least reasonably well in life.

On the other hand, lines which are wavering, broken, looped like the links of a chain or with islands (long loops) in them all show some kind of weakness or uncertainty in the side of the life and character represented by the line.

Narrow, deep lines, well coloured, indicate more vitality than broad, pale ones.

Lines are often forked at their end. This is mainly good, except on the Line of Life, where a fork shows weakened health in old age.

These general points apply to *all* lines, on the palm, and not merely to the three main lines of Life, Head and Heart, which we will now discuss individually.

The Line of Life

The Life Line or Vital Line, as it is sometimes called, starts between the base of the first finger and the thumb and runs down the hand in a wide curve which encircles the Mount of Venus at the base of the thumb. (See Fig. II)

Read the Life Line downwards, starting above the thumb.

On this line you read the general health and constitution of its owner; also certain of the important events of her life. These events should be checked and amplified on the other lines specially relating to them, because the Life Line deals with events only in a rather *general* way.

If this line is long, running well down to the wrist, clearly marked and free from breaks and loops, it shows that old age will be reached and that the health will be mostly good because all the vital organs are sound. Small ailments or nervous troubles, in no way dangerous, as well as accidents and operations, should be looked for (thought it's much wiser, really, *not* to look for them!) on the Health Line (page 34) or other parts of the palm.

The Life Line should have a good curve. The further it sweeps out into the palm of the hand, the better the vitality is. Such people recover well from any ill-health they may suffer, especially if the Line of Mars (see page 34) is shown on the hand.

When the line forks near the wrist, a branch running out on to the Mount of the Moon, there is a great wish to travel. If the branch is deeply cut, the wish will come true. In fact, should this branch line be stronger and clearer than the Life Line is after the forking, the subject will probably emigrate, or at least spend much of her life abroad.

Look for any small lines which start on the Life Line and strike upwards. They are most often found on the upper part of the line, near the Head Line, but may occur anywhere on its length. They are ambition lines, and at the date of each one of them promotion is attained or the subject makes some determined effort to improve her position.

The first (highest) strong ambition line generally leaves the Life Line at the age when the career was first started—or the first definite step taken towards it, as when a scholarship making it possible is won. To know how to judge age on any main line, see page 61.

Beginners in palmistry sometimes announce dramatically, "Your Life Line is broken, and that means death!" Besides being cruel and dangerous to say such a thing—NEVER foretell anyone's death, however unmistakably it may seem to be marked—it is also quite wrong.

I can't emphasise too strongly that a broken Life Line only means death if it is broken in both hands completely, with no new line or repair signs, and *if all the other principal lines*—Head, Heart and Fate—*also break off short at the same age.*

This is seldom seen, because it does not indicate the natural ending of life in old age, but a premature death, which, after all, is not common. There will also be signs of serious disease or accident somewhere in the hand to cause such an early decease.

Much more frequent is a break in the Life Line in *one* hand only, indicating a fairly serious illness. In some cases a new line starts before the old one breaks, runs alongside it for a while, giving the effect of a double Life line and then runs on alone after the break. Unless the new line is much weaker than the old one, this is quite favourable.

It shows a complete change of environment (such as that cause by emigration or sometimes by marriage) or an equally complete change of mental outlook. It was this latter, involving such an alteration of values and viewpoint that it almost amounted to a new life, which occurred to a woman whose hand I once read. The doubling of the line covered the period of years during which her outlook had gradually changed. The break affected the right hand only.

A Life Line break such as this has nothing whatever to do with length of life.

Islands in the line show periods of poor health or of difficult general environment. See page 58 for more details.

The Line of Heart

The Heart Line is the upper of the two big lines which cross the top half of the palm more or less horizontally. (See Fig. II, page 34.) It might more accurately be called the Emotion Line, for it is concerned not only with heart affairs, but with every kind of feeling, such as sympathy, jealousy, and so on.

While, roughly speaking, the Line of Heart runs across the hand under the fingers, it has several different starting points in different palms and must be read accordingly.

Ideally it should begin between the first and second fingers, and be long and clear, without a chained or broken effect. It then shows a loyal, devoted yet well-balanced emotional nature which will bring happiness.

If the line forks at the start, throwing one branch on to the Mount of Jupiter, while the other runs between the first and second fingers, the subject is not quite so well-balanced. She has a tendency to get obsessed, either about people or other enthusiasms.

This is still more the case if the whole line starts on the Mount of Jupiter, high up and near its outside edge. These people are such romantic idealists that they will be reckless in love. The loved one is considered absolutely perfect, and when he shows feet of clay, heartbreak is the result. There is also jealousy and possessiveness. Often the poor man can hardly say "Good morning" to another woman!

With a Heart Line starting only on the middle of Jupiter's Mount, the affection is rather more reasonable, but also a little more calculating. Such folk must still reverence and look up to those they marry, but often in a more literal sense, either by choosing a tall man or one who is higher socially or richer or more successful than themselves. But this Heart Line gives a faithful and honourable person and is considered excellent to have.

Again, the line may be shorter, starting under the Mount of Saturn, when a rather selfish or at any rate self-centred nature is indicated. When this Heart Line is found in the left hand, you should always hope to find a longer one in the right hand, giving more devotion and less inclination to take.

You will see form all this that the Heart Line should be neither too short (denoting coldness and selfishness) nor too long (indicating great jealousy); It should have a horizontal ending on or towards the outside edge of the hand. When it turns up towards the Mount of Mercury money calculations enter too much into heart affairs and then, as occasionally happens, it slopes sharply downwards towards the Mount of the Moon, there will be a morbid element in all matters of emotion.

The Heart Line itself or a branch from near its start, is often found to droop downwards in a curve on to or towards the Head Line. This shows a disappointment in the affections, usually caused by expecting the loved one to reach too high a standard which he or she fails to do.

This mark usually only comes into the hand *after* the event, and in some palms, of this description, there are three or four such lines drooping from the Heart to the Head Line, showing that disappointment has occurred several times because the subject habitually expects too much.

A break in the Heart Line shows what one would expect— a broken heart. Fortunately this is seldom permanent, and you may know a mend has occurred if a new line starts a little overlapping the old one or the broken end is enclosed in a square (see page 59).

A Heart Line which seems dragged down out of place towards the Head Line shows that matters of affection will be influenced by worldly considerations. If a branch from the Heart Line runs down and joins the Head Line, there is always a tussle between the Head and the Heart, and once at least in the lifetime there will be a great struggle between love and self-interest.

To decide which will win, note which line seems to be drawn out of its normal position towards the other. By consulting the other hand as well this often becomes quite clear.

A Heart Line which is chained or tasselled in effect by having a lot of tiny lines running into it, belongs to a flirt who does not take love or men seriously.

An island (see page 58 for islands) on the line foretells a grief of the affections at the age shown. (How to reckon age on the lines will be found on page 61).

The Heart Line is also a guide to the physical condition of the heart, but very great skill, beyond the amateur, is required to unravel this. So it is best to let this side alone and concentrate on matters of feeling, in which most people are far more interested!

The Line of Head

This very important line is the lower of the two horizontal lines running across the upper part of the palm (See Fig. II, page 34), below the Heart Line. The Head Line is our guide to the kind of mind a subject possesses, to her general abilities and the amount of concentration and self-control. Together with the thumb (page 23) it shows the degree of will power.

The Head Line starts from between the thumb and first finger, usually between the Mount of Jupiter and the Mount of Mars. Occasionally it begins low down, on the Mount of Mars itself, below the Life Line. Most often it is joined to the Life Line at the start, but sometimes it rises above that line on the Mount of Jupiter, with a clear space between it and the Life Line.

Each of these three beginnings gives you a definite idea of the personality. The Head Line springing from the Mount of Mars shows the dependent type, timid, over-sensitive and clinging to her family, nervous and uncontrolled to a degree—in fact, the typical Victorian woman who went into a faint on the slighest provocation. Fortunately this start of the Head Line is uncommon nowadays.

The Head Line joined to the Life Line at the start is the sign of someone who develops slowly and is rather lacking in self-confidence. There is a tendency not to strike out for oneself and to remain late in the childhood home. Independence and initiative will develop at the age where the two lines separate. (For age on the lines, see page 61).

When the Head and Life Lines are separated from the start and the Head Line begins on Jupiter's Mount, there is marked independence and even recklessness, more or less intense according to the size of the space. The nature is excitable and precocious, opinionated and a personality right from babyhood. Such people chafe very much at any restrictions on their freedom.

The endings on the Head Line vary as much as its beginnings. The straighter the line runs across the hand, the more practical is the temperament and a straight line is often found on a square hand. Sloping downwards towards the Mount of the Moon, the line shows idealism and imagination; but if the slope becomes a steep decline, the imagination will be morbid.

A moderately sloping line which ends in a fork often gives ability to write. A fork on any type of Head Line shows both practical and imaginative sides to the nature. But there is less concentration than with an unforked line and often a good deal of emotional conflict between the opposing tendencies represented by the branches.

Good memory is indicated by a long line running quite, or almost, to the outside edge of the hand. A definitely short Head Line, denotes a lack of cleverness.

Instead of running level or sloping downward, the line may turn up at its end towards the Mount of Mercury or may send a branch in this direction. At this is the business mount, such a development of the line shows a keen desire for more money.

When the line itself turns upwards, the subject is rather mercenary and anxious to be rich. But if it only throws out a branch, its owner is not a money-grubber, but is forced by having dependent loved ones to increase his income.

Islands on the Head Line show periods of nervous trouble or severe headaches.

Occasionally this line is doubled for part of its length. At the age at which the doubling starts, the personality changes radically. Usually the change takes the form of a person who has hitherto been content to play second fiddle now emerging as a leader, forceful and even domineering.

Clearly marked *small* crosses on or near the Head Line mean accidents, not necessarily serious, to the Head.

One Line only for Heart and Head

In my general remarks on page 34 about the three "main roads" I mentioned that very occasionally—perhaps in one percent of palms—the Heart and Head Lines are replaced by a single line which seems to combine them. This is not as good a sign as when both lines are present and your interpretation of it must be a little tactful.

This single line gives great intensity of purpose, a rare willingness to pay almost any price for the one thing particularly desired. I once read the hand of a man who had this marking. His career was everything to him. For it he gave up the pleasures of social life, family ties and even the girl he loved and emigrated to a distant land. It was only when his position was well established in the new country and he himself was no longer very young, that he thought of the softer side of life and married a girl whom he met in the land of his adoption.

With this single line it is as if both mind and heart are fixed on whatever is wanted and so a tremendous "drive", which always achieves its purpose, is created. The tragedy is that when the heart's desire is gained at so much cost, it does not always satisfy. A person with this line is rather self-absorbed and one-sided—the specialist in ambition and often in abilities, too.

Naturally, if the combined Head and Heart Line is seen in one hand only, this reading will not apply so strongly.

Other Important Lines

Next in importance to the three "main roads" of the palm are three other lines which also reveal a very great deal to the palmist, but not essential to the hand. That is, they are sometimes missing—one, two or all of them—on a quite normal palm.

These three "second-class roads" on the palmistic map are the Lines of Fate, Success and Health. (See Fig. II on page 34 for their positions in the hand.) After reading the Life, Heart and Head Lines in as much detail as you can, you should next study this second trio of lines.

The Lines of Fate or Saturn

The Fate Line (see Fig. II on page 34) runs up the hand more or less vertically towards the Saturn or second finger.

Be careful not to confuse it with the Success Line which runs up towards the Sun (third) finger or the Health Line which runs up towards the Mercury (fourth) finger. All three are shown clearly in Fig. II.

The name of this line is not very apt; for there is no more of "unavoidable fate" shown on the Fate Line than on any other in the hand. As with the rest of the palm, this line to a large extent is what we make it. It records the work and career history of the subject—the story of his livelihood and the events that make and mar it. It does not show any *general* history of its owner, but only the plans and events which affect his work.

As I have said (see page 43) in a certain proportion of hands this line is missing or is only present in a very faint and broken form—often missing in the left hand and dimly apparent in the right. It is our thoughts and plans which produce strong lines in the palm, so it follows from this that the absence of the Fate Line simply shows a drifting, happy-go-lucky person who does not plan or want any job in particular. He just, like Mr Micawber, waits for something to turn up!

Such people may have a happy and interesting life, but will not make money *steadily* or achieve any *sustained* success.

Read the Fate Line upwards. Notice first of all where it begins, for it has several different starting points.

When rising from the lower part of the Life Line, the career will be started by family influence or money, as in the case of someone who inherits a family business or is financed in early difficult years by a relative. The date at which the Fate Line parts from the Life Line shows the age when the subject finally became independent—though with this type of Fate there is a likelihood of family influence all through the career.

If the Line rises from the wrist, the subject will be self-made, owing nothing to influence or luck. This generally means plenty of hard work before success comes and shows grit and determination in the character.

The Fate Line, again, may start from the Mount of the Moon, running more diagonally up the hand than in the previous cases. This is good for careers which depend on the favour of the public—such as the stage or writing—but usually denotes a fair amount of change and uncertainty. Often help is given by one of the opposite sex, not a relative; and if this Fate Line runs to the Mount of Jupiter instead of that of Saturn and ends there in a cross, the career will be "made" by a fortunate marriage.

Sometimes the Fate Line only starts quite high up in the palm, near or even above the Head Line. This indicates a hard fight, or rather a late start at the age at which the line begins. Even later successes may be shown by the Line only rising from the Heart Line.

A good Fate line, wherever it rises, should be clear and fairly deep, without breaks or faint places, and it should run up on to the Mount of Saturn, but not far enough to reach the base of the middle finger. If the line turns instead to any other mount, there will be decided success of a kind connected with that Mount—if Jupiter, a position of power and responsibility, if Apollo, success in one of the arts, and if Mercury, the gaining of wealth.

However, before predicting a big success of any kind verify it on the Success Line, (page 47) for the Fate Line deals not so much with brillancy as with *everyday* results and the gaining of a living.

Bars across the Fate Line show bars or obstacles to the career. Their seriousness depends on the heaviness of the bar and whether the line after it continues fainter than before. A bar coming from the Heart Line shows grief over a loved one adversely affecting work; from the Head Line, nervous trouble or bad judgement; from the Life Line, usually family difficulties; from the Health Line (see page 34) ill-health of some kind.

For islands on this line, see page 58.

Often, particularly in a woman's hand, a sister line will run close alongside the Fate Line (but never touching it) for part of its length. This indicates a second job or absorb-ing hobby (for it need not necessarily be paid work) which is carried on side by side with the main livelihood.

Such a sign is often seen in the palms of women who carry on their work after motherhood, and run the home as well. Or it may indicate someone who has two separate business irons in the fire.

If the Fate Line is full of breaks and overlappings, this indicates an unsettled working life, with frequent changes of job or even of the kind of work done. Breaks that always overlap show that the changes were made without loss or too much strain, but if a line of this type has definite gaps, you can deduce periods of unemployment or real difficulty.

In one hand the Fate Line started with a tiny fork at the wrist, one branch coming from the Life Line. This was the hand of a clever girl who won a scholarship for higher education at school (start due to her own efforts) and intended to become a teacher. To her intense disappointment her dominating mother (family influence from the Life Line), took her away from school at the earliest legal age and forced her to start wage-earning at once.

Sometimes the Fate Line is stopped prematurely. I have seen three interesting examples of this. In the first the rather wavering line was permanently blocked where it met the Head Line, showing bad judgement or lack of ability which closed the working life. In the other two cases the Heart Line formed the barrier.

The second example was interesting, for here a branch from the Heart Line, running to the Mount of Jupiter and ending in a cross there (the sign of a good and wealthy marriage), ended the Fate Line. No more need to work!

The third example showed a very long island on this line, with the line barred by the Heart Line very soon afterwards. This girl was involved in a divorce scandal with a man connected with her work (the island) but as a direct result, happily married someone else and left the job.

The Success Line

The Success, Fortune or Sun Line is the second of the three important lines which can be missing from a hand. It very often is. It runs up the hand, roughly parallel with the Fate Line, but going towards the third (Sun) finger instead of towards the second. It is nearly always shorter than the Fate Line, as in many cases it rises higher in the hand. See Fig. II on page 34 for the position of this line.

The reason for this is that the average career (shown by the Fate Line) begins early but as a rule success and prestige do not come till after years of work and effort. The Success Line, you see, does not record ordinary work for the weekly pay envelope, but only results which are out of the common—real success, distinction, a name. If it is absent, the subject may do quite well and earn a fair amount of money, but will never make a reputation for herself or get into really easy circumstances.

From the date at which the Success Line gets properly started, the Sun begins to shine on that career. More success, more money, more reputation, more luck—all these are brought by the Line of Fortune. To judge the age at which it starts, see page 60.

If it only appears clearly in places and seems to fade out in between, the success will merely be fitful. Sometimes the Sun Line takes the form of two or three parallel lines appearing on the Mount of the Sun only. This is better than no Success Line at all, but indicates that the subject will fall between two or three stools and largely miss her chances. On such a hand you will probably find lack of concentration clearly shown elsewhere by finger-tips mixed in type, a forked Head Line and an uncertain thumb.

One clear mark on the Mount of the Sun shows easier circumstances after fifty, often due to inheriting money—or someone who "gets there" late in life. A long Fortune Line starting from the Life Line shows a similar inheritance, or

early success, this time brightening nearly the whole of the
life.

If the line is doubled at any point by another line running
closely parallel, the good fortune is doubled also. Branches
running upwards from the line showed more marked success
or riches from that date.

When you see a good Success Line in a *soft* hand, predict
money through inheritance or marriage rather than a self-
made success, for such subjects are too lazy to earn
themselves distinction. If the third finger is long, heavy or
standing out by itself the riches may come from some form of
gambling.

Bar lines show setbacks, as on the Fate Line, while an
island indicates some loss of prestige or reputation, in an
otherwise good hand, or disgrace, *if other signs are
unfavourable.* I have seen this sign in a good hand where an
"innocent" party had divorced the marriage partner; also
where people in opposition have set scandal going.

The Success Line has a wonderful power of overcoming
the defects or weakness of the Fate Line in the same period.
In fact, even if the Fate Line should break off short (usually
a serious misfortune) provided the Sun Line continues or
even starts at this point, you need only predict a change—for
the better!

The Health Line

The third of our second trio of important lines is the
Health, Liver or Mercury Line, also sometimes known as
the Hepatica. Fig. II on page 34 shows an *average* position for
this, slanting rather across the hand with one end on or near
the Mount of Mercury and the other on or near the Life
Line.

But no main line varies in position more than this and

at times it may be more or less vertical with one end on Mercury's Mount and the Heart Line. Be careful not to confuse it with the Line of Intuition (see page 52) though this is a rare line, and is always curved, whereas the Health Line is straight.

This is the one main line in the hand which it is nicest to be without, as then the health is well-nigh perfect and never needs to be thought about! Many men have no Health Line in their palms. But it is sometimes not absent from a person's hand, as it is concerned with these minor, day-to-day ailments from which some people suffer more or less, such as headaches,, indigestion and so on.

While the Life Line shows serious illnesses or major ill-health, the well-named Liver or Health Line is a guide to one's fitness or otherwise *at the moment.* In consequence, it varies from week to week and month to month more than any other line, so do not read the signs upon it as being particularly permanent ones.

Some palmists consider that this line should be read upwards; others that it should be taken downwards. But if you use it as I have suggested (and this is the only way suitable for an amateur) as a sort of calendar of health, you will not need to consider which end it starts.

The best Health Line is one which runs more or less vertically down the hand, keeps well away from the Life Line and is unbroken and not too deep. With this line the constitution is sound and any ailments are unimportant ones or purely nervous in origin. When the Health Line rises from the Line of Life (not common), health is likely to be a difficulty all through life.

A chained line shows that the liver is sluggish and needs attention, particularly if the line is yellowish in colour.

When the line is made up of little bits, indigestion causes trouble, while a waviness of outline means biliousness or rheumatism. The subject should avoid rich food.

If the Health Line runs towards and cuts the Life Line, palmists often given an alarmist reading threatening a dangerous illness. It is much more accurate to say that with this formation there is a health condition or weakness present which will probably *ultimately* lead to trouble, if it is not checked.

A red line shows that the subject easily runs a high temperature.

When reading the Health Line, remember to check its indications by the Life Line and the nails.

It is sometimes said that the Mercury Line also shows the money and business prospects, but I have found this to be only true in so far as indifferent health may spoil one's work, while physical fitness enables one to do one's best.

Love and Marriage in the Palm

When you read hands you will find that what women, at any rate, are chiefly interested in, are their love affairs and marriage prospects, or the course of their marriage, if they are already wives.

They will listen more or less patiently while you tell them about their characters, their work and their friends, but it is when you say, "Now about love affairs—" that their eyes light up and they pull their chairs a little closer to yours!

Even so, it is a mistake to begin a hand reading with romantic matters. You see, you will not be able to form a correct judgment as to how they will love and how their love affairs will end, till you know the kind of people they are. Also, a properly balanced reading should deal with the personality and all sides of the life, and I'm afraid if you tell of love and marriage first a good many "clients" will hardly listen to the other points afterwards!

I have already told you that, by a curious and interesting law (we don't know why it happens like this), the ages at which a person will fall in love can be foretold from the very cradle. Apparently certain emotional periods, during which love will enter the life, are fixed from the very moment of birth. Very often, however, the details and outcome of such love affairs do not show in the hand until much nearer the time.

For love affairs, turn the hand partly outwards and examine the edge of it under the little finger between it and the Heart Line. Lying horizontally across this space you will notice from one to five short lines. They are tiny and a magnifying glass will help you to examine them more closely.

These are often referred to, by palmists with only a smattering of the subject, as marriage lines. But as many people have three or four of them and very few have less than two, there would be no spinsters and bachelors and the marriage rate would go up very considerably, if this were true! Actually they are *love affair* lines. Whether any particular one will end in marriage depends on other markings as well.

Each of these lines denotes a separate love affair and according to the length and depth of each line you can judge of the intensity and duration of the romance. The most important-looking line probably shows marriage.

At what age will the love affairs occur? It takes great skill and long practice to give age exactly and one is often a year or two out; but here is a rough guide. Count age upwards from the Heart Line. A quarter up, between seventeen and twenty-four: half-way between Heart Line and finger, twenty-four to thirty: above that, thirty to forty-five.

The number of lines is not always the same on the two hands. This is because the right hand marks people who love you and the left the people you love, and a love affair may, or course, be on one side only. So, if a love line on the left hand has no matching one on the right, try to put the man out of your head, for he will not return your affection.

A good many love affairs, unfortunately, never come to a happy ending. To judge if any particular one will end in marriage, you must also examine the influence lines on the Mount of Venus (See Fig. III) and see if one of these is connected to the love line by a line running across the hand, the Marriage Line, also shown in Fig. III.

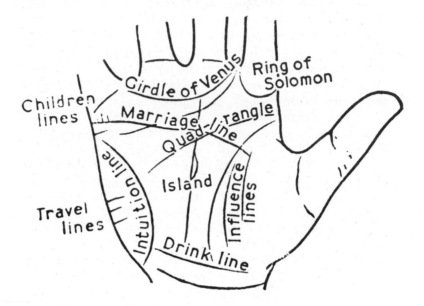

Fig. III

Some minor lines and markings.

Often this connection line only begins to grow across after the two people concerned have actually met, and for this reason it is usually not possible to be sure about a marriage very long beforehand. Of course, signs of change on the Life and Fate Lines, at the same date as the Love Line, strongly suggest a wedding!

Influence Lines on Venus. —If you look closely at the Mount of Venus, you will see that various fine lines run down it, rising usually from the Life Line and continuing more or less close to it (Fig. III, page 52). These are called influence lines and each one denotes a person who is linked in close affection to the owner of the hand.

Do not think, though, that the number of influence lines shows the number of lovers, because close friends, or relations who have played a large part in the life are also shown by influence lines. In fact, if you see one which does not start from the Life Line, but is parallel to it from the very beginning of the life, you may safely judge that it is an older person (most likely one of the parents, but sometimes a nurse, an older brother or sister or other relative) who has had a profound influence during the childhood of the subject.

However, many of the influence lines on this Mount do show a person the subject has fallen in love with, and it is when there is a line linking this person to a "falling in love" line under the little finger that you will be safe in predicting marriage. This is not always a legal bond, by the way; a marriage in fact, without any actual ceremony, is marked in the same way on the palm.

Influence lines coming from the Mount of the Moon also run into the Fate Line in some hands, but in my opinion these relate to help given with the career by friends of the opposite sex and do not necessarily imply marriage. Of course it may be the spouse who gives the help—or, again, it may not!

To see what will be the general trend of a love affair, either ending in wedding bells or otherwise, examine closely its tiny line under the little finger. One that terminates in a droop shows grief or widowhood, while one which ends in a fork indicates separation by distance or estrangement. This separation is not necessarily permanent. The mark is found in the hands of many married women, for instance, whose husbands were overseas in war-time for two or three years.

A break in the line shows a break-up of the relationship

during the time the gap lasts. The end of the line is the part nearest the middle of the hand.

If a love line is level and unbroken, the romance or marriage is happy. When a vertical bar ends the line usually one party is married already, or there is some serious religious barrier. But should the love line push right through the bar in both hands, some way out is found in the end.

If the bar is in the left hand only, the obstacle is on the side of the owner of the hand; if in the right hand only, it is connected with the other person.

Read the signs on the Mount of Venus influence lines in the same general way. If an influence line, after being close to the Life Line, gradually separates more and more widely from it, this particular friend will play less and less part in the subject's life. Broken influence lines show quarrels or separations, islands illness or trouble (usually illness) overtaking the friend indicated by the line.

By the part of the Life Line at or near which the influence line starts, you can judge at what age the friend came into the life.

The Marriage Line itself (that joining the love line to the influence line) should be clear and well-marked for happiness. If it, or a branch from it, joins the Line of Success, the marriage will be to a rich or distinguished person.

Children Lines

You will find when reading hands that nearly all women and most men want to know about their prospects of parenthood. Here a magnifying glass will be in demand, for children show as minute upright lines rising from the love line which ends in marriage (see Fig. III).

Don't mistake for portents of babies fine vertical lines which cut through *all* the love lines on the Mount of Mercury.

True children lines rest on one love line only and do not touch any others there may be. Each clearly marked line indicates a healthy child.

Thin wavering lines show babies who will probably not survive or who will be weakly. An island in a child line also shows ill-health for that child.

It is said that the lines are strong boys and weak for girls, but these points are so difficult to discern on such tiny lines that I should not bank on them, if I were you! It is never wise, unless you have exceptionally good sight, to be too confident in making predictions concerning children.

By the distances between the lines, reading from the outside of the hand inwards, you can judge how many years apart the babies will be.

Check any predictions about children by looking also at the Bracelets (see page 57 and Fig. II).

Minor Lines often Missing

There is a number of fairly unimportant lines which are in no way essential to a normal, well-balanced palm. Most people, however, have one or two of them, though probably no one has them all. They give what we might call specialized information as to some particular side of the personality of life.

The Intuition Line (see Fig. III) is rare. It might be mistaken for a semi-circular Health Line—but the Health Line never *is* semi-circular. The Intuition Line curves round the Mount of the Moon.

It is most often found on a conic, mixed or psychic hand, particularly the last. It shows that its owner has occult gifts and great intuition, a very sensitive, highly strung nature and often second sight. Most hands with this line belong to women.

The Line of Mars (see Fig. II) is also known as the Inner

Life Line, a name which suggests both its position on the hand and its nature. It is somewhat rare, but when present is found running parallel to, and inside, the Life Line. Do not confuse it with an influence line. It is heavier, more closely parallel to the Life Line and altogether more of a semi-main line than an influence line can ever be.

This line backs up and strengthens the Life Line. If the latter is weak or broken, the presence of the Mars Line shows that the subject's vitality is strong enough to overcome any health troubles. It will not prevent illnesses shown on the Life Line, but it will ensure good recovery from them.

Added to a *good* Life Line, the Line of Mars indicates ardour in love, excellent health and a rather reckless, fighting disposition, with plenty of enthusiasm. It is most often seen on square or spatulate hands.

The Gridle of Venus (Fig. III) is not, as you would expect, near the mount of that name, but is a semi-circular line enclosing the Mounts of Saturn and the Sun. It is often much broken up, or clear in one hand and broken in the other.

In bygone days some very unpleasant characteristics were attributed to the possessor of this line. However, these extreme readings are seldom right and most modern palmists agree that the traits of this line are best summed up in the phrase, "So temperamental!" The subject is full of moods, highly nervous, artistic and pleasure-loving and is likely to suffer from fits of depression.

If the line is weaker in the right hand than in the left, these traits have been largely overcome.

The Via Lasciva or Drink Line is another line (rare), which, as its name suggests, formerly had a very bad character. It has various positions. Sometimes it forms a semicircle connecting the Mounts of Venus and Luna. In other cases it runs straight from the lower part of Luna towards the wrist (Fig. III, page 52).

People with this line have so much vitality that they

find it difficult to use it all up. Hence there is a temptation to squander some on drink, drug-taking or other undesirable sensations—but it is only a *tendency* and may never mature. Advise these people to use up their surplus energy in real hard work or in sports and all will be well, especially if the hand is hard.

The Bracelets or Rascette (Fig. II, page 34) is the name given to the three lines which form rings round the wrist. They are often not clearly marked and there may be only two or even one. Three lines, well marked and unbroken, show that their owner will live to be a good old age and will be fortunate over money. If there is a fourth bracelet, as occasionally happens, then you have a future centenarian!

A woman who has the bracelet nearest the wrist rising up into a sort of arch at the base of the hand is not so likely to have children.

Travel Lines, like love lines, are short horizontal marks lying across the outside edge of the hand, but in this case on the Mount of the Moon, below the Heart Line. (See Fig. III, page 52).

They are much longer than the love lines, and the longer they are the longer or more important the journeys will be. Quite short lines usually indicate no more than brief holidays abroad. On the other hand, people who, like sailors, are constantly travelling, often have only one or two journey lines in early life.

After that travel becomes so normal to them that it makes no impression on the hand! Such a person usually has a Fate Line starting from the travel part of the palm —the Mount of Luna. Judge the ages when journeys are made in the same way as the ages of love affairs.

If a travel line joins the Heart Line, that journey will be on behalf of someone loved or in connection with a romance.

The Ring of Solomon is a rare semicircular marking which encloses the Mount of Jupiter (see Fig. III, page 52). It gives the power of becoming an adept in occultism and psychology, and denotes wisdom.

The Quadrangle

This name is given to the space on the palm lying between the Head and Heart Lines (Fig. III, page 52). If it is fairly wide and clear of small lines, the owner will be generous and tolerant, with an honest, intelligent nature.

When the Quadrangle is narrowed by the Head and Heart Lines lying rather close together, it shows an undecided and somewhat timid person. A too-large Quadrangle indicates rather a reckless disposition and if the space is much lined there is a good deal of worrying and restlessness.

Small Signs

There are numerous small signs which may appear on any mount or line in the palm. Below are given their general meanings and these must be interpreted according to their position on the hand. For instance, on the Fate Line they refer to work, on the Health Line to Health, on the Life Line to general events, on the Success Line to distinction, on the Head Line to judgment, nerves or the mental capacities and on a particular mount to the qualities governed by that mount.

The Island (Fig. III) is a long, narrow loop, nearly always on a line. It shows some type of trouble according to the line it is on, the position and length of the loop telling you when the trouble will occur and how long it will last. Islands do not show a crisis or acute trouble so much as a difficult period.

One special note. This mark on the Fate Line is often said to denote a double life or disgraceful love affair. But that cannot be, since the Fate Line shows the career, not love. Read this sign, then, as financial difficulty. This *may*, of course, be brought about by a love entanglement, but in that case there will be a line joining the island with the Heart Line, or an affection or influence line.

The Cross is another common small sign. Disregard it if it is merely two longer lines crossing. But if there is a distinct and separate small cross, usually on a mount, there will be a setback or personal fault of some kind. In the Quadrangle is occasionally seen a well-formed and favourable small cross known as the *Mystic Cross* which denotes psychic power. But this sign is rare.

The Star may be found anywhere in the hand. Its formation may be irregular, but is has definitely more "spokes" than a cross. This sign is exceptional in coming in only *after* the event, which is a physical, mental or emotional shock—quite unexpected and overwhelming at the time.

The Grille is the name given to a criss-cross of lines, nearly always on a mount. It indicates obstacles and lack of success, generally because the subject shows the faults instead of the virtues of that mount. A grilled Mount of Venus indicates an intensely worrying temperament, for instance, whereas the Venus nature should be bright and carefree.

The Spot shows as a tiny dent or dot, usually on a line. It denotes a temporary stoppage of the side of life represented by the line.

The Square is an excellent sign, for it shows preservation from previous trouble or difficulty when it is found enclosing a break, cross or weak spot anywhere. Read the square as "The worst is over and things are slowly but surely on the mend." It is not prophetic, only appearing when the healing process has actually begun.

The Medical Marks (vertical) are a special sign found only on the Mount of Mercury, close to the love lines, but a little farther in from the edge of the hand. This is a common sign, showing ability for medicine, nursing or science in general. There are several close together.

How to Judge Age

Judging the age at which events will occur is one of the most tricky parts of palmistry, as it must be done mostly by eye and a space the size of a pin's head may cover a year or two in the life. You will need a lot of practice before you can estimate age well, and even then warn your subjects that you may be a year out either way.

It is no good attempting to get nearer than the year of

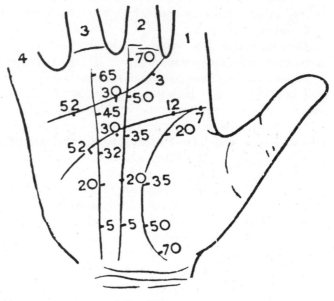

Fig. IV.

How to judge age on the hand.

an event; months and weeks are impossible to estimate. Judge ages also only on the five main lines (excluding the Health Line).

Remember:

The Life Line is read downwards.
The Fate Line and Success Line are read upwards.
The Head and Heart Lines are read from the thumb side of the hand.

Fig. IV will serve as a guide.

Life Line. Where this line separates from the Head Line in normal hands is from seven to ten years old. Downwards from the space between the first and second fingers, eighteen to twenty. Where the greatest outward bulge occurs, forty-five to fifty. Fit the other ages between these key points by eye, with Fig. IV to help you.

Fate Line. Where it crosses the Head Line, thirty-five; where it crosses the Heart Line, fifty. Another useful point is level with the most outward bulge of the Life Line—five to ten, according to where the bulge occurs.

Success Line. Level with the Life Line bulge, five to ten; where the Head Line is crossed, twenty-eight to thirty-five; where the Heart Line is crossed, forty-five to forty-eight.

Head Line. Where it leaves the Life Line, seven. Measuring straight downwards, from between first and second fingers, twelve; from between the second and third fingers, thirty; between the third and fourth, fifty-two.

Heart Line Measuring straight downwards, from between the first and second fingers, three to six; between other fingers as stated above for the Head Line.

These age indications are given for a hand with the main lines normally placed, as in Fig. IV. If any of them are out of the usual position, such as a high Head Line, a low Heart Line or Life Line curving out less than usual, you must mentally adjust the fingers to fit it. This is one of the reasons why age is difficult to judge.

The Best Way of Reading the Hand

When reading a friend's hand you will get better results and find it less tiring both for yourself and her if you make the best arrangements before you start. These are very simple, but important.

In the first place, the light must be good, for the lines on the hand are fine and small and you have to study them closely. I would like to say, "Read hands only by daylight and then near a window". But this is not always practicable, as the time when most people have leisure for palmistry is in the evening.

So let us say, read preferably by daylight and if not, by a good reading lamp placed close to you. Strip lighting is also good. You will only strain your eyes and make lots of mistakes if you attempt palmistry by much diffused light, or illumination that is high up or far away.

If possible, be quite alone with your subject, as then he or she will relax the hand more and you will be able to speak more freely. If someone else is present, be much more careful what you say, even if that second person is a marriage partner, or close relative. It is often just their nearest and dearest that people have most secrets from, you know!

It's advisable not to read a hand in a public place such as a restaurant. Even if nobody overhears you, in my experience it attracts an uncomfortable amount of attention.

Of course, if you are fortune-telling at a party, part of the fun often is for the others to sit round and hear the reading of the person you are doing. In this case the whole thing is only an amusement. You must not take too long over each hand and it is advisable to give the very surface readings, chiefly character with one or two past and future events not at all of a private kind.

Generally speaking, however, it is best not to hurry over a reading, so see that both you and your subject have comfortable seats and are warm enough. As it soon becomes very tiring holding the hands out for your inspection, provide a cushion to rest them on, placing this preferably on a small table between you, or otherwise on your knee.

Have ready a magnifying glass for examining fine lines such as the love and children lines.

Begin by telling your subject to place the hands naturally, palms uppermost, not arranging them in any set way. Study the shape and size of the hands, determine the type they belong to, feel them for the amount of firmness, then turn them over and glance at the nails. Turn them back to palms uppermost and look at the main lines in a general way and at the thumb and fingers.

Do not say anything up to this point, but now give her an outline of her character as you have gleaned it so far.

Go on to study in detail each main line, examining it in both hands and noting any important differences. When reading any particular line, before telling of events, whether past, present or future, check them by reference to other lines concerned. For instance, if the Fate Line shows a change of work, look elsewhere to see whether this is brought about by improved capacity (better Head Line from that date) a move to another district (Life Line) a love affair (Heart Line) or health (Health Line).

If you do this careful checking up you will get more details, often striking ones, and you will not be likely to make any bad mistakes.

When foretelling the future, bear in mind the character of your subject as you have already summed it up. For instance, if you see indications of some course of action which needs strong will power (giving up drinking, for instance) and the thumb and Head Line show a weak nature, you will be more accurate if you say that the course of action is contemplated but it is doubtful if it will be carried out.

Go on to read the minor lines and signs in the same way. At the end of your reading, if it is a long one and difficult for the subject to remember, she will like it if you give a brief summary of the chief character points and events. Let her have an opportunity, too, to ask any questions and put forward any problem. A palmist is as much a sympathiser and consultant as a seer, and it is often a great relief to people to unburden their minds to her.

Just one more reminder never to predict death, madness or any serious misfortune. At most, give a warning as to guarding the health or nerves. And never emphasise people's faults—they are usually quite conscious enough of them already! They will not thank you to present them absolutely perfect, of course, but stress the good points and touch in the defects only lightly.

This should be especially the case if other people are present.

Linked Readings

You will find it most interesting—and so will your sitters—to make comparative readings of the hands of two or more people who are closely linked either by blood or affections. Thus, if you can, read one after the other the hands of a parent and child, two or three brothers and sisters, an engaged or married couple.

In people who are close relations it is absorbing to try to trace the family traits which appear in two or all of them. There is especially likely to be similarity between a mother and son or father and daughter, as children tend to resemble most the parent of the opposite sex.

Note particularly the similarity of the thumbs, the way that both fourth fingers stand apart from the others and the marked likeness between the two forked headlines.

In the case of marriage partners or close friends, see if you can find the characteristics in each which have attracted the other. They will be thrilled to be told about these in addition to the ordinary reading and you yourself will learn a lot, too. In all linked readings, look also for the points of strain and discord. Then you can give a warning to the parent inclined to be too possessive with a son or daughter or to the fiancée who may wreck a promising engagement by jealousy, or ruin wedding life owing to extravagance which a thrifty husband will resent.

Points like these make palmistry extra helpful and extra interesting, both to the subjects and to the palmist.

One last point. When examining the hands of babies or young children, remember that their little hands are still growing and their characters not yet fully formed. Therefore don't be so positive about what you see in the case of older people. Grown-ups "are" so-and-so but children merely "may be" this and that. It is the difference between promise (which may or may not be fulfilled) and accomplishment.

Taking Impressions of Hands

Sometimes you may want to do palmistry for people who are a great distance off, and the only way then is to get them to send impressions of both their hands. These are not as satisfactory as flesh-and-blood readings, but they do tell you a great deal, and have the advantage over real hands that you can file the impressions away for future study!

The easiest way of taking an impression is to pass a firm sheet of paper to and fro over a candle flame till it has a thin film of soot all over it. Naturally this must be done quickly and skilfully, or the paper will catch alight instead of blackening.

Put the blackened paper on the table and firmly press the hand, palm downwards, on to it. Hold it there while someone runs a pencil round the outlines of the hand, in order to give its size and shape accurately. The pressure of the hand on the sooty film will reveal all the lines marked in white, though any very hollow part of the palm may fail to "register."

Fix the impression by spraying it with gum through an aerosol; otherwise it will smear when touched. Handle carefully, as the blackening over the flame makes the paper rather brittle.

Remember when reading from impressions that the hands are reversed; that what appears to be the left hand is the right and vice versa.

IN WHICH MONTH WERE YOU BORN?

NOW we come to another way of fortune-telling—a very easy way, based on astrology or the study of the stars. Astrology proper—the accurate casting and judging of a horoscope—is explained on pages 89 to 137. But this is rather difficult. It takes more time than can be spared by the average woman who is merely interested in knowing a little about the fortunes of herself and her friends. For her the solar horoscopes, as they are called, which are given here, are quite easy and cause plenty of fun and excitement!

Solar horoscopes are based merely on the position of the sun at birth, not taking any notice of the other planets. As no doubt you know, the sun passes through one of the twelve signs of the Zodiac each month and every sign gives its own special characteristics to those born under it. So by merely knowing the month and day of birth we can get a rough-and-ready idea of a person's character and some events of the life. It *is* rough-and-ready, of course, because we are ignoring the hour of birth and the other planets and their influence. But as the sun is so very important, you will find that solar horoscopes are reasonably accurate, four times out of five, as far as they go, and serve as very useful general guides to personality.

It is necessary to know the day of the month as well as the month of birth itself, because, as you will see under each individual horoscope, the influence of the Zodiac signs does not begin on the first of the month but about the 21st. So each sign includes part of two months and each month, according to the birth date, comes under two different signs.

Solar horoscopes are handy for giving the fortune of anyone you happen to meet or perhaps at a party, when you want to tell a number of fortunes quickly. So I have put the main characteristics of each month into easily learnt rhymes.

You will soon get these by heart and then will be able to produce the character reading merely by turning on the tap, as it were.

For times when you can refer to this book, additional information is given in notes at the end of each rhyme. I have written these jingles in the feminine gender, because I find it is mostly women who are interested in this quick way of telling character. But naturally the traits suggested apply equally to men born at the same time of year.

Remember that for the first week of a new sign—that is, from about the 21st to the 28th of each month—the disappearing influence of the previous sign is mingled with that of the one just starting. So for people born on one of these dates you will need to add a certain amount from the previous sign.

Thus, when making a solar horoscope for Mary, born on March 22nd, which is almost at the start of the Aries sign, allow also for the influence of waning Pisces, which will give her a fair slice of Pisces characteristics as well. If her birthday were on March 28th, though, the Pisces influence would be so slight as to be hardly worth considering.

In astrology the year starts in spring, when Nature revives from her winter sleep. Therefore Aries is considered the first of the twelve signs and I am giving it first here.

The Aries Person

The planet Mars and the sign of the Zodiac Aries (the Ram) rule birthdays falling between March 21st and April 20th.

> At the season of the year
> When the daffodils appear,
> Comes the sign of Aries—clean,
> Spotless as the new spring green,
> Every Aries girl seems made
> For the laundry's snowy trade,
> For, if she can have her way,
> *Every* day is washing day!

In her home there's sure to be
Lovely bath, with h. and c.:
And, with recklessness her sin,
Hot water she is always in!
In her dress you'll surely find
Marks of an artistic mind.
In her ways you'll surely see
How impatient is this She.
She's so lively, vital, sweet,
That all men worship at her feet;
And if her love-affairs are brief,
"Oh," says Miss A, "what a relief!
Why to old ways and people cling?
The king is dead. Long live the king!"

Additional traits: Hot-tempered and cruel when angered, but it is soon forgotton; always wants to lead; impulsive, without much self-control; decided, good-natured, generous.

Her life: Many brief love affairs before settling down. Aries women usually marry men who make little money, so they go on earning themselves. They have small families.

The Taurus Person

The planet Venus and sign Taurus (the Bull) rule birthdays falling between April 21st and May 20th.

May Day crowns its annual queen
In a pageantry of green,
And Queen Taurus, truth to tell,
Empress fain would be as well!
For, from early days at school
All through life, she loves to rule.
To her subjects sweetly kind,
Those who fight her always find
Stubborn as a bull she'll be.
Little tact or grace has she,
And to mind the saying pops—
You know—of bulls in china shops!
With Miss Taurus argue never;
You will not convince her ever,
And she'll, without more ado,
Talk much more—and loud!—than you.

> But by love, when all is said,
> Is this leader quickly led.
> Home, sweet home's the place for her,
> Thence she seldom wants to stir,
> And the menfolk, one and all,
> Come there at her beck and call,
> For, in her imperious way,
> She's charming Queen of May.

Additional traits: Hospitable and good hostess, frank and outspoken; very devoted to those she loves; rather dominating; fond of food, drink and comfort.

Her life: Very attractive to men, has several chances of marriage and almost always does marry. Often has a large family and a numerous household with relatives or friends living with her. If widowed, she soon marries again.

The Gemini Person

The planet Mercury and the sign Gemini (the Twins) rule birthdays falling between May 21st and June 20th.

> As spring days into summer pass
> Comes Alice through the Looking Glass.
> For so I dub this changing elf
> Who to all folk adapts herself;
> So many-sided, versatile,
> That she is different all the while
> And like a mirror she reflects
> Whatever mood her world expects.
> 'It makes a change!' is e'er her song.
> She's everything—but nothing long!
> In not one thing is she a dunce.
> She often goes both ways at once!
> Two minds within one body she,
> For Gemini means 'twins,' you see—
> And twins who never once agree!
> Oh Gemini, what fun you are,
> What a bewildering, quick-change star!
> You·were in front, beyond a doubt,
> When speed and wit were given out.
> You dazzle men, you airy fay,
> You beckon all of them your way.
> They love you (though illusions pass),
> Gemini of the Looking Glass!

Additional traits: Fanciful, contradictory; she learns rapidly but hates drudgery or long, concentrated effort; often foolish, but usually forgiven for her charm; extravagant, dashing.

Her life: She tries everything and regrets nothing, so her days are full of change, excitement and often unconventionality. She does not fall intensely in love but marries for adventure and companionship. Her children must have the best of everything, whether she can afford it or not!

The Cancer Person

The Moon and the sign Cancer (the Crab) rule birthdays falling between June 21st and July 20th.

Give Cancer's girl the smallest chance,
She'll prove her middle name Romance.
For her brave knights on horseback prance,
And in the moonlight fairies dance.
The sea she loves, 'twill never fail her,
She's the nice girl who loves a sailor!
Love at first sight's the only love,
And in a cottage sweet will prove.
Thus, in a glamorous defiance,
Miss Cancer makes a *mésalliance,*
And then, alas, repents at leisure
Of following her romatic pleasure.
At best, she marries Peter Pan
(Perpetual boy); at worst, a man
Who will not work with any spur
And leaves the kiddies all to her.
Oh, then Miss Cancer up and fights
To give her children all their rights!
For them, she puts aside her dreams;
For them she works, endures and schemes.
For, taking one thing with another.
She is the year's most splendid mother!

Additional traits: Must have plenty of appreciation; moody, easily discouraged; discreet and diplomatic; sympathetic but not very helpful; very domestic.

Her life: Born rover and loves long distance travel, especially by sea; she often makes rather an odd marriage, with someone foreign, much older or much younger, or in a different social rank.

The Leo Person

The Sun and the Zodiac sign Leo (the Lion) rule birthdays falling between July 21st and August 20th.

> Ring up the curtain! Start the play!
> Let minor actors strut away
> A little while. Then—breathless stir!—
> The limelight plays direct on HER,
> Leaving all else subdued and shady,
> And enter—centre—Leading Lady!
> Bows to applause 'ere she can start,
> Magnificently plays her part,
> Then at the curtain's final fall,
> With thunderous claps, she takes her call!
> Oh Leo Girl, that is the bit
> Of life you like, now isn't it?
> No one was ever more efficient,
> More calm, and capable, proficient
> In all a girl should know and do,
> More apt at carrying big things through!
> Child of the sun, as is but fit,
> How you do love your place in it!
> A place, of course, bang in the centre,
> And yet you win it when you enter,
> For you're so generous, loyal, true,
> That we all fall in love with you!

Additional traits: Idealistic; defender of the weak; logical, persistent, reasonable; often has dramactic ability, wit and gaiety; very large-hearted; hot-tempered.
Her life: She is suited to the Civil Service or work in a bank. Often poor when quite young, but properous all through

middle life—in fact, lucky in most things but not very fortunate in love.

The Virgo Person

The planet Mercury and the sign Virgo (the Virgin) rule birthdays falling between August 21st and September 20th.

> In young Miss Virgo's lucid sight
> 'Most everything is black or white.
> Grey is a colour that, I ween,
> She's never heard of, much less seen!
> And there's a line, drawn hard and strong,
> For her, between what's right and wrong.
> She never doubts what's best to do,
> Or hesitates, like me and you,
> And people (so her fancy paints)
> Are utter rogues or perfect saints!
> With her clear sense of what is right.
> She loves reforming all in sight,
> And when, as oft, she speaks her mind,
> She mostly has an axe to grind,
> And yet—how loyal she can be!
> (Her friends are always right, you see).
> How vivid, full of life and fun,
> How quick to get the hard work done!
> And in her softer moments she
> Is full of charm and sympathy
> A charm that draws men to her side!

Additional traits: Inclined to be critical and fault finding; methodical, judging by externals; very practical, not to say earth-bound; active and restless; philosophical.

Her life: She is not specially inclined to marriage, though attractive to men. Usually a broken engagement (broken by herself) precedes her wedding. She stays young and young-looking far into middle age.

The Libra Person

The Planet Venus and the sign Libra (the Balance) rule birthdays falling between September 21st and October 20th.

Chills sweep across October's path,
Bright fires are welcome on the hearth;
And by the hearth, domestic, staid,
Sit Cinderella, Libra's maid.
While sisters type and act and teach,
While brothers have their training each,
Somehow, when Libra's turn is here,
There's no cash left for her career.
Is Libra filled with blank dismay?
No! While she longed to sing or play
(She's musical) her thoughts are bent
On sheltered ways and home content.
Domestic tasks don't make her wince.
Her dreams float softly round a prince,
And she will gladly spend her life
Being a helpful, thrifty wife.
She really *loves* to polish up
A bit of brass or wash a cup.
And if her chatter chiefly rings
Of brass and cups and such-like things,
Of Mother's cold and Baby's fall,
And why the baker didn't call,
She's still—and so we always tell her—
Our loving, winsome Cinderella!

Additional traits: Generally pretty; timid and dependent; merciful; very sympathetic; harmonious; very intuitive; inclined both to save and to borrow money.

Her life: She is a real homebird and the one who looks after old parents or the family invalid. Often both career and marriage are thus sacrificed. If she weds she makes a good, though rather house-proud wife.

The Scorpio Person

The planet Mars and the sign Scorpio (the Scorpion) rule birthdays fall between October 21st and November 20th.

> The Amazons of long ago
> Where women warriors, we know,
> And doubtless ruled by Scorpio;
> For each Miss Scorpio feels it right,
> In every circumstance, to fight!
> Life is to her a battlefield,
> And not one inch she'll ever yield.
> Weakness is not among her sins,
> So when she fights she mostly wins.
> She fights her family at first
> (A struggle where they come off worst),
> She fights each week and day and hour,
> But most of all she fights for power,
> And she'll, in this great warlike race
> Cut off her nose to spite her face!
> She's full of love and full of hate,
> Her talent's always very great.
> Her Amazonian charm and wit
> Draw men, there's no doubt of it,
> But she's so keen to strive and harry,
> She often hasn't time to marry!
> And fighting still, brave, firm and gay,
> Pursues her single-minded way.

Additional traits: Very determined; rather secretive and silent; inclined to over-do everything; ambitious; reliable; self-possessed.

Her life: It is not an easy one, but her grit brings her success rather late in life. She has a magnetic appeal for men and if she doesn't marry it's not because she couldn't!

The Sagittarius Person

The planet Jupiter and the Zodiac sign, Sagittarius (the Archer) rule birthdays between November 21st and December 20th.

> Riding an early morning ride,
> With graceful figure set astride,
> Swimming the Channel (well, not quite!)
> Dancing with zest half through the night,
> Playing tennis, swift and strong,
> Hiking the country lanes along,
> Sculling a boat through sleepy water,
> You'll find December's agile daughter.
> An active maiden she will prove,
> And one who's always on the move,
> For, when her sports don't keep her busy,
> She'll do, do *something*, till you're dizzy!
> She crowds up each and every day,
> Works hard, then goes as hard at play.
> And that's not all. For, between whiles,
> She's helping lame dogs over stiles,
> And teaching, to each limping rover,
> Just *how* a stile should be got over!
> A fairy godma, wise and gay,
> The best of helpers, any day,
> If she can help folk on her way!
> A wee bit bossy. But how true,
> How kind, how quick to dare and do,
> Dear Miss December, here's to you!

Additional traits: Optimistic, though easily discouraged temporarily, rather finicking and fault-finding; anxious to advance education and causes generally; very affectionate; impulsive.

Her life: She often marries twice and likes to keep on her work—or unpaid public work—after marriage. As she wants to get to the top, her husband is generally Somebody with a big S. Not always happy in marriage, but invariably opposes divorce or separation.

The Capricorn Person

The planet Saturn and the sign Capricorn (the Goat) rule birthdays falling between December 21st and January 20th.

> A quiet girl is she who's born
> Beneath the sign of Capricorn.
> Pleasures to her make small appeal.
> In leisure hours she'd rather feel
> She was acquiring information,
> For she just worships education!
> Language and other evening classes
> Are filled with Capricorn's keen lasses.
> She's of the British bulldog breed,
> Entirely true in word and deed.
> For very few folks' love she'll try,
> And for those few she'll die—or lie!
> If she had lived in days of yore,
> A hermit she'd be cut out for.
> Alone within a simple cell
> She'd live on twopence—and live well
> In her opinion, though *we'd* find
> Her fare but little to our mind.
> Love in a cottage makes her happy,
> She's ne'er discouraged, bored or snappy!
> And he who takes Miss Cap. to wife
> Will find her loyal all his life.

Additional traits: Prudent; a book-lover; inclined to pessimism and the blues; very good at concentrating; strictly represses her emotions; patient and self-reliant.

Her life: A career usually means more to her than marriage, but if she weds, unless she waits until middle age she is usually not very happy. She shuns social life and often lives alone.

The Aquarius Person

The planet Uranus and the sign Aquarius (the Water Carrier) rule birthdays falling between January 21st and February 20th.

Small Miss Aquarius, years ago,
Set up her dollies in a row,
And taught them all that they should know!
For February's girl, you'll find,
Has a maternal, teaching mind.
In school or out, by pen or classes,
She'll tend and educate the masses.
Yet seldom is she one of those
Regular schoolmarms, specs on nose,
For, of all girls the year around
Most beauty's in Aquarius are found.
When she was born a fair star shone—
She's easy (most!) to look upon!
Old times, old things, old customs too
She likes, and rather fears the new
Just change your hair, and she will say,
"How ugly when it's done that way!"
But in a twelvemonth change again,
The *nice* last way she'll beg for them!
Still, of all folk, Aquarius seems
Most moderate, free from all extremes,
A perfect friend, an ideal wife
To give some man a happy life.

Additional traits: Can lead but usually hasn't enough energy to; decidedly musical; a devoted, faithful friend; seldom expresses her feelings, owing to deep reserve.

Her life: It is seldom she does not marry—happily, too, but she is much the better for some career or active social work after marriage and usually seeks it. Friendship plays a very large part in her life—so do her children.

The Pisces Person

The planet Jupiter and the Zodiac sign Pisces (the Fishes) rule birthdays occurring between February 21st and March 20th.

> The Pisces girl, with brains to spare,
> Is sometimes mad as a March hare,
> For she'll pursue some craze or fad
> Until you really think she's mad,
> Till of the subject you're so sick
> You'd like to shoot or drown her—quick!
> (Choose drowning, please, for March's daughter,
> For she's mermaid of the water,
> And, though you try to end her in it,
> She'll swim her way out in a minute!)
> To every fortune-teller she
> Will run as fast as she can flee,
> The future and its plan to see.
> Oh, *how* untidy is this girl!
> Her room is always in a whirl,
> And half her leisure speeds away
> In finding things lost yesterday!
> Yet none can be more brave and kind,
> A harder worker you won't find.
> Miss P. is generous with her pelf,
> And thinks of others 'fore herself.
> Suitors come soon and make it snappy!
> They know her husband will be happy.

Additional traits: Active and restless; a great worrier; romantic and rather given to moods: intuitive, with occult ability; very reliable; rather pessimistic.

Her life: More than one disappointment in love, but she often marries early and has a large family. These women are more apt to be widowed (not necessarily prematurely) than those of any other sign. Money conditions are mostly easy, though they are seldom rich.

THE MAN FOR YOU!

CERTAIN signs of the Zodiac and, consequently, certain months of the year, are naturally sympathetic to one another. This sympathy is very real and strong and is based on the division of the twelve signs into Earth, Air, Fire and Water groups, as explained on page 85.

So remember this natural sympathy when the boy friend comes into your life. For real happiness and harmony in marriage you will do well to find out his birthday and see if it comes under one of your affinity signs. If it does, he will have the characteristics you admire and you will get on well together and nothing in the world can cause a permanent breach between you. I have found this to be always true in my experience.

Here are brief descriptions of the men of each month. A man, of course, should take them as thumb-nail sketches of possible wives.

JANUARY MEN (born between December 21st and January 20th) do most things rather slowly. So if your boy is one of these, do not expect a lightning courtship of a very speedy marriage—though if born before December 28th he will go a little faster. Let him do all the wooing himself, for he likes to be the leader, and to make up his own mind.

Don't look for him to be a picturesque wooer. He won't often call you pet names or tell you he loves you. But to the right girl he shows a deep devotion, expressed in deeds of kindness rather than in words.

He is very ambitious. Nothing and nobody (including yourself) must stand in the way of his career. Take a real interest in his work if you want to win and keep him.

The girls who are happiest with January men are those born under the Zodiac signs of Taurus, Virgo and his own sign of Capricorn.

THE FEBRUARY MAN are those with birthdays between January 21st and February 20th. You are quite likely to meet this boy in a club or institution, for he is interested in all such things and will like you to be.

He is rather pessimistic. But he is fascinating, companionable, trustworthy and a very good father. Expect financial ups and downs if you marry him, for his fortunes vary a good deal. The girl who weds him should preferably be born in his own sign, Aquarius, or in those of Gemini or Libra.

THE MARCH MAN (born between February 21st and March 20th) makes an almost ideal lover, for he is romantic, deeply affectionate, unselfish and very generous. If he loves a girl he will adopt her opinions, spend his last penny on her and do everything in the world to show his devotion.

At the same time, such a blind love exacts constant attention in return.

He adores travel and often meets his future wife while on a journey or staying abroad. He hates long engagements. As he is usually lucky with money when young, the wedding bells are likely to ring soon.

As a husband he is not quite so successful. He continues to spoil his wife thoroughly in little ways and to be easily influenced by her; but in big things she must shoulder all the responsibility, for he will not. So he should marry a girl who likes taking the lead.

The ideal wife for him is one born under the signs of Cancer or Scorpio, or failing these, in his own sign of Pisces.

THE APRIL MAN is a real "he man" and falls for an intensely feminine type of girl. He loves his mate, but she will find him hard to influence, very headstrong, ambitious and inclined to quarrel.

He is the man who is always right. There's a tip for you if you want to win his love!

He is brave and adventurous and likes travel. He won't make the homebird type of husband, but will be very much the master of the house. As his children grow he is likely to disagree with them, for they will resent his "bossy" ways.

The girls who will be happiest with him is one born in his own sign, Aries, or in those of Leo or Sagittarius.

MAY MEN (with birthdays between April 21st and May 20th) are, of all males, simply born to marry! They have the husband instinct. They are not philanderers. When they court a girl they really mean business.

They are very affectionate, but can also be extremely stubborn when opposed. Don't marry a May man unless you are sure you see eye to eye—for he is the hardest of people to convert to different ideas. He is devoted to home and expects his wife to be, for he likes plenty of her company.

He is really interested in the domestic wheels—and *can* be rather a nuisance interfering in the house. He is very healthy, very musical and a good money-maker as a rule.

The girl best suited to him is one born under Capricorn, Virgo or his own sign, Taurus.

JUNE MEN, who are born between May 20th and June 21st, unlike their May brothers, flit from flower to flower. They take sudden fancies and cool off just as quickly. So don't reckon on your June man till you've had him for a good while.

When he marries, though, he generally settles down. Make up your mind you will get on well with your "in-laws," for this husband likes to see a lot of his brothers and sisters, nephews and nieces and to entertain them in his own home.

It takes a girl born under the signs of Aquarius, Libra or his own sign, Gemini, to handle the June man really well.

JULY MEN have a compelling charm. You may thoroughly disapprove of their laziness and improvident ways, yet you can't help adoring them!

If you boy is a July man (born between June 21st and July 20th, that is) *you* must be the practical one and think of ways and means, for he won't. He'll fervently swear by love in a cottage, but not like it quite so well when it means hard work and getting up early!

He is the real romantic—the one-woman man, who finds his wife as lovable when she is old and grey as in her pretty youth. She may be sure that he will never tire of her.

The girl who will be happiest with the July man is born under the signs of Pisces, his own sign, Cancer or Scorpio.

AUGUST MEN (born between July 21st and August 20th) feel like royalty and look for rather the same deference! An August husband expects to be a little king in his own home. He has a great sense of dignity, so never, *never* make him look ridiculous.

He likes an artistic, well-run home, first-class cooking and a wife who is an excellent hostess.

The girl best suited to him is one born under Aries, Sagittarius or his own sign, Leo.

SEPTEMBER MEN with birthdays between August 21st and September 20th) never go crazy about you. At the same time, in a level-headed way a September boy may love you dearly and want to spend the rest of his life in your company. He marries for companionship and affection rather than for romance.

He is a wonderful comrade, always interesting and lovable. Try to be tidy and methodical when you wed a September man, for he believes there is a plan, a time and a place for everything!

You will find him a generous husband and a very good father.

The girl who will be happiest with him is one born in his own sign, Virgo, or under those of Capricorn or Taurus.

THE OCTOBER MAN (with a birthday between September 21st and October 20th) has Charm—with a capital C. He simply captivates you with his gaiety and he is always a social success. Don't be disappointed if he often wants to join a party when you would rather be alone with him.

He is a devoted and tender lover, very chivalrous and kind. You must not expect him, after marriage, to change into a masterful he-man! He will always be inclined to leave the big decisions to you. He hates quarrels and will do almost anything for peace.

He makes the happiest marriage with a girl born under his own sign of Libra, or under those of Aquarius of Gemini.

NOVEMBER MEN (born between October 21st and November 20th) are, frankly, a handful! If your boy friend has a birthday this month, you will never have a dull life with him—but seldom a peaceful one either!

He is a masterful, attractive lover, a strong personality, very capable in providing for wife and family.

If you can get your way by guile and are willing to absorb yourself in your own interests—for work takes most of *his* time—you will find him well worth while.

You will be happiest with him if you were born under Pisces, Cancer or his own sign Scorpio.

DECEMBER MEN (born between November 21st and December 20th) are destined to prosperity. You need not fear poverty or hard drudgery if you marry one of them. The good things of life will be yours—if not actual wealth, at least you will have sufficient to travel and entertain and to indulge in the social pleasures that appeal strongly to him.

He makes a kind, cheery, restless husband. Let's hope you enjoy travel and can cook well when at home, for he loves to wander and to have the pleasures of a good table.

He will want to provide the best without being extravagant in doing so, and to be well dressed on a moderate allowance. Yet, though he likes value for money, he is generous rather than mean.

He is rather moody, at times very sociable and jovial, at other times inclined to solitude and philosophy. He has high ideals and a great desire to help the world forward.

The girl who suits him best is one born under the signs of Aries, Leo or his own sign Sagittarius.

For the dates corresponding to all the signs mentioned here, see pages 68 to 79.

WHO ARE YOUR FRIENDS?

AS mentioned on page 91, the twelve signs of the Zodiac are split into four groups. Each group is ruled by one of the four Elements—Earth, Air, Fire or Water—and consists of three signs in the same group are always naturally sympathetic to one another and will never quarrel permanently.

Perhaps you go to a party or to a new job and are introduced all at once to a number of fresh people. For no reason that you can give, you feel drawn immediately to one or two of them. Perhaps even before you hear their names you like them instinctively. Later, when you known them better, you will almost always discover that these folk you "fell for" at first sight have birthdays which bring them into your own Element group.

Think of your chief friends and you will find that a majority of them have birthdays in your own sign or the other two signs of your group. Or it may be that they were born in the sign exactly six months round the year from your own. Thus, if you have a Capricorn birthday—the January sign—you are likely to be attracted to those born under Cancer, the July sign.

Opposite signs like these never come into the same Element group, so here the attraction is one of contrasts. It is specially favourable for marriage or business partnership, as each will strengthen the weak points of the other.

The Element grouping is particularly concerned with friendship, though it is also a very happy omen for matrimony. Personally, I have always found it wonderfully accurate for these two relationships, explaining many apparently capricious likings.

"Own month" attractions are not quite so good for marriage as for friendship. Though they give a very close harmony and understanding, the faults and virtues of the pair will be too similar to make a good partnership—and what is marriage but a partnership, after all?

All these Element attractions take no account of birth, nationality or age, because they are based on the two people having the same general outlook on life, whatever their individual differences. Owing to circumstances, these two people may never become close friends—though they often do under favourable conditions—but they will always feel strongly in sympathy with one another when ever they *do* meet.

Remember, the three signs in each group have their own differing character traits, but are drawn together by a common outlook.

Earth people have a practical outlook.

Air people have a mental outlook.

Fire people have an idealistic outlook.

Water people have an emotional outlook.

The Three Earth Signs. These are Capricorn (December 21st to January 20th), Taurus (April 21st to May 20th) and Virgo (August 21st to September 20th).

Earth people are practical and scientific. They always ask of a new idea, "Will it work?" or "What will it accomplish?" Above all, they *do*. They are slow, sure and patient and keep their feet firmly planted on the earth of reality. They learn only from first-hand experience.

They are honest and trustworthy, straightforward and hard-working. The world would be a poor place without their truthful accuracy and sturdy common sense. They prefer the practical professions, such as business and those connected with the earth, like farming or coal-mining. They also enjoy hobbies which keep contact with the earth, such as walking and gardening.

The Three Air Signs. These are Aquarius (January 21st to February 20th), Gemini (May 21st to June 20th) and Libra (September 21st to October 20th).

The Air group is specially linked with the mind and mental things. So Air people, above all, *think*. When a new idea or experience comes, they ask. "Is it intellectually sound? Is it logical?" Consequently they are not particularly practical. Their feelings and their spiritual side must bow to intelligence. They are natural teachers, philosophers and reasoners and their heads gain the victory over their hearts.

Because they reason everything out, they are very fair-minded and moderate, without being cranky or over-enthu-siastic. They are calm, gentle and a little slow, but very thorough and systematic. They like to do one thing at a time and not be hustled or interrupted.

They succeed in the brainy jobs. Education is their special field and they also excel in clerical work. Their hobbies are books or pastimes connected with air, such as flying and the study of birds.

The Three Fire Signs. These are Aries (March 21st to April 20th), Leo (July 21st to August 20th) and Sagittarius (November 21st to December 20th).

Fire people are idealistic and spiritual. Their test of a new proposition is, "Is it right? Will it make the world better?" They always look for the uplifting element as they go through life, just as fire itself leaps up towards heaven. Because of this, Fire people sometimes lose sight of the practical point of view, and so they may fail to reach their ideals by being too visionary.

They are artistic and creative, seldom mere routine workers. They always want to excel and be important and admired. They have much charm and popularity, and, above all, they *dream*.

Being children of Fire, they have fiery (but quickly over) tempers, and they often take up jobs in which fire, furnaces or firearms play a part. They like fiery and sunny hobbies, too, such as camping (complete with camp fire), cooking and sunbathing.

The Three Water Signs. These are Pisces (February 21st

to March 20th), Cancer (June 21st to July 20th) and Scorpio (October 21st to November 20th).

Water people are very emotional and sympathetic. In them, feeling is stronger than action or thought, and this makes them romantic and very pliable with those they love, though they can be obstinate and self-willed with others. "How do I like it? How will it feel?" is their test of a new experience. They are big-hearted and their hearts will usually triumph over their heads.

In every way water plays a large part in their lives. They should, if possible, live near their own Element, either a river, canal, lake or the sea. They are restless and often make long voyages. They drink plenty of water and indeed, liquid generally, and as children they are prone to tears.

They take everything intensely, for, above all, they *feel*. They therefore suffer and rejoice more than most folk.

Work connected with water suits them best. They should be employed by the local Water Board or in a laundry, water the streets, be swimming instructors or have river or sea jobs. Their hobbies are of the same type—rowing, swimming, cruises and so on.

HOW TO CAST A HOROSCOPE

ON pages 67 to 79 you will find quick and easy ways of getting to know a certain amount about people's characters from solar readings—that is, considering only the month and day of the month on which they were born. These give rough-and-ready results and are very useful more or less for fun or for immediate use. But as solar readings don't take into account either the year or the time of birth (both important factors), they can really only rank as the child's play of astrology.

To get detailed and accurate astrological results about a person's character and the events of his life you need to cast his horoscope—that is, to make a map of the heavens and the positions of all the planets in them at the exact moment of birth. When the map is made, then you must know how to interpret it. You could not find your way somewhere by a map unless you already knew what symbols represented roads, woods, towns and so on on maps. The same is true of horoscopes, which are the maps of astrology.

Here I want to give you a warning. The solar readings already given have only to be read and the rhymes, perhaps, memorized. They are a small portion of astrology made foolproof. But casting and reading horoscopes is rather a different matter. They take quite a lot of time; they can't be dashed off in a hurry at a party and for the casting some aptitude for figures is needed. So, unless you have plenty of patience and an ability to calculate, you'll be well advised to stick to the solar readings already given and skip this section of *Book of Fortune Telling*.

However, if you do decide to give the time necessary for

astrology proper, you will find that you get results which are much fuller and more satisfying than is possible with solar readings. You will have at your command an absorbing hobby from which you can learn an immense amount about yourself, your friends and human nature in general.

First you must know what we may call the alphabet of astrology—the twelve signs of the Zodiac, the various planets and the symbols for all these. Horoscopes would be inconveniently large and take an extra long time to do if the names of the signs and planets had to be written on them in full. Therefore each has a symbol which takes no longer to put on paper than one letter of the alphabet—and no more space.

The Zodiac, as you probably know, is an imaginary belt round the earth through which, when seen from the earth, the Sun and Moon (called the luminaries in astrology) and

Zodiacal Sign.	Its Symbol.	Planet Ruling the Sign.	Planet's Symbol.
1. ARIES (The Ram)	♈	MARS	♂
2. TAURUS (The Bull)	♉	VENUS	♀
3. GEMINI (The Twins)	♊	MERCURY	☿
4. CANCER (The Crab)	♋	MOON	☽
5. LEO (The Lion)	♌	SUN	☉
6. VIRGO (The Virgin)	♍	MERCURY	☿
7. LIBRA (The Scales)	♎	VENUS	♀
8. SCORPIO (The Scorpion)	♏	MARS	♂
9. SAGITTARIUS (The Archer)	♐	JUPITER	♃
10. CAPRICORN (The Goat)	♑	SATURN	♄
11. AQUARIUS (The Water-Carrier)	♒	SATURN	♄
12. PISCES (The Fishes)	♓	JUPITER	♃

The three recently discovered planets, URANUS, NEPTUNE and PLUTO, do not rule any signs alone. But they may be considered as junior partners and co-rulers—URANUS with SATURN over Aquarius, NEPTUNE with JUPITER over Pisces, and PLUTO with MARS over Aries. Their influence should always be taken into minor account with these three signs. Their symbols are: Uranus ♅ ; Neptune ♆ ; Pluto ♇ .

the other planets appear to travel. Another name for it is the Ecliptic. This belt or circle consists of 360 degrees (written 360°) and is divided into twelve signs of the Zodiac, each containing 30°.

In astrology the year starts in early spring, and the first sign is therefore Aries, which the Sun enters on March 21st each year. Aries contains the first thirty degrees, those numbered from 0° to 30°, the next sign, Taurus, those from 30° to 60°, and so on all round the Zodiac.

On page 90 is a useful table showing the signs of the Zodiac, the Planets ruling them and their symbols. The symbols seem rather alike and confusing at first. But after a little practice in writing them you will name and distinguish them from each other just as easily as you do the letters of the alphabet.

The signs are divided up into four different groups, which you will also soon memorize. These are:

1. *Northern* (0° to 180°) = Aries, Taurus, Gemini, Cancer, Leo and Virgo); *Southern* (180° to 360°) = Libra, Scorpio, Sagittarius, Capricorn, Aquarius and Pisces.

2. *The Elements* (Earth, Air, Fire and Water). Three signs in each element, as explained on page 85 to 88.

3. *Positive and Negative.* These alternate, beginning with Aries, which is positive; so also are Gemini, Leo, Libra, Sagittarius and Aquarius. The remaining signs, Taurus, Cancer, Virgo, Scorpio, Capricorn and Pisces are negative.

4. *Cardinal, Fixed and Mutable* (sometimes called Common). Each of the four seasons begin with a Cardinal Sign—Aries, Cancer, Libra, Capricorn. Fixed signs mark the middle of each season—Taurus, Leo, Scorpio and Aquarius—and Mutable or Common signs the end of spring, summer, autumn and winter, with Gemini, Virgo, Sagittarius and Pisces.

Fig. V shows these four different groups clearly as they affect each sign and can be consulted in a moment at any time.

Fig. V.

The Signs in Rhyme. Here is an old jingle which will help to fix the order of the signs in your memory:

> The Ram, the Bull, the Heavenly Twins,
> The Crab and next the Lion shines,
>   The Virgin and the Scales;
> The Scorpion, Archer, then the Goat,
> The Man that holds the Watering-Pot,
>   The Fish with glittering tails.

The Aspects. These are the angles which the various signs and planets make to each other when placed in the map—or, to put it in another way, their distance part by signs or degrees. The aspects and their symbols are:

Aspect.	Symbol.	Distance or degrees apart.	Degrees of operation.	Influence.
1. Conjunction ...	☌	Same degree or area.	7°	May be good or Bad.
2. Semi-sextile	⚺	1 sign (30°)	2°	Slightly good.
3. Semi-square ...	∠	1½ signs (45°)	3°	Slightly bad.
4. Sextile	✳	2 signs (60°)	7°	Good.
5. Square	☐	3 signs (90°)	7°	Very bad.
6. Trine	△	4 signs (120°)	7°	Very good.
7. Sesqui-square ..	⚼	4½ signs (135°)	3°	Somewhat bad.
8. Quincunx (Inconjunct) .	⚻	5 signs (150°)	3°	May be good or bad.
9. Opposition	☍	6 signs (180°)	7°	Usually bad.

The meanings of the terms used in this table will be explained later. Meanwhile you can grow familiar with the various aspects by studying Fig. V. From this you will see that Capricorn, say, is in opposition to Cancer, in sextile to Pisces and Scorpio, in square to Aries and Libra, and so on. While the houses or divisions of the horoscope are numbered counter-clockwise, as you will see by the figures at the centre of Fig. V, aspects are reckoned both ways, either forward or backward.

As the signs are divisions of the Zodiac, no two can ever occupy the same space, and so there can be no conjunction between two signs. But conjunction occurs between planets, several of which, as you will discover later, may be placed close together in a horoscope.

Other Astrological Terms. To complete your alphabet of astrology, here are some other terms you will need to know.

Cusps. The twelve houses or fixed divisions of the Zodiacal circle (the signs being twelve similar moving divisions, which pass over or through the houses in a steady progression) are divided, as Fig. V shows you, by lines which are known as cusps. (For house numbering see the small centre circle in Fig. V.)

The *Ascendant* (marked Asc. in Fig. VI) is the name given
to the cusp of the first house; the sign occupying the first
house at birth is also often referred to as the *Ascendant* or
the *Rising Sign.* In Fig. V the Rising Sign is Aries, but of
course it can be any other of the twelve signs, according to
the year, day and time of birth. In Fig. VI, for example,
it is Pisces.

The *Ruling Planet* (don't confuse this with the Rising
Sign or Ascendant) is the planet which rules the Rising
Sign, whether it happens to be placed in it in the horoscope
or not. Thus, in Fig VI, the Ascendant is Pisces. Look
up Pisces in the sign and planet table on page 90 and you
will see that it is ruled by Jupiter. So Jupiter is the Ruling
Planet for a Pisces Ascendant. The *Sun Sign* is the sign in
which the sun is placed at birth and can be determined by
the month and day of birth, without reference to year or
time. Solar readings (see page 67) are based on the Sun Sign
only.

In the reading of a full horoscope all these, the Ascendant
or Rising Sign, the Ruling Planet and the Sun Sign are very
important. So also is the *Midheaven* (the cusp of, and the sign
occupying, the tenth house). In Fig. VI, where Sagittarius is
on the tenth cusp, the Midheaven is marked as M.C., from
the initials of its Latin name. Try to get these four names
and what they stand for firmly into your head, for you will
need them a lot.

Requirements for Casting a Horoscope. To give a brief solar
reading (see page 67) you require no information but the
birthday of the person concerned—say, May 14th or
September 1st. For a horoscope, which is far more detailed
and exact, you must also have the year and time and place of
birth—thus: May 14th, 1926, 10.10 am., London, or
September 1st, 1949, 4.30 p.m., Birmingham.

You will need in addition Raphael's Ephemeris for the
year of birth, 1926 in the first instance we have given, or
1949 for the second. An ephemeris is a sort of time-table
of the movements in the heaven during a particular year.

Just as you could not know—if for some purpose you required to—just how the trains ran between London and York in 1930 by consulting a railway guide of the present year, so one ephemeris only will not serve you for the horoscopes of people born in different years. You must buy a separate one for each year you require.

A good atlas is also needed.

Raphael's Ephemeris for any year you are likely to need may be obtained from Foulsham & Co., Yeovil Road, Slough, Bucks.

Books of blank maps for use when casting horoscopes may also be bought there, or you can make your own map forms very easily with a ruler and a pair of compasses.

Making a Map Form. On a sheet of paper describe a circle with your compasses—one with a radius of three inches in a convenient size. Mark the centre with a pencil dot, so that you can find it again easily. Using the same centre, make a circle with a radius of 2½ inches inside the first. Now with a radius of only ½ inch make a third tiny circle in the centre. (See Fig. VI.)

Next, with a radius of only half of the second circle—that is, 1¼ inches if you used a 2½-inch radius for that second circle—mark off your twelve houses. To do this place the compass point on this second circle, at its highest point. Keeping the 1¼-inch radius, cut the circle wherever the pencil comes to the right. Place the point now at this new pencil mark, cut again to the right and so on till you have six pencil marks on the inner circle. Join each of these cuts to the centre point in the middle of the map, continuing the line straight across till it touches the inner circle on the other side. You now have twelve equal divisions of the inner circle for the twelve houses. Rub out the circle-cross of lines inside the tiny centre circle and use it for printing there the birth data of the person whose horoscope you are casting, as in Fig. VI (page 103).

Exact Birth Time Not Known. People who want their horoscopes done often do not know the exact minute of their birth. They may say, "Oh, about seven o'clock", "between ten and half-past", "some time in the evening," or, perhaps, "I haven't the faintest idea". What are you to do then?

All you *can* do is to use the most exact time you have. For example, if you are told "between ten and half past", cast the horoscope for 10.15—but be very sure whether it was 10.15 a.m. or 10.15 p.m. Should you get the reply, "Some time in the evening," pin it down as closely as you can. Horoscopes which are not accurate to the minute of birth will not be quite so reliable as those which are, but they will still be exact enough to give a great deal of help.

If the time is not known at all, the rule is to erect the map for sunrise of the birthday, because the position of the heavens at sunrise has a general influence all through the day. But don't expect the results to be so right and revealing as when you have even an approximate birth hour.

The time of sunrise for every Sunday in the year is given in the Ephemeris for that year, usually on or about page 40. From the difference between one Sunday and the next, which is only a few minutes, you can easily calculate sunrise time for any day in the middle of the week.

Now we come to the actual casting of a horoscope.

Taking quite a simple instance to begin with, let us erect a map for a person born in Skipton (Yorkshire) on June 10th, 1947, at 2.45 a.m. First problem is that in England in 1947 Double Summer Time was in operation. In fact, all summer births in Britain between 1916 and 1968 took place during either Summer Time or Double Summer Time (Double Summer Time operated from 1941 to 1947). This means that summer births in Britain from 1941 to 1947 were recorded at times two hours fast by Greenwich Mean Time, and in the other years mentioned at times one hour fast. The heavens take no account of such man-made alterations in reckoning as Summer Time, and therefore adjustment has to be made when horoscopes are being cast so that the time of birth is expressed in Greenwich Mean Time (G.M.T.

for short). On page 138 is a Table which lists the dates during which Summer Time has operated since 1921.

It will be seen that on June 10th, 1947, Double Summer Time was in operation, and therefore we must deduct two hours from the time of birth (2.45 a.m.) of the person in our example to convert it to G.M.T., which means that for horoscope calculations, the time of birth was 0.45 a.m.

Similar conversions to G.M.T. will have to be made to account for different time zones throughout the world. The earth is divided into 24 time zones, and there is an international date line which marks the point where one day becomes the next. The time zone conforming to Eastern Standard time (U.S.A.) is five hours slow in comparison to G.M.T., therefore a person born at 6 p.m. in New York has a G.M.T. birth time of 11 p.m. Central European Time is one hour fast by comparison, so that a G.M.T. birth at 11 p.m., a New York birth at 6 p.m. and a Munich birth at midnight all happen together. All birth times must be converted to G.M.T., whatever the reason for the deviation.

Sidereal Time of Birth. The next step is to find the Sidereal (Star) Time of Birth. This is usually written S.T. for short. The pages of tables given at the beginning of the Ephemeris and headed with the names of the various months give the required information. Turn to page 12, which is for June and look back at the lower half of the page, below the heavy black line. In the first two narrow columns each day of the month and week is given (headed respectively D.M. and D.W.) and then follows a wider column headed Sidereal Time. The times given are always for noon of the date stated. Noon on June 10th would, however, be too late for a birth which took place 45 minutes after midnight, so we will take the S.T. for noon of the *previous* day, June 9th and add on the time between that and 0.45 a.m. For a birth occuring *after* noon, we should use the noon of the actual birthday instead.

"H.M.S." just under "Sidereal Time" at the head of the third column stand for Hours, Minutes, Seconds, so we see that S.T. for June 9th, 1947 was 5 hours 8 minutes and 3 seconds, written, for horoscope purposes:

$$
\begin{array}{ccc}
\text{H} & \text{M} & \text{S} \\
5 & 8 & 3
\end{array}
$$

The time which elapsed between noon on June 9th and 0.45 a.m. on June 10th was 12 hours and 45 minutes, so this must be added to the S.T. For reasons which are complicated and unnecessary to explain, a slight correction must be made in this elapsed time period. This is; make the correction by allowing 59 seconds for each complete period of 6 hours, 10 seconds for each complete hour (beyond or less than the six-hour period or periods) or 1 second for each 6 minutes.

This sounds complicated but you soon get used to it and can make the correction rapidly. Thus, in our particular case, 12 hours 45 minutes contain two complete six-hour periods, so allow twice 59 seconds = 1 minutes 58 seconds. Allow 1 second for each 6 minutes of the 45 minutes remaining = 7½ seconds. Any time less than a second is too trifling to matter in this calculation, so add 7 seconds to the one minute 58 seconds and you have a total of 2 minutes and 5 seconds. Add the elapsed time and the correction to the S.T. already obtained. Below you see it set out sum-wise for quick reference.

	H.	M.	S.
Actual birth time (when two hours are subtracted for Double Summer Time).........................	0	45	0 a.m.
S.T. at previous noon (June 9th)........................	5	8	3
Add time elapsed since previous noon.....................	12	45	0
Add correction		2	5
	17	55	8

Should the answer be over 24 hours (it isn't here) subtract 24 hours from it.

The last figure, 17 hours, 55 minutes, 8 seconds, gives us the correct S.T. for a birth at 0.45 a.m. (G.M.T.) on June 10, 1947, at Greenwich, London, Lewes, Louth, Cambridge, Havre, Angoulême, Tarbes (France) Castellon (Spain) or any other place in any country which is on or close to the 0 degree of longitude. Look in your atlas and you will see this and the other lines of longitude as vertical, numbered lines running straight down the map at equal intervals). All time is reckoned from the 0° which passes through Greenwich. Hence the expression, Greenwich time.

But our map is for a birth at Skipton, in Yorkshire, which is *not* on the 0 meridian or longitude line. As of course you know, local time varies as one travels east or west of Greenwich, because the sun's noon or highest point, as it moves westward, is seen earlier east of Greenwich than west of it. Every degree of longitude that is passed going either east or west from Greenwich makes a slight difference—four minutes—in local time. Skipton is almost exactly on the second meridian or longitude west of Greenwich. Therefore one must reckon twice 4 minutes = 8 minutes difference in time. Now, will Skipton time be slow or fast of Greenwich time?

The rule is simple and easily remembered. For every meridian counting (either way) from 0°, reckon 4 minutes difference in time. For all places west of Greenwich subtract this difference from the Sidereal Time already obtained. For all places *east* of Greenwich add the difference to the Sidereal Time already obtained. In *either case,* if the answer comes to over 24 hours, as it does with some maps, subtract 24 hours from the result.

(Naturally, if the birthplace is somewhere between two degrees of longitude, as very often happens, you will make a corresponding time allowance—2 minutes, 5 minutes, etc. according to the position of the birthplace in the atlas.)

Skipton is west of Greenwich, so we add a bit more to our sum shown on page 98, thus:

	H.	M.	S.
Sidereal time already obtained	17	55	8
Subtract longitude difference		8	0
S.T. at birth	17	47	8

But suppose with the same date and time of birth, the birth-place had been Toulon, in the South of France. This is almost exactly 6 degrees of longitude *east* of Greenwich as the atlas shows us. Allowing 4 minutes per degree, that gives a total of 24 minutes, which must be added to the Standard Time. Thus the sum in that case would be:

	H.	M.	S.
Greenwich Time	17	55	8
Add difference of longitude		24	0
Summer time at birth (Toulon)	18	19	8

These two examples, incidentally, show you how it is that two people born at the same moment on the same day of the same year, but in different places, would have considerably varying horoscopes, because the S.T. for the two places, when worked out, is not the same.

Remember when making calculations for maps that there are 60 seconds in a minute, 60 minutes in an hour, 24 hours in a day; and, when you come to them a little later in these pages, 30 degrees in a sign of the Zodiac.

Finding the Ascendant. Now that you have calculated the corrected Sidereal Time for the exact hour and place of birth, turn to the Tables of Houses which you will find almost at the end of the Ephemeris. You will notice that there are three of these, for London, Liverpool and New York respectively. You use whichever one is nearest in latitude to the place of birth of your particular subject. Look again at your atlas and you will see the latitude lines running *across* each map at regular intervals, crossing the downward longitude lines already mentioned. You look, therefore, to see whether your particular place is *horizontally* nearest to London, Liverpool or New York.

Broadly speaking—latitude in a horoscope is not reckoned nearly as exactly as is longitude—you use the Tables for Liverpool for northern places, the Tables for London for places between north and south and the Tables for New York for southern places. Skipton, of course, is nearest to the Liverpool Table and you will find a helpful list on the cover of the Ephemeris of places covered by each of the three tables. All these are north of the Equator. For places south of it—say in Australia—the same tables are used but with a difference.

Southern Latitude Birth Places. Reckon the Sidereal time just as already described but when you have found it, add twelve hours to it. Having done this, whichever of the three Northern Tables is nearest in latitude to the southern birth place will be correct and you find the nearest S.T. in it just as explained on page 97. Then erect the map—but with this difference. Start with the Fourth House and place against it the sign given in the Table for the Tenth, on the Fifth put the Eleventh House sign and so on. Afterwards fill in the opposite signs just as for a Northern map but similarly reversed.

This, however, is running ahead. To go back to the finding of the Ascendant for our sample map. For Skipton we must obviously use the Tables for Liverpool. Turn to the double page in the Ephemeris which give them. You will see that the wide column headed "Sidereal Time" contains rows of figures graded within the twenty-four hours of a day. Taking the S.T. you have calculated for your June 10 birthdate—17 47 8—look for the nearest time to it in the Liverpool Table. This is 17 46 55. Directly in line with this time, to the right, are six further columns of figures, five narrow and one broad, headed at the top of the page with the numbers of six of the houses in a horoscope and the sign in each. Thus:

Sidereal	10	11	12	Ascen.	2	3
Time	♐	♐	♍	♍	♓	♉

The Ascendant is, of course, the First House, so begin
with this. The Ascendant for S.T. 17 46 55 is 21 degrees 27
minutes (written 21° 27″ ′) of Pisces; for though the Ascendant column, as quoted above, is headed Capricorn, by the

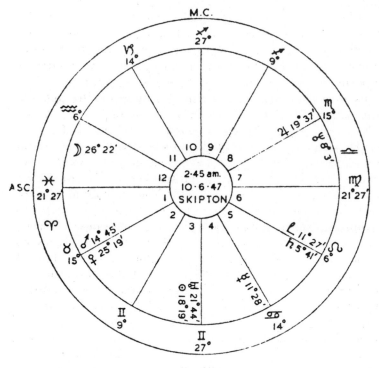

Fig. VI.

Sample map.

time we have got as far down it as our particular S.T. the
signs have changed twice. (Always take the number parallel
with the S.T. and the nearest sign *above* it.) Thus, enter on
the cusp of the first house of your prepared map form   ✕
21° 27′, as in Fig. VII. This diagram shows you, too, how

you take the sign and number of degrees for each house in turn as given in the narrow columns, 10, 11, 12, 1 and 2 and place them, with their number of degrees (only the Ascendant has minutes as well) on the corresponding cusps of the map.

Filling in the 3rd to 9th Houses. This is very simple. As you will see by Fig. VI, each house has an opposite one exactly half way round the circle from it. Thus the Seventh House is opposite the First or Ascendant, the Fourth is opposite the Tenth and so on. Similarly, if you number the signs in order, Aries 1, Taurus 2 and so on through the twelve, you will get these six pairs of opposites: Aries-Libra; Taurus-Scorpio; Gemini-Sagittarius; Cancer-Capricorn; Leo-Aquarius; Virgo-Pisces. All you have to do is to put the opposite sign to each of the six you have already, on the opposite cusp to it, giving it the same number of degrees as its opposing sign has. Now the map is as in Fig. VI.

Intercepted Signs. Go round your signs, naming them in order. You will find that although all twelve cusps are filled, Gemini and Sagittarius occur on two cusps each and consequently two other signs, Aries and Libra, are missing. Signs like these, for which there is no cusp, are called intercepted signs. They only occur in some maps, including the one we are doing, not by any means in all. There are no cusps for the missing signs but put them in (without degrees, for they haven't any) in their correct places inserted or intercepted between their two neighbouring signs—Aries between Pisces on the first cusp and Taurus on the second, in this particular case and Libra opposite between Virgo and Scorpio. Now the map contains, as it must, every one of the twelve signs.

Finding the Planet's Places. The next step is to discover the exact position of each of the planets in the heavens at the moment of birth, so that they can be inserted in the map in their correct positions. On page 26 of the 1947 Ephemeris you will find tables showing the distance each planet moves from one noon to the next throughout the year. Every planet has a different rate of motion.

To find the places of the luminaries (Sun and Moon) and those of the planets Mars, Venus and Mercury—that is, all the faster-moving planets—there is a definite rule which you should keep always in your mind. This rule is:

Add the log. of the planet's daily motion to the log. of the time from the nearest noon and the sum will be the log. of the planet's motion during the number of hours required by the particular horoscope. Add this to the planet's place at noon, if the birth was an a.m. one, but subtract for a p.m. birth. When making this calculation, use the G.M.T. of birth.

This rule probably sounds like Greek to you at the moment! So let's explain by working out the position of the Sun in our sample horoscope for June 10, 1947, 2.45 a.m.

This birth took place in Double Summer Time and its G.M.T., as we have already seen, is 0.45 a.m., almost exactly half way between the noon dates of the planet's daily motions given on page 27, 1947 Ephemeris. However, we must work to the *nearest* noon, which is June 10th. Had the birth been an hour earlier, at 11.45 p.m., the nearest noon would, of course, have been that of June 9th.

Logs. This is the abbreviations used for Proportional Logarithms, a useful set of ready-made calculations which occupy the last page of the Ephemeris. They work like the fare tables you see in some buses, only the logs give degrees or hours in the downward columns and minutes in the crosswise ones. They serve as a sort of horoscopical ready reckoner when finding the planets' places.

To find the Sun's place for June 10th, 1947 at 0.45 a.m., look in the June section on page 27, in the Sun column and you will find that on June 10th the daily motion, between that noon and the next noon, was 57 minutes 21 seconds (printed 57' 21".) For these planetary calculations we only work to the nearest minute and as 21 seconds is less than half a minute, we call the D.M. (daily motion) 57'. To find the log. of this, turn to the end log. page in the Ephemeris and run your pencil down the 0° (degrees or hours) column—since 57' contains no degrees—until it meets the 57 (minutes) crosswise column at 1.4025. Write this figure down.

The time from noon is 11 hours 15 minutes and to find its log. proceed in the same way, finding the junction of the 11 (hours or degrees) column with that of the 15 (minutes) crosswise column. The figure you get is 3291. Note this down also. You will need it for all five of these fast-moving planetary calculations.

Next set down the little sum, thus.

Log. of Sun's D.M., June 10th.....................	1.4025
Log. of time from noon	3291
Add together, making	1,7316 = 0.27

It saves turning to and fro later if at this stage you do as I have done above, "translating" your sum total, by again consulting the logs. back into degrees and minutes—in this case, only 27'. This is the sun's movement between 0.45 a.m. and noon. As the time is earlier than the noon taken, this sum must be subtracted from the noon position to get the actual position of the sun three-quarters of an hour after the previous midnight.

The noon positions of the planets for every day in the year are found in the early pages of the Ephemeris, starting with January on pages 2 and 3, in the section you have already consulted for the S.T. Use the Longitude column for each planet, ignoring those for the Sun and Moon which are labelled Dec. The sun's noon position on June 10th was 18° 46' of Gemini and from this we must subtract the log. of its motion, which we have already turned into degrees in the little sum above.

Here is the remainder of the calculation.

Sun's noon position, June 10th...................	18	11	46'
Subtract log. of planet's motion			27'
Sun's position at 0.45 a.m.	18	11	19'

Remember when making these calculations that there are 60 minutes both in one hour and in one degree of longitude. Remember also that you always *add* the log. of the time from noon to the log of the sum's daily motion (first sum, page 105). But when dealing with the planet's noon position (second sum, page 105) you *subtract* the log. of the planet's motion if the time of birth is an a.m. one, but *add* these together if the time of birth is p.m. I emphasize these points because the calculations of planets' places seem very complicated and confusing at first but once you understand the rules and the use of the log-tables they can be done with fair speed and ease.

Now, working out exactly similarly the Moon's position for the same map, we get this sum:

Log. of Moon's D.M., June 10th (12° 18' nearest
minute) 2,903
Log. of time from nearest noon 3,291
_____
Add, thus obtaining log. of Moon's motion ....   6,194 = 5° 46'
_____
Moon's noon position, June 10th ....2° ♓ 8'
Subtract Moon's motion ....5°   46'

Here we meet with a difficulty that sometimes occurs in these calculations—you can't subtract a larger sum from a smaller one. Obviously, if at noon the Moon had only reached 2°8' of Pisces and it had travelled 5°46' less at 45 minutes after midnight, it would then still be in the last degrees of Aquarius. Therefore, add 30° (the number of degrees in a sign) to the noon position, subtract the Moon's motion and then, to counteract you adding, put the result into the *preceding* sign. Thus:

Moon's noon position, June 10th ....2° ♓ 8'
Add 30° ....30°   0'
_____
32° ♓ 8'
Subtract Moon's motion .... 5°   46'
_____
Moon's position at 0.45 a.m. ....26°♒22'
_____

Mars, Venus and Mercury. Find the positions of these three planets exactly as already explained and worked out for the Sun and Moon.

Jupiter, Saturn, Uranus and Neptune. These four planets move so slowly in a day (in fact Uranus makes no measurable movement at all) that their correct places can be calculated easily in your head, without any need for sums or logs. For example, Jupiter moves only 6′ in the twenty-four hours concerned and so 0.45 a.m. is very nearly half way between one noon and the next, you have only to take the half way point between its position on June 9th—19° ♏ 37′ and that on June 10th—19°♏31′—which gives you 19°♏34′ as a sufficiently correct result. Reckon similarly for Saturn and Uranus, while for Neptune, whose position is the same for both days, you need only put down the position given in the Ephemeris.

You will find these planets' daily positions for June, 1947, not under "Daily Motions of the Planets," but in the lower half of page 13 of the Ephemeris.

Pluto moves so slowly that its position is only given every ten days, not with the other planets already mentioned, but at the foot of page 39 of the Ephemeris. Our date, June 10th, is one of those for which its position is given. For other dates, some very simple mental arithmetic will give you the approximate result.

NOTE.—I have worked out in the examples here and placed in the map (Fig. VI) the positions of the planets, with minutes as well as degrees. Actually, as you will find after a little practice in doing horoscopes, you can safely ignore the minutes altogether, as the difference they make is so trifling. But it occasionally happens, as you will see when we come to inserting the planets in the map, that even a difference of a few minutes may bring the planet over a cusp into another house or sign. Therefore you should know how to calculate the minutes as well as the degrees and always include them if you see that the planet's position brings it very near the junction of two signs or houses.

Similarly, with the slow-moving planets, Jupiter, Saturn, Uranus, Neptune and Pluto, for practical purposes their positions are accurate enough, in nine cases out of ten, if they are entered on the map as they appear in the Ephemeris for the appropriate day. But in the tenth case, when you see that a planet's position is very close to a cusp or the end of a sign, you must reckon it more exactly. This is because Saturn, say, in the first house means one thing and in the second quite another and the same applies if it is placed in the wrong sign.

ANOTHER NOTE.—You are reminded that the Ephemeris page numbers so far given, when working out the sample horoscope, are for the 1947 Ephemeris. But if you are using the one for any other year, at any rate in recent times, you will find the various tables and calculations you need either on the same pages or on corresponding ones if the Ephemeris happens to be a little differently put together.

Inserting the Planets in the Map.—Each planet must be placed in the map not only in its correct sign but in its right house, too. This is quite simple and only needs a little care. Let us take Mercury, which we have calculated to be in 11 degrees 28 minutes of Cancer. On the cusp dividing the Fourth and Fifth Houses (the House numbers are placed round the small centre circle and run, you remember, counter-clockwise) is 14 degrees of Cancer. Thus the cusp dividing the two houses cuts almost midway across the sign Cancer, splitting it into roughly equal halves, the early degrees in the Fourth House, the latter ones in the Fifth. Mercury is in the 11th degree, which is less than the 14th degree on the cusp. Therefore it must be placed in the Fourth House and not the Fifth, which contains only those degrees of Cancer from 14 onwards. As, however, 11 degrees are not very much less than 14, we place Mercury quite close to the cusp, though on its Fourth House side.

The same applies to all the planets. If you notice the degrees of the signs on the cusps and follow them round the map counter-clockwise in their correct order, you will find inserting the planets correctly quite a simple matter. Study Fig. VI, which shows all ten planets inserted in our sample map.

There are one or two special points to note, if you are to keep your maps neat and easy to read. First, two or more planets often fall in the same house—see the Sun and Uranus in Fig. VI, which both come in the Third House. Note here the correct way to place them. Twenty-seven degrees of Gemini are on the fourth cusp. Uranus, which is in 21 degrees, is therefore placed nearer the cusp than the Sun, which has 18 degrees (I have omitted the minutes for brevity). So, before inserting a planet in any house, look to see if there are others in the same house, so that you can place them in their proper sequence.

Again, when a map contains intercepted signs—in ours, Aries and Libra are intercepted—thy have no space of their own and it may not be clear, with the ordinary placing, whether a planet is in the intercepted sign or in one of those on the neighbouring cusps. So insert any planet in an intercepted sign against that sign and *parallel with the inner large circle,* instead of in the usual position parallel to the cusps. Note how this has been done in Fig. VI, making it clear at a glance that Neptune is in intercepted Libra and cannot possibly be confused with Jupiter, near by, in Scorpio.

In the small centre circle it is convenient to put the name or initials of the owner (native, in astrological terms) of the map, with the place, date and time of birth.

Now the map is completed and ready for reading, as in the simplified beginner's version of astrology I am giving here I am leaving out of account certain minor points, such as the Dragon's Head and Tail and the Part of Fortune, which are not very important, but entail separate rather wearisome calculations.

It is a good plan, however, before starting on the reading of the horoscope, to tabulate the aspects handily for easy reference during the reading. This should be done preferably in astrological ''shorthand'' on the same piece of paper as the map; but if there is not room, use a separate sheet and clip the two together.

All about the Aspects

The Table of Aspects given on page 93, with remarks immediately following and Fig. V (page 92), will help you to grasp this section of astrology. Of the nine aspects listed in the Table, you should begin by getting familiar with the five major ones, namely, the conjunction, sextile, square, trine and opposition. The other four, though useful, are of less importance.

The table gives you the number of signs apart planets must be to form the various aspects and also their degrees of operation (or orbs of influence, to use the techical term). These orbs, as you will see by the table, vary from 2 to 7 degrees, according to the aspect.

Signs are in aspect by their position in the Zodiac only —thus, Taurus is in trine to both Virgo and Capricorn, because it is four signs apart (backward) from Capricorn and four signs apart (forward) from Virgo. But planets in Capricorn and Taurus, or in Taurus and Virgo, are only in trine to each other if they are also within the degrees of operation (orbs of influence), which, for the trine aspect (in fact, for all five major aspects) are 7 degrees.

Thus, in our sample map (Fig. VI) the Sun and Uranus are in Gemini, the Moon in Aquarius and Neptune in Libra. These three signs, Gemini, Libra and Aquarius, are trine to each other. But of the four planets in them, not all are in aspect. The Moon in 26° of Aquarius is within 7° of Uranus in 21° of Gemini. But between the Moon and the Sun in 18° of Gemini, also between both

Moon and Sun and Neptune in 8° of Libra, the number of degrees in each case is too great for a trine aspect.

Take another example, this time the conjunction. Uranus and the Sun are both in Gemini and within 3 degrees (Sun 18°, Uranus 21°) of each other. As the conjunction has an orb up to 7 degrees, these two planets are easily in conjunction.

To find several of the major aspects quickly and easily here are some aids to memory.

(a) The Fire Signs (see Fig. V) are all in trine to each other. The Air Signs (see Fig. V) are all in trine to each other. The Earth Signs (see Fig. V) are all in trine to each other. The Water Signs (see Fig. V) are all in trine to each other.

(b) The following pairs of signs are in opposition to each other: Aries is in opposition to Libra; Taurus to Scorpio; Gemini to Sagittarius; Cancer to Capricorn; Leo to Aquarius; Virgo to Pisces. The houses in which they are placed (numbered in Figs. V and VI) are similarly in opposition to each other.

(c) Now refer to the list of Cardinal, Fixed and Mutable signs given on page 91. Each sign in the Cardinal group is square to the sign after and before it—thus, Aries is square to Cancer and Capricorn and Cancer is square to Aries and Libra. Each sign in the fixed group is similarly square to the Fixed sign before and after it and the same applies to the signs in the Mutable (Common) group.

(d) Positive and negative signs are listed on page 91. Each positive sign is sextile to the next positive sign before and after it—thus, Gemini is sextile to Aries and Leo. Each negative sign is similarly sextile to the next negative sign, both forward and back, e.g., Pisces is sextile to Taurus and Capricorn.

The four minor aspects—the semi-sextile, semi-square, sesqui-square and quincunx—present one aspect very simple to spot at sight and three which are more difficult than the major aspects.

The semi-sextile—one sign away in either direction, is simplicity itself. Thus, Libra is semi-sextile both to Virgo and to Scorpio. For the quincunx (five complete signs) the easiest plan is to find the opposition sign (see (b), page 111) and then count one sign *backward*. Thus, Leo is in opposition to Aquarius; count one sign back to Capricorn; Capricorn is therefore in quincunx aspect to Leo.

The semi-square and sesqui-square each involve half a sign (semi-square, 1½ signs; sesqui-square, 4½ signs). A sign contains 30°, so half a sign is 15°. Add these 15° on first to the number of degrees of the planet concerned, then count forward one complete sign for the semi-square or four complete signs for the sesqui-square. For example, on our sample map, Neptune in Libra 8° looks as if it might be in sesqui-square to the Moon in Aquarius 26°. To make certain, first add 15° to Libra 8°, resulting in Libra 23°. Four complete signs forward from this gives as Aquarius 23°. The orb for this aspect is up to and including 3°, so the Moon in Aquarius 26° is just in sesqui-square with Neptune in Libra 8°.

Remember, by the way, that the orb of influence of any aspect is *up to and including* the figure given for it in the table on page 93. A square aspect, for instance, need not be exactly 7 degrees—it may be 7° or any less number, but *not more*.

The Meaning of the Aspects.—The Aspect table (page 93) gives the general result of each aspect, whether good or bad, slightly or markedly so. But for a good reading of the map you need to know just how and in what direction the various aspects affect the horoscope. Here are important points to note. (They work, of course, through the nature of the planets, signs and houses involved in the particular aspect.)

The Conjunction and Opposition have an intensifying effect, bringing into a prominence which may be good or bad, but cannot be ignored, the matters denoted by the planets, signs and houses concerned.

The Semi-Sextile has a mildly beneficial effect, bringing some development and increase.

The Semi-Square denotes a certain amount of friction, which will prove irritating and may cause impatient, impulsive action.

The Sextile brings opportunities or the power to create them. Whether they are made use of or not depends on the horoscope. With this aspect seize your chance, don't just wait for something to drop in your lap.

The Square sets up formidable barriers to progress which are not easily overcome and make the native feel limited and frustrated. This aspect calls for firm, patient effort, not sitting down under so-called "bad luck."

With the Trine, things go your way and luck is with you. Under this aspect good things *do* drop into your lap and you have only to catch and use them.

The Sesqui-Square relates chiefly to the feelings. The native tends to be hindered by his own emotional disturbances. He is inclined to quarrel and finds it difficult to make wise decisions. Calmness and patience should be cultivated under this aspect.

The Quincunx is rather like the Semi-Sextile, with this difference—that if the Sun, Moon, Mercury, Venus or Jupiter are concerned, the results will be mildly good, as with the Semi-Sextile. But with Mars, Saturn, Uranus, Neptune or Pluto the results will be somewhat unfavourable, though with Saturn, concentration and with Neptune, ability to make use of helpful suggestions, will minimise the difficulties.

But aspects, though explained here for convenience, come only at a fairly late stage of reading a map. We will start now at the beginning and arrive at them in their turn.

How to Read a Horoscope

You have cast your map or horoscope and now you must interpret it. This is naturally far more interesting to most people than making the preliminary calculations, and it is in the interpretation or reading of a map that an astrologer uses his or her experience and shows his or her skill. Every sign, house and planetary position and every aspect has several possible interpretations and the astrologer must use his judgement and knowledge to decide which is the truest one that best fits the particular nativity on which he is working. A balanced mind and a sound knowledge of human nature are just as important to good results as accurate calculations and remembering all the rules.

Above all, PRACTICE is needed. Don't be discouraged if your first few maps take hours to work out and your first few readings of them are even longer, because you have to keep looking things up. Speed, ease and sureness of judgment all come with experience.

The Order to Follow.—You will get the best and easiest results by working to a definite plan. Always read the character first, before the events of the life, because character, to quite a large extent, determines what the native will do with his or her opportunities and difficulties.

For character, consider, in the order given:

(1) The Ascendant or Rising Sign.
(2) The Ruling Planet, with its house and sign positions.
(3) The Sun Sign (or Solar Sign).
(4) The Moon Sign (or Lunar Sign).
(5) Mercury's Sign.

These five points in the horoscope give you the basic character of the native and therefore form, as it were, the firm foundation of your reading. Afterwards (and only afterwards) you should study the various houses, with the signs and planets in them, and the aspects, to get an idea of the run of the native's life and his good fortune or otherwise in career, money, marriage and so on.

Don't try to pick out titbits, such as love affairs, or legacies, at random. What is given in the following pages about any particular planet, house or sign can only be assessed reliably if it is considered in perspective, so to speak, to the life as a whole.

The Ascendant or Rising Sign. —(Really, Rising Sign is the better term, because the Ascendant can also mean the whole of the First House, whereas the term Rising Sign always means the sign on the cusp of the First House and nothing else.) The Rising Sign is the most important of the five indications listed on page 114 for judging character. You must modify its indications by those given by the other four, but it always remains predominant.

The Rising Sign gives a picture of the native's temperament and instinctive attitude towards life when alone and free to express himself without outside interference or the pressure of other personalities. It also describes in a general way the personal appearance, though this will be modified by the sign in which the Ruling Planet is placed and also by the Moon's Sign.

The Signs of the Zodiac

For character studies of the twelve Signs, see the pen pictures given in easily memorised rhyme for Solar Horoscopes, on pages 68 to 79; also the Additional Traits listed below each jingle. But ignore the "Her Life" paragraphs, which are too generalised to apply to the individually cast horoscopes with which we are dealing here.

Below is the sort of physical appearance likely with each sign rising, though it may be modified considerably by the traits of the Moon's Sign and that in which the Ruling Planet is placed.

Aries Rising. —A rather thin body of medium height, large-boned and with strong arms and legs and rather broad shoulders. Hair brown or red-brown, usually wavy, skin dry and dark or florid, eyes usually brown.

Taurus Rising. —Short, plump figure, with short, thick neck. Dark, rather curly hair, a full face with wide mouth and nostrils. Full lips and rather dark skin.

Gemini Rising.—Figure tall and held very straight, with long arms and thin hands and feet. Quick, bright eyes, usually hazel, and other colouring rather dark.

Cancer Rising.—Of medium height and rather broadly built. Features small and colouring usually subdued—dull brown hair, pale complexion and rather small grey eyes.

Leo Rising.—Medium height and broad shoulders, with a good carriage and much dignity. Enthusiastic eyes, generally brown or hazel and thick, fairish hair, with a round or oval face.

Virgo Rising. Slender, of middle height, with a good figure and neat appearance. A noticeably long nose in a pleasant, rather high-coloured face.

Libra Rising.—This sign of all others gives beauty to women. The height varies from medium to rather tall, with a graceful figure. Round, well-shaped face with beautiful clear complexion, fine large eyes, either blue or green. Smooth, well-burnished hair, usually blonde, but occasionally black.

Scorpio Rising.—Strong, stocky body of medium height, with rather gliding, snake-like walk. A square or wide face, thick dark brown hair, with shrewd-looking eyes of brown or grey.

Sagittarius Rising.—Rather tall and well-formed, with good, athletic bearing. Face noticeably long, with a high forehead and long nose and a good skin. Light brown or reddish-brown hair, and brown eyes, which are normally round and wide-open.

Capricorn Rising.—This sign seldom runs to good looks. The body is short and slender, but not graceful, the chest narrow and the knees weak. Thin neck, long, protruding chin and very dark brown or black hair.

Aquarius Rising.—This sign confers good looks, especially on men, but to a lesser extent on women. Strong body of medium height, with a long face. Clear, rosy and delicate skin, hair blonde or light brown and attractive blue or hazel eyes.

Pisces Rising. —Short and broadly built, with a tendency to round shoulders. Large, pale face, very expressive, with a clear skin. Eyes (usually dark blue or grey) rather prominent, hair rather dark and a soft voice.

The Ruling Planet, as explained on page 94, is the planet which rules the Rising Sign. As you will see by the table of signs and their rulers (page 90), if the Rising Sign is Pisces, as in our Sample Map in Fig. VI, the Ruling Planet will be Jupiter, with Neptune as a "junior partner," whose influence is also taken into account. But most of the signs, as the table shows, have only a single ruler each.

All the planets appear in every horoscope, but the Ruling Planet is of more importance in judging character than any others, except the Sun and Moon. So special attention should be paid to its characteristics, as given below. If the Sun or Moon should also happen to be the Ruling Planet, then its effect becomes even greater.

The aspects made by the Ruling Planet should be specially noted, as their influence is strong. Good aspects to it bring out its virtues, whereas bad aspects intensify its faults.

The Sun

Physical Appearance. —Large, lion-like head with thick mane of hair, though baldness often comes early. Large, rather protuberant eyes, skin generally sunburnt or freckled.

Characteristics. —Very proud, ambitious and firm-willed, with a tendency to showing off generally and dandyism in dress. Vain, ardent, enthusiastic, able to organise and lead. Marked ability for arts and handicrafts.

Health. —The Sun shows the vitality and natural strength of the constitution. Its weak spots, where disease is most likely to occur are the circulation, the heart and the eyes.

Occupations. —Government or Local Government employment. Running own business or where authority and organisation are required.

Finance. —Usually good and steady, with money coming

by favour of superiors, by legacy from the father or by wise investment.

Love and Marriage. —There may not always be harmony in wedlock, which often occurs rather late. But the marriage brings financial and social advancement.

Travel. —Long journeys, especially by land and to hot countries.

The Moon

Physical Appearance. —Pale, round face, short limbs, small hands and feet. Often a jerky walk and one eye a little larger than the other.

Character. —Fond of change, variable in mood and easily influenced, yet capable of great tenacity. Imaginative, sociable, loving ease, peace and home.

Health. —The Moon governs functional ailments rather than organic ones. Weak spots are the stomach, breasts and (in women) the womb. Health is best when the Moon is in a negative sign.

Occupations. —Those dealing with women are concerned with liquids or domestic affairs. Publicity and advertising.

Finance. —There are many ups and downs in income. Legacies may come from the mother or women relatives.

Love and Marriage. —Moon people often have difficulty in deciding to marry, but wedlock usually turns out happy, though the marriage may not be considered financially or socially very good.

Travel. —Home is generally preferred to getting about, but there may be some long voyages.

Mercury

Physical Appearance. —Spare in figure, quick and nimble in movement. Long face with sharp nose and bright, hard eyes. Thick hair.

Character. Good mental ability, with quickness, ingenuity and some secrecy or slyness. Inquisitive and rather superficial. Restless, a good talker yet reserved. Often more head than heart.

Health.—Mercury governs the hands and arms, the respiration, the nerves and the mental faculties, such as memory. These are all possible weak spots.

Occupations.—Methods of communication, such as the railways, postal and telephone services. Clerical work, teaching, journalism, printing and bookselling.

Finance.—Best where the turnover is quick or for work done on commission or piece-work, rather than a settled salary.

Love and Marriage.—The marriage partner is likely to be younger and the match based on affection and companionship rather than romantic love.

Travel.—There is a decided liking for travel and holidays abroad and some long journeys are likley.

Venus

Physical Appearance.—Beautiful when Venus is on or near the Ascendant. Otherwise a rather short, graceful person with good legs. Soft dewy eyes, with eyebrows darker than the hair and a small red mouth, usually with dimples.

Character.—Fond of beauty in any form, including personal adornment, jewellery and perfume. Kind, jealous, very sociable, careless and artistic.

Health.—Venus governs the veins and venous system. These are weak spots, also the throat, ovaries and kidneys.

Occupations.—Those concerned with pleasure, entertainment luxury, such as music, the theatre, jewellery, perfumery and the arts. Also banking and finance.

Finance.—Usually money prospects are good and wealth or, at least, prosperity, tends to flow to Venus subjects, whether through their careers, investments in firms dealing with luxuries, legacy or a fortunate marriage.

Love and Marriage.—The marriage is generally both

happy and good in a worldly sense, and children bring much bliss with them.

Travel. —Whether for pleasure or profit, travel, specially to beautiful places, is much enjoyed.

Mars

Physical Appearance. —Rather stocky, muscular build, with prominent jaw, giving a rugged look. Often a ruddy complexion, red or reddish hair and grey eyes. The face lines early.

Character. —Energetic, fearless, a good fighter, independent and quick-tempered. Plenty of ardour and impulse and any kind of regimentation is much disliked. Often lacking in self-discipline and tact.

Health. —Usually ample bodily vigour and strength, but when out of sorts the tendency is towards fevers, muscular troubles, injuries, such as burns, or ailments of the nose.

Occupations. —Mechanical and constructional occupations, such as engineering, the Army, athletic jobs, medicine (especially surgery) or work connected with fire, such as smelting, Fire Service or blacksmithing.

Finance. —A good and quick earner, but extravagance and carelessness with money often cause financial difficulties. Mars people should not lend to others.

Love and Marriage. —Love affairs are apt to be violent and short-lived, and the union to suffer from the proverb about marrying in haste. Wedlock usually comes early and sometimes twice.

Travel. —On the whole this is not very fortunate.

Jupiter

Physical Appearance. —Bulky figure, becoming stout in later life, with long feet. High forehead, clear skin, fine large eyes and big teeth.

Character. —Very dignified (sometimes pompous), optimistic, jovial and conventional. Popular, kind and generous, with a strong respect for the law, religion and ritual.

Health. —Jupiter governs the arteries and the digestive system and the liver. Illnesses most likely to occur are boils, gout, pleurisy, diabetes or apoplexy.

Occupations. —Professions, particularly the Church or the law and businesses connected with foreign countries, or the food and clothing trades.

Finance. —Very little risk of poverty and often considerable wealth, especially through travel, shipping, the land and inheritance.

Love and Marriage. —The partner is often older and may have been wedded before. Marriage should be very happy and prosperous and children bring contentment.

Travel. —Short journeys, especially, are very happy and profitable. Success is likely in foreign lands.

Saturn

Physical Appearance. —Tall, broad-shouldered figure, with large feet and often a slow, shuffling walk. Serious face, mostly downbent, skin dark and without colour, lips rather thick.

Character. —Cautious, with plenty of endurance, steadfast and a person of habit. Plenty of patience, perseverance and frugality, with a tendency to pessimism. An old character, even in youth, and therefore at its best in old age.

Health. —Saturn governs the bones, the spleen and the knee-cap and tends to cause obstruction, showing in such ailments as constipation, deafness, colds, tuberculosis, bad teeth and rheumatism.

Occupations. —Those connected with the land, such as farming and mining, also politics and commerce.

Finance. —Gains come through plodding, hard work and by investment in land, but money is only acquired slowly and with effort.

Love and Marriage. —If badly aspected, there may be on

marriage, or a late one. The partner, if marriage takes place, will probably be older.

Travel.—Apt to be disappointing or undertaken for sad reasons rather than for pleasure or profit.

Uranus

Physical Appearance.—Tall, slender and long-limbed, moving erratically and quickly, with plenty of nervous energy. Noticeable eyebrows.

Character.—Original, unconventional and rather eccentric, with strong opinions and a liking for out-of-the-way interests. World-wide and idealistic views, capable of heroism, abrupt and sarcastic in manner. In brief—an oddity.

Health.—Uranus gives a tendency to shock and accidents, spasmodic diseases, rupture or stricture.

Occupations.—Unusual careers, especially in science, mathematics, astronomy, astrology, wireless and advertising.

Finance.—Violent monetary ups-and-downs and it is always the unexpected that happens.

Love and Marriage.—Plenty of romance, often an unconventional union or an unexpected marriage, perhaps followed by divorce.

Travel.—There is a liking for travel and change, and for setting some distance from the home of childhood. Journeys will often be sudden and unexpected.

Neptune

Physical Appearance.—Slim when young and often beautiful. Artistic looking, with fine pointed fingers and a dreamy manner. The face wrinkles badly at a comparatively early age.

Character.—Indecisive, changeable, romantic and sensitive. Often lazy, without much self-control, but full of inspiration and psychic gifts. Emotional, intuitive, difficult to understand, artistic and musical.

Health.—There is some tendency to suffer from poisoning,

drug-taking, sleep-walking, obsession and nervous disorders which are not well understood and are difficult to
cure.

Occupation.—The drug and film trades, photography,
psychiatry, an artistic career using inspiration, or one
connected with liquids, particularly oil.

Finance.—Money may be made in strange ways, but there
is a likelihood of trusting others too much and so being
exploited or defrauded, or of just frittering money away.

Love and Marriage.—There is a tendency to fall in love with
people blind, lame or in some way afflicted, and to bring
great romance and idealism into marriage, or perhaps make
it only a platonic union.

Travel.—Strange experiences occur during journeys and
they are not always favourable.

Pluto

This planet was discovered so recently (1930) that not
very much is known about its influence, but the following
suggestions will be helpful.

It is believed to control annihilation and transformation
and to govern the atom and atomic energy. It has a general
Mars-like tendency, on a larger and more violent scale. Its
influence of human horoscopes seems to be generally
disturbing. But the disturbance is not necessarily bad
however upsetting it may be at the time. It may destroy
conditions which have outlived their usefulness and yet
which we have not the courage to break away from and
bring unforeseen new developments which will alter the
whole of life for the better.

On page 114 I gave five main points to consider in assess-
ing character by the horoscope. Having dealt with the
Rising Sign and the Ruling Planet, we now come to the
third of these, the Sun or Solar Sign.

The Sun Sign.—The sign in which the Sun was placed
at birth—it was in Gemini, in our sample horoscope
(Fig. VI)—shows the inner or private individuality

and corresponds to the Heart Number in a Numberscope (see page 164). Your Solar Sign represents the you that only you know. It is seen partly, perhaps, by your marriage partner and one or two intimate friends, but remains secret from the world in general. According to his Sun Sign, you, as astrologer, may lift the veil and see a person as he is in his inmost heart, his true feelings and his real ideals and wishes for himself.

Study the rhymed Solar Horoscopes, with their Additional Traits given below each (see pages 68 to 79) to find this important hidden keynote to the character of the person whose horoscope you are reading.

Fourth of our five main pointers to character is the Moon's Sign or Lunar Sign.

The Moons's Sign is, of course, the sign in which the Moon is placed at birth. In our sample horoscope, for instance (see Fig. VI), the Moon is in Aquarius. The Lunar Sign shows a person as he exhibits himself to the world—not his inner self, indicated by the Sun Sign—but the mask he wears in public to cloak that inner self. It is this mask which is seen by people, who only know him slightly or not at all and only gradually, as he makes friends with people, that he gives them glimpses of his Solar Side. The Moon's sign may therefore be said to indicate personality.

Here are brief indications of the Moon's influence in each of the twelve signs.

MOON IN ARIES. Great love of change, fits of enthusiasm which do not last, much restlessness, ambition and independence. You need to curb the emotions and develop patience and stability.

MOON IN TAURUS. Here the Moon is well-placed and should bring happy and lasting friendships and good money conditions. You are sociable, patient and quietly firm, but need to be more adaptable and to restrain jealousy and obstinacy.

MOON IN GEMINI. You are good at detail and thought interests you more than feeling. You like writing, books, literature and having two or three irons in the fire. Cultivate more tact.

MOON IN CANCER. You are very sensitive and a great lover of peace and harmony, rather thrifty and careful, hating waste. You probably resemble your mother a good deal in character, are domesticated and yet love change and travel.

MOON IN LEO. Strong-willed, self-reliant, ambitious, anxious for success and authority. You are imaginative and generous and a good friend; but be more methodical and spend less on dress and pleasures.

MOON IN VIRGO. You are very practical and orderly, fitted to work under others rather than to command. People like you. Adapt yourself to them rather than them to you and don't worry so much.

MOON IN LIBRA. You are popular and sociable, likely to be well in the public eye and to marry fortunately. You are artistic and could succeed in interior decorating but need to be more energetic.

MOON IN SCORPIO. Plenty of will-power, energy and impulse with the Moon in this sign and you take violent likes and dislikes. Don't be quite so set in your ways and cultivate diplomacy.

MOON IN SAGITTARIUS. You're quick, impetuous and restless in all you do, inclined to overwork, with some talent for art or music. Try to be thorough as well as quick and to develop more staying-power. You are likely to travel and change your occupation, perhaps more than once.

MOON IN CAPRICORN. You are patient, persevering and cautious, rather self-contained and often appear cold to others. There is good business ability and you should work with or for a number of people rather than a few. Let yourself go more and develop greater optimism.

MOON IN AQUARIUS. You possess intuition, originality and independence and many friends. Social success comes to you and you may cultivate psychic ability. Politics and education draw you.

MOON IN PISCES. Emotions and sensitivity are strong

and you easily react to your surroundings. You like change, particularly changes of residence. You are easy-going but need more energy and persistence.

The fifth and last character indication is the sign position of Mercury. This is important because it show's your type of mind and abilities, which in turn will influence your personality, your choice of a career and your success in it.

Here are some pointers to Mercury's effect in each of the twelve Signs.

MERCURY IN ARIES. Your mind is restless, quick, witty and aggressive, with an ability for books, writing and public speaking. You can decide quickly and argue cleverly. Try to curb sarcasm and exaggerations.

MERCURY IN TAURUS. Good concentration but the mind works rather slowly and is not adaptable enough. Persistence and determination are your main assets, with musical or artistic skill. Business and finance also make an appeal.

MERCURY IN GEMINI. Here's a quick clever person who can profit by higher education—but what a Jack of all trades! Try to concentrate more and decide things more promptly. You like travel, especially short journeys and could succeed at astrology, science or teaching.

MERCURY IN CANCER. Yours is, above all, a practical mind—you want everything to work, be useful and advantageous. Even your intuition and imagination are used practically. A job which calls for travel, study or some kind of writing would suit you.

MERCURY IN LEO. You are dramatic, strong-minded, firm and far-thinking and could succeed in the theatre, the educational world or in a public body or concern. Don't, however, overlook small but important details.

MERCURY IN VIRGO. You learn easily and will repay a really good education—educate yourself if other opportunities are lacking. You are versatile and could succeed in many directions—clerical or secretarial work, music, a travelling job, science or perhaps literary criticism.

MERCURY IN LIBRA. You have intuition, good taste

and are very sociable, so choose a job in which you deal directly with people. Preferably it should be of a scientific kind.

MERCURY IN SCORPIO. You are determined, tactful and active-minded, with both shrewdness and prejudice in your viewpoint. You concentrate well and show ability for drawing, engineering, chemistry, science, languages and medicine.

MERCURY IN SAGITTARIUS. Yours is a deep and philo-sophical mind, interested in religion and history, but you are inclined to take up too many studies and not persist long enough with each. You should work with one or more others rather than alone.

MERCURY IN CAPRICORN. Your memory is good, your mind clear and you easily accumulate information, which comes in very useful. You have a practical, tactful outlook and ability for business or politics. Don't overdo caution.

MERCURY IN AQUARIUS. You're always in the forefront with new ideas, especially about education. You think for yourself, memorise easily and have ability to succeed as a teacher, an agent, manager or scientist or in the aviation world.

MERCURY IN PISCES. You are intuitive and easily know how people are thinking and feeling, which gives you ability for the stage, films, music, nursing or as a detective. You like to do two jobs at once and need more concentration.

Contradictions of Character. When working out character indications in a horoscope, through the five points which I have given, you will often find that one indication seems to contradict another. Your subject appears to be, shall we say, both energetic and lazy or tactful according to one indication and blunt according to another.

Well, people *are* contradictory. No one is consistent all through. Look round among your family and friends and you will see how true this is. An astrologer must accept these contradictions, balance one against the other and try to fit them reasonably into the character as a whole. It's no good saying, "That *can't* be right!" and throwing overboard some trait which seems to you not to fit but is really an integral part of your friend's make-up.

Look in the signs and houses to see in what departments the opposing traits operate. Thus, a person lazy at work may be most energetic in sport or someone who works hard in the office may be slack and indolent when it comes to washing up at home! Again, the lady who is tactful with her boss may speak her mind rather too frankly among her friends, where there is no fear of losing her job; and so on. In another case a friend may be diplomatic or the reverse by fits and starts, according to the mood of the moment.

You will find a character reading for our sample horoscope on page 133 and by following it you will see how the various points I have explained are combined and weighed against each other to form a clear idea of the personality.

Now, having summed up character, we look to see what the horoscope tells us of the events of a person's life.

Happenings shown in the Horoscope

There are no two moments in life when your horoscope (or anyone else's) is exactly alike. The Signs, at their appointed season, move round to the same positions in the houses as they held at birth or some other given time. The Planets also have their unchanging orbits. But because they all move at different speeds, they are continually in different positions in relation to each other, even when they get back to the same spots in the Signs or Houses. Thus a person's life never exactly repeats itself, although generally similar conditions may come back at stated intervals. This perpetual variety, within a familiar framework, means that astrology is always fascinating and never becomes monotonous.

The Twelve Houses

While the Signs and the Planets indicate character and the type of events which are likely to happen, the twelve

Houses through which the Signs and Planets move show the department of life in which the events or personality will manifest themselves. Remember, by the way, when considering the Houses, that through them the Signs move counter-clockwise; and the Houses themselves are numbered in the same way. But the planets progress always in the reverse direction—clockwise.

In some respects the twelve Houses correspond with the twelve Signs, the First House with Aries, the Second with Taurus and so on. But as the Signs move through the Houses while the latter remain stationary, each Sign will at one time or another go through every house. Therefore, when reading a horoscope, you must always consider the influence of the Sign in the particular House in which it is placed at the moment; also the influence of any planet or planets in the same part of the heavens not merely as themselves, but as they will operate through that particular sign and house.

The departments of life covered by each of the twelve houses are given below:

First House. This house contains the Rising Sign and therefore shows the temperament; also the physical appearance, though this, as explained on page 115, is often modified by the signs in which the Ruling Planet and the Moon are placed. It has to do with the general course of the life and much concerns health. Then it indicates the part of the body—the head—which is chiefly liable to illness or injury. Think of it mainly as the Personality House.

Second House. This is the principal money house and from it, more than any other, you judge of a person's financial standing during life and his or her attitude towards money. The Fifth, Eighth and Eleventh govern particular aspects of finance, so consider them also, but to a lesser extent. In health matters, this House governs the neck and throat. But think of it mainly as the Money House.

Third House. Its province is your own relatives, particularly brothers and sisters, neighbours, local affairs, short journeys, letters and papers and your mental abilities.

From the health standpoint it governs the arms, shoulders, nerves and lungs. Think of it mainly as the (things and people) Close-to-You House.

Fourth House. This governs the home and family affairs, the immediate conditions surrounding you (environment) and the end of things—whether death or any other form of finality. Thus it indicates what conditions will be in old age, as life closes. The parts of the body under its control are the chest, breasts, liver and stomach. Think of it mainly as the Home House.

Fifth House. It broadly governs two departments of life—pleasure and creation. Pleasure includes such things as the theatre and other entertainment, gambling, food and cooking, bathing, etc. Creation, in its widest sense, embraces not only the children we bring into the world but creative work—in the arts, for instance. New enterprises and *speculative* money affairs are also included. On the health side the heart and back are chiefly concerned. Think of this mainly as the House of Pleasure.

Sixth House. This house is concerned with servants, employees or those inferior to you generally, also the routine or drudgery part of daily life, service for others, superstition and small annoyances. In a general way it shows your health and in particular it govern the bowels and solar plexus. Think of it mainly as the Service House.

Seventh House. Partnerships, whether business or marriage ones, come into this house. So do public affairs, laws and lawsuits and open enemies. The parts of the body it rules are the kidneys, veins and bladder. Think of this mainly as the Marriage House.

Eighth House. This governs death and money connected with death, such as inheritance or legacies; also the marriage or business partner's money as it affects yourself. There is a secret aspect about the eighth, which is concerned with secret wishes, secret undertakings and, from the health standpoint, the secret parts of the body, the sex organs. Think of it mainly as the House of Death.

Ninth House. With the Third, it covers travel, the Third denoting short journeys, while the Ninth governs long ones. It has much to do with overseas affairs. It also controls intellectual, "high-brow" matters, such as religion, science and philosophy and the expansion of the mind by travel and study. In health the Ninth governs the thighs and (with the Third) the nerves. Think of it mainly as the Travel House.

Tenth House. This is a very important house, corresponding to the Mid-Heaven or highest point of the horoscope. It rules honour, ambition and the career and in a general way shows how far you will get in realising your ambitions and how high your reputation will stand. It also governs your father, employers and superiors generally and (in health matters) the knees and bones. Think of it mainly as the Career House.

Eleventh House. This has to do with social life (friends and acquaintance) and also work associates. It governs your wishes and hopes and, financially, the money you gain from your occupation. The parts of the body ruled by it are the ankles and the blood. Think of it mainly as the Friends House.

Twelfth House. Astrologers often give this house a very bad name and ascribe to it nothing but misery. Actually, like any other house, it has its good and bad points. It is concerned chiefly with the private and inner you, which is often difficult to understand (hence, perhaps, its unfavourable reputation) and the troubles which, wittingly or unwittingly, you bring on yourself by being what you are. It governs solitude, secrecy and restrictions (all of which may bring benefits as well as draw-backs) secret enemies, the acquiring of wisdom and institutions such as hospitals and prisons; also the feet. A mixed bag, decidedly, but think of it mainly as the House of Growth.

Above and Below the Earth. The first six houses are said to be below the earth—that is, out of sight. When signs and planets are in these houses, their force is felt chiefly in your own self and, so to speak, behind the scenes. When you have many planets below the earth you will feel neglected and unrecognised and that your life and work are being largely wasted.

The other six houses, from the Seventh to the Twelfth inclusive, are above the earth, where they can be seen and receive the warmth of the sunshine, as it were. Then their influence is felt in the outside world and you receive recognition, attention, popularity and reward for what you have achieved so quietly in the preceding period below the earth.

It is usually when Saturn emerges into the Seventh that life becomes more public and rewarding and when this planet enters the First that a period of dull (but growth-making) obscurity begins. Remember, a plant must be firmly rooted out of sight under the soil before it can spring up into the sunshine and flower gloriously.

The Aspects must now be taken into account. They were fully explained earlier (pages 92 and 110), so refer back to this part of the book. They show, of course, how one event or circumstance affects another, helping it, hindering it or neutralising it, according to which aspect it is. Nothing that happens in our lives stands by itself—it is pushed or pulled or affected in some way by other happenings or by influences outside ourselves or in our own personalities. Interpret aspects in this kind of way, judging the type of event from the planets and signs concerned, the department of life affected by the houses concerned, and the influences at work by the aspect or aspects.

It is wise when doing your first two or three horoscopes to simplify things for yourself by considering only the three or four most important aspects you find in the map—those to the Sun, Moon or Ruling Planet and/or the "Big Five" among aspects, which are the Conjunction, Opposition, Sextile, Trine and Square. The other four, which only affect the life in a much smaller way, may be left out of account until you have had more experience in reading a map.

In fact, this applies all through astrology. Start with the most important things in a reading, picking out thus a few high lights. Then, as you gain confidence with practice, you can delve into the details as well and so make your reading fuller and better balanced.

Brief Horoscope Reading of Sample Map (Fig. VI)

Person born at Skipton, June 10, 1947, at 2.45 a.m.

You are kind, sympathetic and emotional. In childhood you will have probably shown good imagination and creative ability for music and acting. You should learn tidiness and to curb your moods (Rising Sign, Pisces). You tend to be a little greedy, thinking you can never have too much of a good thing, but you have plenty of enthusiasm and generosity. You are law-abiding and want to do the accepted thing socially but are a bit lazy. (Ruling Planet, Jupiter, with Neptune as "junior partner.")

At heart you are versatile, loving movement and change and feel that you would rather persuade than command, rather sell than manage (Sun Sign, Gemini). But to other people you seem essentially an executive, with considerable ability to lead and teach and you will probably sooner or later find yourself at the head of affairs (Moon in Aquarius). You are both practical and intellectual, using even your imagination in a practical way to get results (Mercury in Cancer). With Cancer in the Fourth (home) house you would make an ideal head-master or head-mistress of a boarding-school. There is also talent for secretarial work, writing or the printing trade.

Though you seem calm, you are highly strung and much inclined to day-dream and worry. Relax as much as possible to offset this tendency (Sun conjunction Uranus).

Your life will be much controlled by the actions of others and also by deaths in the family or around you. Your emotions and secret wishes play a powerful part, too (Ruling Planet in Eighth).

Money prospects seem good, though rather fluctuating. You need to work hard for what you make and should save—but you are not of a saving nature and your love of good living and comfort tends to extravagance (Moon square Jupiter). You should profit through women or feminine affairs or through people met socially. You probably receive legacies from business associates but there will be some intrigue or trickery over these. Financial benefits (perhaps a pension) is likely through some Government, municipal or trade union source.

Marriage looms very large among your life influences and there will be much romance about it, but also some coldness. You will meet your partner, an intellectual, critical and rather changeable person, who needs a great deal of understanding, in your home circle (Virgo on cusp of Seventh; Neptune in Libra in Seventh).

There seems deep pain or trouble connected with your children, but you should also gain financially through them (Saturn in Fifth).

Travel is very favourable to you and you will benefit both through journeys and in foreign lands or affairs (Sagittarius in Ninth). You will meet important people while travelling, but find it hard to settle down again on returning. Most of your journeys will be sudden and unexpected (Sun and Uranus in Third House).

Your constitution is sound and your health good on the whole, but you may suffer from blood disorders owing to self-indulgence and in later life from heart trouble (Leo on cusp of Sixth, Sun conjunction Uranus). You will probably live until your middle or late sixties. (Rising Sign and Sun's Sign both mutable, indicating longevity, but Ruler's Sign and Moon's Sign fixed, suggesting death in the sixties.)

Future Prospects

Now you know how to cast a map for the exact time of birth and read it from a person's character and the general run of his or her life. But you may also want to know more precisely what is likely to happen to yourself or anyone else this year or next year or five years ahead. You can find this out by what is called Progression.

To do this easily we must remember that the signs are always moving round in the houses and so, as the years go by, one sign succeeds another on the Mid-Heaven or highest point of the map. The rate of movement or progression is, nearly enough, one degree (1°) per year—though, as this is not quite exact, allow slightly less after middle age, say 59 at age 60. Then see what aspects are made by the new (Progressed) Mid-Heaven to the planets in the Map. From these you can judge the outlook for that particular year.

To illustrate: taking our sample map in Fig. VI, suppose we want to see what will be happening to this person at the age of 25. The map shows us that 27° of Sagittarius were on the Mid-heaven at birth, so we must add 25° to this, remembering that each sign contains 30°. The end of Sagittarius would have been reached at three years old, therefore. Add 22 more degrees to bring us to age 25 and we find the Mid-heaven is now past the middle of the next sign, in 22° of Capricorn. It is a good plan to jot this down beyond the original Mid-heaven, just outside the outermost circle.

Now see what aspects this new Mid-heaven, Capricorn 22°, makes to the planets in the birth map and judge by them whether the year will be a good or bad one (by the aspects) and in what directions or departments (by the planets, signs and houses involved.)

In Progression the various aspects have the following meanings:

Conjunction. To Sun, Moon, Mercury, Venus or Jupiter, good progress; to Mars, progress but upsets also; to Saturn, new responsibilities, but also a risk of serious setbacks; to Uranus, sudden good or bad changes; to Neptune misfortunes or setbacks.

Semi-sextile. To any planets, slight progress.

Semi-square. To any planet, slight adverse.

Sextile. To any planet, there is progress through personal effort and the recognition it brings.

Square. To any planet, serious difficulties and reverses.

Trine. To any planet, decided progress due both to luck and to having deserved it.

Sesqui-square. To any planet, sharp but temporary troubles.

Quincunx. To Sun, Moon, Mercury, Venus or Jupiter, slightly favourable; to Mars, Saturn, Uranus, Neptune or Pluto, slight setbacks; to Saturn and Neptune, progress from one standpoint, difficulties from another.

Opposition. To any planet, reverses caused by opposition from other people or from outside events.

Special Points to Remember

Finally, here are some miscellaneous points to bear in mind when reading *any* map, not merely a progressed one.

Marriage Indications. I have said (page 130) that the Seventh is the Marriage House. This is true in a general way, and when considering the marriage prospects you should always look first at the planet which is nearest to the cusp of the Seventh; or, if there is no planet there, at the planet which rules the Seventh and the actual sign position of that planet.

For a business partnership these points are all you need consider. From them you can judge whether the partnership will be a success or not. But for a marriage partnership you should also consider the position and aspects of Venus, the planet of love (since there can be love without marriage or marriage without love). Also, in a woman's horoscope, the Sun and its aspects and in a man's map, the Moon and her aspects.

Thus, for example, an opposition of Saturn to the Sun may deny a woman marriage, even if Seventh House positions seem favourable. As the Sun represents the father, spinsterhood would probably be caused by opposition or too possessive a love from him.

Interpreting the Chief Planets. The planets which have the most important influence on the life at any given time are the slow-moving ones, Jupiter, Saturn, Uranus and Neptune, because they stay a long time in one place. A brilliant modern American astrologer, Grant Lewi, gives them these general interpretations, which I personally have found to work out accurately:

Jupiter's house position at any date shows the department of life in which opportunities and luck will occur.

Saturn's sign position at any date indicates the point of duty, the responsibility that must be undertaken, the necessity that must be accepted.

The sign position of Uranus at any date shows where self-expression is possible, where one can, so to speak, let oneself go.

Neptune's sign position at any rate gives the thing we take for granted, the fundamental fact that underlies all our planning.

Mars, which moves quickly, is the day-by-day indicator, the minute hand on the clock of life where the other four represent the hour hand.

Intercepted Signs lend a special importance to the houses in which they are placed, so emphasise the traits of these houses when giving your reading.

Now I have told you in fair detail how to cast and read a horoscope. When either writing out or speaking your findings, it is best to use the simple, direct "you" style. "You are generous and independent." "Difficulties may occur in your marriage" and so on. A reading is far more vivid and interests people more keenly if they are directly addressed in this way than if you say, "The native is generous." "Difficulties may occur in the native's marriage." And after all, having done all the work a horoscope entails, you do want it to interest the person it concerns, don't you?

Dates of Summer time (Daylight Saving) in Great Britain

For ordinary Summer Time the clock was put forward one hour at 2 a.m. on the date given below and put back one hour at 3 a.m. on the second date in the same year: In some years during and after the Second World War Double Summer Time (two hours ahead) operated during a shorter period each summer (lower table).

Table A

Year.	Summer Time started.	Summer Time ended.	Year.	Summer Time started.	Summer Time ended.
1921	Apr. 3	Oct. 2	1945	Jan. 1	Oct. 7
1922	Mar. 26	Oct. 8	1946	Apr. 14	Oct. 6
1923	Apr. 22	Sept. 16	1947	Mar. 16	Nov. 2
1924	Apr. 13	Sept. 21	1948	Mar. 14	Oct. 31
1925	Apr. 19	Oct. 4	1949	Apr. 3	Oct. 30
1926	Apr. 18	Oct. 3	1950	Apr. 16	Oct. 22
1927	Apr. 10	Oct. 2	1951	Apr. 22	Oct. 7
1928	Apr. 22	Oct. 7	1952	Apr. 20	Oct. 26
1929	Apr. 21	Oct. 6	1953	Apr. 19	Oct. 4
1930	Apr. 13	Oct. 5	1954	Apr. 11	Oct. 3
1931	Apr. 19	Oct. 4	1955	Apr. 17	Oct. 2
1932	Apr. 17	Oct. 2	1956	Apr. 22	Oct. 7
1933	Apr. 9	Oct. 6	1957	Apr. 14	Oct. 6
1934	Apr. 22	Oct. 7	1958	Apr. 20	Oct. 5
1935	Apr. 14	Oct. 8	1959	Apr. 19	Oct. 4
1936	Apr. 19	Oct. 4	1960	Apr. 10	Oct. 2
1937	Apr. 18	Oct. 3	1961	Mar. 26	Oct. 29
1938	Apr. 10	Oct. 2	1962	Mar. 25	Oct. 28
1939	Apr. 16	Nov. 19	1963	Mar. 31	Oct. 27
1940	Feb. 25	Dec. 31	1964	Mar. 22	Oct. 25
1941	Jan. 1	Dec. 31	1965	Mar. 21	Oct. 24
1942	Jan. 1	Dec. 31	1966	Mar. 20	Oct. 23
1943	Jan. 1	Dec. 31	1967	Mar. 19	Oct. 29
1944	Jan. 1	Dec. 31	1968*	Feb. 18	Oct. 27

*Between October 27th, 1968 and October 31st, 1971, British Standard Time, also 1 hour ahead of G.M.T., was kept.

Table B

Year.	Double Summer Time started.	Double Summer Time ended.	Year.	Double Summer Time started.	Double Summer Time ended.
1941	May. 4	Aug. 10	1944	Apr. 2	Sept. 17
1942	Apr. 5	Aug. 9	1945	Apr. 2	July 15
1943	Apr. 4	Aug. 15	1947	Apr. 13	Aug. 10

WHAT DO THE CARDS SAY?

Egyptian Rhymed Fortunes

THIS is a very simple method of finding the luck of the
seven days immediately ahead of you and is specially
suitable to amuse a large party of people. It consists of a set
of ancient rhymes, each of which is linked with one of the
playing cards in a pack. Fascinating results can be obtained
if you use the rhymes rightly, for they come from the Land of
Mystery, Egypt—country of the Sphinx and the
Pyramids—and have been used there for many centuries by
the wise old Eastern seers. They have been specially
translated into English verse for readers of this book.

Use them in conjunction with a pack of ordinary playing
cards from which the tens—considered unlucky in this
method—have been removed. This gives you a pack of
forty-eight cards

Make a circle round the table. Each person in turn takes
the pack, shuffles it and draws one card without looking at it.
All the cards drawn are then turned face up on the table and
the rhyme belonging to each is read. If liked there may be a
second round, after the pack has been put together again
and re-shuffled. But two cards must never be drawn by any
one person at the same time, nor should more than two be
drawn on any one day.

Here are the forty-eight rhymes.

Ace of Diamonds.
> A song of love, a kiss that burns,
> And your luck on the Ace of Diamonds turns.

Ace of Hearts.
> Your fate is sealed on a Friday night,
> 'Midst music, song and pure delight.

Ace of Clubs.
> Two hearts entwined on the trunk of a tree—
> The man who cut it is true to thee.

Ace of Spades.
> If hearts be true, then naught can stay
> Love's arrow on a coming day.

Two of Diamonds.
> A spider spinning on the wall
> Shows he'll be brave and strong and tall.

Two of Hearts.
> The viper's tongue, the sting of lies,
> Beyond dark clouds are blue, blue skies.

Two of Clubs.
> The Priest of Isis scans your fate—
> Your true love waits at the old church gate.

Two of Spades.
> Though sorrow come with parting pain,
> He shall come back to you again.

Three of Diamonds.
> Three words of love in a garden fair—
> He shall be waiting for you there.

Three of Hearts.
> The third hour of the third day,
> The King of Hearts shall win you away.

Three of Clubs.
> Wealth, good health and a lover true,
> These are the three in store for you.

Three of Spades.
> Queen of his heart you'll ever reign,
> If you should meet him in a train.

Four of Diamonds.
> Under your pillow, place a rose
> For luck to your lover where'er he goes.

Four of Hearts.
> As you sit in the firelight glow,
> His name is writ in the embers low.

Four of Clubs.
> A gipsy woman will tell you the truth—
> You are fated to marry the love of your youth.

Four of Spades.
> A letter written in purple ink,
> Will bring you more than you can think.

Five of Diamonds.
> If a large black cat you see,
> 'Twill bring good luck 'twixt one and three.

Five of Hearts.

> Five this week's your lucky number,
> And fortune comes to you in slumber.

Five of Clubs.

> If when the moon is full you kiss,
> It will lead to married bliss.

Five of Spades.

> On a summer's day, by the deep blue sea,
> You'll have luck if you count to fifty-three.

Six of Diamonds.

> If you would be a rich man's wife,
> Cut a silken cord with a silver knife.

Six of Hearts.

> If a blue butterfly you see,
> It is your luck to go over the sea.

Six of Clubs.

> The six of clubs will bring you hope.
> Make three knots in a piece of rope.

Six of Spades.

> His heart is gold, his eyes are grey,
> You'll meet him twice on Saturday.

Seven of Diamonds.

> Three men, three men in love with you,
> The first and last will ne'er be true.

Seven of Hearts.

> On Tuesday you may look to find
> A lover who is true and kind.

Seven of Clubs.

> His words are fair, his heart is black,
> So turn to one whose name is Jack.

Seven of Spades.

> Your lucky colour is apple green,
> And your lucky number, twice fourteen.

Eight of Diamonds.

> Should you doubt his love for you,
> Place a golden bead in your left shoe.

Eight of Hearts.

> A twilight kiss and a dream of bliss—
> A little black dog will lead you to this.

Eight of Clubs.

> Someone is waiting, someone you know.
> You will have luck when you meet in the snow.

Eight of Spades.

> At ten in the morning on Wednesday,
> You will be travelling far away.

Nine of Diamonds.
>Two days from now, take care what you say,
>'Twill bind you, 'twill bind you five years and a day.

Nine of Hearts.
>A whisper of love, a whisper of hate,
>Tie a silk thread to the garden gate.

Nine of Clubs.
>Love, wealth and happiness will be yours,
>If every night you lock three doors.

Nine of Spades.
>For love and luck, when the sun goes down,
>Rub a new penny and change you gown.

Knave of Diamonds.
>A butterfly wing set in a ring,
>This to you good luck should bring.

Knave of Hearts.
>Beware of Cupid and his darts!
>Your fate is held by the Knave of Hearts.

Knave of Clubs.
>Two eyes of blue and hair of gold,
>And two strong arms about you fold.

Knave of Spades.
>If his name begins with G,
>You will ever happy be.

Queen of Diamonds,
>This week or next will likely bring
>Good luck and an engagement ring.

Queen of Hearts.
>The Queen of Hearts, the King of Love
>A ring, a rose and a silken glove.

Queen of Clubs.
>A lover's knot that none shall break,
>Two shall ask, the third shall take,

Queen of Spades.
>A kitten, a kitten as white as snow,
>By her to-morrow your luck you'll know.

King of Diamonds.
>When bees in honeysuckle sip,
>Love shall be sealed with a scarlet lip.

King of Hearts.
>A lover true now waits for you.
>Don't say "No," whate'er you do.

King of Clubs.
>A kiss within an hour of noon
>Will bring a wedding very soon.

King of Spades.
>When Friday dawns a golden morn,
>You'll thank the stars that you were born.

You will see from these rhymes that they deal chiefly with love affairs and are more suited to women than men. If you want a prophecy that does not concern itself with romance shuffle the pack well and then draw a card which corresponds with the day of the week on which you were born. For example, Sunday is the first day of the week, so in this case you would take the top card. If born on Thursday, the fifth day, you would draw the fifth card, and so on.

Here are the meanings for each day of the week and the card drawn to correspond with it. There are two meanings for each day according to whether the card drawn is high or low. Ace, Two, Three, Four, Five and Six count as low; Seven, Eight, Nine, Knave, Queen and King count as high. (Remember that the tens are not used in this Egyptian method.)

Sunday.	*Low.*	A relative who will make mischief.
	High.	A joyful message from afar.
Monday.	*Low.*	A gift of money or increase in income.
	High.	Gossip about you spread by a false friend.
Tuesday.	*Low.*	You will cross water before long.
	High.	Difficulties removed by a new home
Wednesday.	*Low.*	A good business offer comes unexpectedly.
	High.	An unexpected visit from an old friend.
Thursday.	*Low.*	A disappointment which proves a blessing in disguise.
	High.	A change of surroundings shortly
Friday.	*Low.*	Promotion will come your way
	High.	An unlooked-for holiday proves very enjoyable.

Saturday.   *Low.* You will find something lost long
                             ago.
                   High. You have a gay time socially and a
                             short journey.

According to Egyptian soothsayers, it is unlucky for a
person to try this "day-you-were-born" method more than
once in any one month.

Fortune Telling with Ordinary Playing Cards

There are many methods besides the Egyptian ones given
above of reading the future with an ordinary pack of playing
cards. You will find this foretelling very popular at a party,
and as it does not take long to do, a number of fortunes can
be told in one evening.

Of the many different systems, the following pages give
you some of the best and simplest. The card fortune-teller
needs a good memory, as the meaning of each card, and also
of various combinations of cards, must be carried in the
head; and although some methods use only part of the pack,
others require the whole fifty-two cards!

If you like you can keep a special pack in which you have
written the significance of each card on that card. This is a
very good way of teaching yourself and getting the meanings
memorised, but if you use a marked pack for telling other
people's fortunes, I'm afraid it does not sound so impressive
when they can read the prophesies for themselves!

In any case, if you use marked cards when reading for
others, keep the Spade cards unmarked and memorise these
meanings. The reason is that most Spades are unlucky, and
it is advisable to be able to omit or soften these meanings if
required.

If, however, you want a very quick method and one that
won't tax your memory much, try the first one, "Queens
of Fortune" given below. It gives character more than
events, but is a good method for lightning readings if time

presses or you feel lazy. It also enables you to "fortune tell" for friends of friends, by their merely describing the colouring of the absent one to you.

Queens of Fortune

In all card-reading methods the first thing the fortune-teller does is to pick out one of the four queens to represent the woman whose future is being foretold, or one of the four kings in the pack in the case of a man. And she chooses which queen or king it shall be by the colouring of her subject.

So that if you know the colour of someone's eyes, hair and skin you can make quite an accurate estimate of her character and the kind of fortune of which she will be queen.

To decide whether you subject's colouring belongs to Diamonds, Hearts, Clubs or Spades, go by the tint of the hair and eyes. If these clash—for instance, if you find fair hair with brown eyes—take the skin as a third choice. Thus: white skin, Diamonds; medium fair skin, Hearts; medium dark skin, Clubs; really dark, Spades.

And if even then you are puzzled (which will rarely happen), classify in the same way the fairness or darkness of brows and lashes. For these do not always correspond with either skin or hair, especially in these days when colouring is so easily altered by make-up and hairdressers.

You may wonder what you are to do if a girl who, you know, really has Heart colouring, suddenly appears as a dazzling platinum blonde. Well, you can either go by the "best of three" plan already suggested, and decide that her Heart eyes and skin outweigh her Diamond hair, or you can equally truly consider that a girl who has taken the trouble to turn into a Diamond type must have, at any rate for the time, some marked Diamond characteristics.

In either case, give a rather modified reading—either Hearts with a dash of Diamonds or Diamonds with a good dash of Hearts. You will be correct, for such a girl has to some extent a dual personality.

A Queen of Diamonds is a real blonde, with golden, flaxen or bleached hair, white or delicately pink and white skin and definitely fair brows and lashes. To come under this heading, the eyes must be really blue, not verging at all on grey. Also red-heads of the red-gold or "carrots" tinge belong to Diamonds, provided they are white-skinned and blue-eyed.

The Diamond woman is essentially fascinating, and gets on in the world more by her power to attract men than by her own energy, for she loves comfort, is rather dreamy and is not fond of drudgery.

But she is so pretty, sweet-tempered and appealing that she has little difficulty in finding other people—chiefly men —who are delighted to protect and pet her. She is made for the ornamental side of life and loves dress, jewels, flowers and all forms of beauty—including her own!

She's fickle, I'm afraid—plenty of men for her and none long!—but very kind-hearted and a splendid hostess.

If her hair tends to red she will have more energy and driving power, but not the same gentle appeal; and she may be rather jealous.

Blue and white are her best colours, and she will be luckiest in the morning, in spring, and before the age of twenty-five.

A Queen of Hearts has golden brown or light brown hair, dark blue, grey or hazel eyes and a rather fair skin.

She fits her name, for she is popular everywhere, among both men and women, for her charm, her freshness, her warm heart and her general sanity of outlook. She is rather too sensitive and sentimental, and perhaps over-influenced by the opinions of others.

She adores travel and will wander. But her love of home and children will always bring her back again, prepared in the long run to settle down. She's a little self-centred, though her pleasant manners often disguise this.

Pink and green are her best colours. She will be luckiest about mid-day, in summer and between twenty and forty.

A Queen of Clubs has medium brown or Titian red hair, brown eyes and rather a dark skin.

She is sociable and sympathetic, generous and enthusiastic. She has good driving-power and is true and steadfast. She works hard, either mentally or physically, or both, and is generally optimistic. Perhaps she's a wee bit conceited, but she really has cause to be, don't you think?

She is good-natured and good-hearted, but lacking in tact, and so is apt to make enemies in spite of her many splendid qualities.

Her best colours are yellow and red. She will be luckiest in the afternoon, in autumn and between thirty-five and fifty-five.

A Queen of Spades has dark brown or black hair, brown or black eyes and a definitely dark skin.

She is "true unto death." You will never hear of her deserting a friend and hardly ever of her forgiving an enemy. She is intense, jealous and rather fanatical, often inclined to be some kind of crank.

But she is very patient and has more grit in going after a thing than the other three Queens. It would be an advantage if she laughed more, for she is rather pessimistic. She loves the country and outdoor life, religion and simplicity.

Her best colours are brown and black. She will be luckiest in the evening, in winter and after forty-five years of age.

Men are Kings of Fortune, naturally, in just the same way.

So far, of course, you can use this method of character-reading without having a pack of cards at all and you may wonder why I have included it under Card Reading.

The reason is this.

Having described your consultant as already explained, according to colouring, take a pack of cards and spread them out until her particular Queen is exposed to view. Ask her to take it—do not hand it to her yourself. Then, holding the card tightly in her hand, she must wish silently and concentrate on anything she specially wants to know, while you count twenty slowly. Do not do this out loud or it will distract her from her concentration.

Then take the card from her and press it against your forehead, making your mind blank of everything but your consultant and her personality. If you are at all psychic, after a minute or two additional descriptive points or prophecies about her will "come into your head" and in this way you will be able to amplify your reading.

Playing Card Readings—General Rules

Sometimes the whole pack is used, sometimes only thirty-two cards, and there are as many different methods as there are weeks in the year! But you should begin by knowing some general rules which apply in every case, unless specially stated otherwise.

These rules are:

(1) The consultant, while shuffling or cutting, must concentrate on the points on which she wants information. She should wish when asked to do so, but never *tell* her wish.

(2) In order to put the pack of cards "in touch" with the consultant, she must shuffle them and cut when asked. Cutting must always be done with the left hand.

(3) Never read the cards for the same person, yourself included, more than once in any twenty-four hours. It is definitely unlucky to do so.

What is called the English system of card-reading uses the whole pack of fifty-two cards. What is known as the Continental method uses only thirty-two cards, omitting all those with pips below seven, but including the Aces. The pack thus consists of the Aces, Kings, Queens, Knaves, tens, nines, eights and sevens of all four suits.

As the smaller pack gives fewer meanings to remember, I will explain its meanings and some of its methods first.

Continental Pack (32 Cards) and Their Meanings

In general, many Diamonds in the lay-out of the cards show money matters uppermost; many Hearts, love affairs and friendships; many Clubs, work and business; many Spades, Fate (what you cannot avoid), trouble and disagreements. Picture cards stand for people, according to colouring, as explained for Queens of Fortune on page 145. Queens are women, of course, Kings are elderly or married men and Knaves are young men.

Some fortune-tellers take Kings to represent men in general and Knaves as depicting thoughts or intentions of the corresponding King. There are so many of these alternative readings in the cards that it is better to try both ways for yourself and adopt the one which seems to give you the best results.

The picture card representing the consultant simply represents *her* and during that reading loses the characteristics given for it in the list below, unless these correspond with the consultant's.

Here are the meanings of each card:

Diamonds

Ace. A ring or paper money.

King. A fair or white-haired man, rather fickle, obstinate and unfriendly.

Queen. A fair, flirtatious woman who likes admiration and society.

Knave. A near relative of the consultant, a rather selfish man.

Ten. A good sum of money.

Nine. A surprise connected with money, or, if next to a Heart, about a love affair.

Eight. A late marriage bringing ups and downs.

Seven. Rather unfavourable—either a small money loss or unfriendly gossip.

Hearts

Ace. This card shows generally for your own home or residence, and what happens there. The happenings will be according to the neighbouring cards. If these are other hearts, love and friendship; if diamonds, money comes or news of distant friends; if clubs, happy social or domestic events; if spades, quarrels or misunderstandings at home.

King. A kind affectionate man of medium-fair colouring, enthusiastic but indiscreet.

Queen. A lovable, rather fair woman with much faithfulnes.

Knave. This card may represent either man or woman and is usually the consultant's best friend, but according to some card-readers stands for Cupid.

Ten. General good luck, wiping out the evil of any bad card on either side of it.

Nine. The wish card. If this comes out favourably the consultant's wish is granted. If also brings luck in money and social affairs.

Eight. Good food and pleasant society.

Seven. A false friend who may make mischief.

Clubs

Ace. Wealth, prosperity and a peaceful home atmosphere.

King. A medium-dark man who is honourable and faithful.

Queen. An affectionate woman with plenty of sex-appeal and rather a man-chaser.

Knave. A generous and reliable friend who will do much to help the consultant.

Ten. Money comes suddenly through a death.

Nine. Friction caused by opposing the wishes of friends.

Eight. Love of money and a hankering to gamble or speculate.

Seven. Happiness and good fortune, especially through the consultant's own sex.

Spades

Ace. A death or other misfortune.

King. A man, dark in colouring, who is successful and ambitious.

Queen. A brunette, often a widow, who is an unscrupulous vamp.

Knave. A friend who means well but often makes mischief.

Ten. Bad luck of some kind, either robbing neighbouring favourable cards of their good omens or bringing grief or confinement.

Nine. Illness, family quarrels or a money loss; none of these necessarily very serious.

Eight. Be careful in connection with any enterprise just going through.

Seven. The loss of a dear friend brings grief.

Six-pile Method

This is quick and simple. Pick out of your pack of thirty-two cards the King and Queen representing the consultant, according to the colouring rules given under "Queens of Fortune" on page 145. Place this card face upwards in the middle of the table.

When the consultant has well shuffled the pack, as explained on page 148, wishing as she does so, take the pack from her and deal out the first six cards in a circle round the centre card. Deal out six twice more, making six piles of three cards each and as each is dealt call out this formula:

1st Pile: For yourself.
2nd Pile: For your house.
3rd Pile: For your friend.

4th Pile: For your work.
5th Pile: What lies nearest your heart.
6th Pile: What comes soonest.

These phrases give the part of the consultant's fortune with which each pile deals, the six piles covering respectively her own personal events, home affairs, friendship, work, the wish nearest her heart and the first even that will happen.

Now turn up each pile of three cards and in turn and read them according to the meanings given on page 149 and in connection with the side of life they refer to.

For instance, suppose Pile 2 shows the Ace of Diamonds, the Queen of Hearts and the Seven of Clubs. You would interpret this trio of cards: "A member of your own household, a lovable, rather fair woman will receive a ring or paper money and through the gift to this woman happiness and good fortune will reign in your home."

If the Wish Card (Nine of Hearts) appears in the fifth pile, the consultant's dearest wish is assured. If it appears in any other pile, some minor wish concerning the part of her life dealt with by that pile, will be granted. When the Wish Card is not turned up at all, interpret matters concerning the wish according to the cards in the fifth pile.

More about wishes will be found under "Will My Wish Come True?" on page 159.

The Gypsy Method

This also uses the thirty-two-card pack, with the sixes to twos inclusive omitted.

Ask the consultant to shuffle the pack and then cut it with the left hand into three piles, which need not be all the same size. Take up the centre pile, place over it the right-hand pile and over this the left-hand cut.

Turn the pack to face towards you, and look at the first three cards. Pick out the one of highest value (whatever its suit), keep it, but put the other two aside for the next deal. Continue taking the highest out of every three and laying aside the remaining two all through the pack.

Shuffle all the laid aside cards together. Look through them, and if there are any threes, either three of one suit or three of the same kind or number, such as a trio of Kings or three Eights, take them out and add them to the special retained cards. Spread all these out in a row in the order in which they were picked, with any threes at the end of the row.

Read the cards from left to right, according to the meanings given on page 149. If the Nine of Hearts is among them the wish will be granted.

The English Pack of Fifty-two Cards

There are many good fortune-telling methods using the whole of a pack of cards, but where a separate meaning is attached to each card, it is no easy job to remember them all! So I am giving you here for preference some simple ways of reading the future with fifty-two cards which do not depend on fifty-two separate meanings.

They have also the advantage of not taking very long to do.

The Eastern Pyramid

Shuffle the pack thoroughly and cut it once with the left hand. Taking the larger of the two piles, lay out one card on the table, face up. Below this place two cards and below this three and so on, increasing one in each row, so that you obtain a pyramid formation.

When your pile is exhausted, finish any uncompleted row from the smaller pile, but do not start any further rows, unless you have less than seven, in which case seven rows should be completed.

Now pick up from each row the last card laid down in that row. This means, of course, that the top row,

containing only one card, will vanish altogether. This does
not matter, as we are only concerned with the seven cards
thus taken up.

Sort these seven cards into suits and see which suit claims
the most. If Hearts are in a majority, the luck will be very
great; if Clubs, ordinary good luck, if Diamonds, middling
luck; if Spades, a lack of luck. This reading is for one month
ahead.

Should the two foremost suits have the same number of
cards in each, draw one card at a time from the discarded
ones left after making the pyramid, until you turn up one
from either of the tying suits, to settle the matter. If there
should not be a card of the right suit in the discarded pile,
which does not often happen, you must build the pyramid all
over again.

Rhyming Fortunes

This method uses fifty-two different meanings, but each is
in rhyme, and is not required to be learnt by heart. It can
just be read out from this book according to the card drawn.
This very simple method makes plenty of fun and laughter at
a party.

Spread a whole pack of cards face downwards on the
table. Each member of the party in turn must close her eyes,
hold her *right* hand (not the usual left hand of card-reading)
over her heart and say,

> "A reading true I seek to find,
>   And take what comes with quiet mind."

Then with her left hand she draws from the spread cards
any one she likes, shows it, and its rhymed meaning is read
by whoever is holding this book. The the next person takes
her turn, after the card drawn has been replaced and the
pack shuffled round so that this particular card cannot be
detected.

Here are the rhymes for the whole pack.

Diamond Rhymes

Ace.   If this Ace should be your gain,
You'll marry one with wealth and brain.

King.   Pleasure and profit come to you,
Where sun is gold and skies are blue.

Queen   Fate sometimes breaks and sometimes bends,
But you'll be helped by all your friends.

Knave.   Fate has been a mistress stern,
But from to-day your luck will turn.

Ten.   The charming maid who draws the ten
Will wed, but nobody knows when.

Nine.   With this nine good luck attends
And in a week your income mends.

Eight.   However great may be your ruth,
Fortune will come through speaking truth.

Seven.   When mystic seven doth appear,
Strange happenings will soon be here.

Six.   Be on guard, says Number Six,
'Gainst enemies and crafty tricks.

Five.   If asked to travel, please say "No,"
'Twon't bring you any luck to go.

Four.   A holiday that's full of fun,
Is coming ere a month is done.

Three.   Great honour comes to you and yours,
For very good, sufficient cause.

Two.   Whatever pain you have to-day,
This card will draw it all away.

Heart Rhymes

Ace.   Love is trumps and you will find
              A sweetheart greatly to your mind.

King.   Stand still, consider, if you can,
              Or you may love a married man.

Queen.   Take heed, for one you think your friend
              Of happy plans may make an end.

Knave.   A new acquaintance you shall meet,
              And find his friendship very sweet.

Ten.   Did you think love was at an end?
              Ah no! For broken hearts will mend.

Nine.   If these nine pips to you appear
              You wedding day is very near.

Eight.   Yours is a lucky working life,
              Quite free from poverty or strife.

Seven.   If the seven you obtain
              Be sure you will not love in vain.

Six.   An enemy will show you spite,
              But everything will soon come right.

Five.   Across the sea you're bound to roam,
              But after several years come home.

Four.   From any trouble troubling thee,
              The next six months will set you free.

Three.   More haste, worse speed, is now your fate,
              Better to linger and be late.

Two.   With him you love do not be wroth,
              Or troubles may beset you both.

Club Rhymes

Ace.   A jolly party, full of mirth,
Within the next week shall have birth.

King.   An old acquaintance you will see
And be much in his company.

Queen.   A woman who is middling fair
Is jealous of you, so beware!

Knave.   Money is coming, so take heed
And use it wisely for you need.

Ten.   In work promotion comes to you
Within a month—more money too.

Nine.   Marriage and money—happy twins
Of luck, quite soon your fortune wins.

Eight.   Your next proposal don't disdain
Or you may ne'er get one again.

Seven.   A little loss may come your way.
Don't fret, 'tis only for a day.

Six.   This six you've drawn will bring you soon
A beau who sets the world in tune.

Five.   For motherhood your name is cast,
And your first child won't be the last.

Four.   Work hard if you success would win,
Your lucky time is coming in!

Three.   If now you love with might and main,
Look further, miss, and love again.

Two.   To-day you get the answer "No."
Tomorrow it will not be so.

Spade Rhymes

Ace.   A disappointment dims your eyes,
             But proves a blessing in disguise.

King.   A trusty friend will help you to
             Prosper much in all you do.

Queen.   A jealous woman—please take care!
             You'll know her by her silver hair.

Knave.   You're thinking this year to be wed,
             Please put if off till next instead.

Ten.   What to-day is bringing sorrow,
             Will bring you happy smiles to-morrow.

Nine.   This week your fortune will be fine,
             Since you have drawn of Spades the nine.

Eight.   Please change your business methods or
             You'll have small trade to change them for.

Seven.   You'll wed and soon, we must declare,
             But not with any trousseau fair.

Six.   Take heart of grace, for you will find
             Next winter far more to your mind.

Five.   Try to avoid a bitter strife
             Which may darken your gay life.

Four.   If you insist on your own way,
             You'll likely live to rue the day.

Three.   You've surely drawn a lucky Spade,
             Money and pleasure to you, maid!

Two.   Small troubles bring you many a sigh,
             But all comes right, lass, by-and-by.

Will My Wish Come True?

Everyone has a dearest wish—something she's simply longing for! If you want to be hugely popular among your friends, help them to discover whether they will gain their wishes. And if there's something *you've* set your heart on, too, you'll love to know the prospects or otherwise of getting it, without needing to tell your whole fortune by one of the ways already given.

Wish methods are all quick and easy, and nearly always use the thirty-two card pack (see page 149 for details of this). Use this small pack for the following ways. Always the consultant must wish hard but silently while shuffling and during the manipulation of the cards. Concentrate on one wish only.

Which Comes First?

There are only two cards which count in this method, the Nine of Hearts (the Wish Card) and the Ten of Spades (disappointment). The consultant must shuffle the pack while wishing.

Take the cards and deal them out one at a time, face upwards. Should the Wish Card turn up first, congratulate the wisher. But if the Ten of Spades appears before the Wish Card, it is likely that the wish will be long delayed, come in some unsatisfactory way or not be fulfilled at all.

Three Questions

This way is a little more complicated, but it answers three questions, one of which may concern that dearest wish of your heart.

From the pack of thirty-two cards, as before, lay out in a row, face downwards, the first three cards that come after the consultant has wished three wishes while shuffling the pack.

In a second row deal out the next five cards and in a third row the next seven.

Turn up the first row of three cards and note their numbers; if they are picture cards, their number value; thus, Knave is eleven, Queen twelve and King thirteen. The lower the value, the less the opposition to the wish. Ace counts as one and is luckiest of all. The wish is certain if one of the three cards is an ace.

Turn up the second row of five cards and judge in the same way. An ace and a seven in this case guarantee a favourable answer; for the third row of seven, two aces are necessary for *certain* success. But in any row several sevens and eights are considered a very hopeful sign.

Seven Days a Week

First pick out the consultant's personal card according to the colour rules given on page 145. Put it in the centre of the table. The consultant must shuffle the pack, wishing as she does so and then cut the cards once with her left hand.

Take up the cards, placing the cut portion on the top, and deal them round the consultant's card in seven piles, going round thrice so that each pile contains three cards.

The first pile dealt stands for Sunday, the second for Monday and so on through the week. Turn up each trio of cards in turn and note if the Wish Card (Nine of Hearts) is among them. If not, the wish will not come true.

But if the Wish Card turns up, say, in the third pile, the wish will come true on some Tuesday (third day of the week) within one month, if it is the first card of the three; within two months, if it is the second; or within three months if it is the last.

Four Aces

The foregoing wish ways are for one person at a time. Suppose you are with several friends and all want to test their wishes at once. This can be easily done.

Four people can try this, one definite ace being allotted to each. Each of the four shuffles the pack in turn, silently wishing.

Now one of them must deal thirteen cards face upwards. If any ace is among the thirteen, the person who was allotted that ace will have splendid good fortune and her wish within three months.

Put the ace aside. Place the other dealt cards back in the pack and reshuffle all round. A second person now deals a second thirteen cards and the owner of any ace turning up in them will have good luck and her wish granted within six months.

If aces still remain in the pack, a third dealing by a third person is allowed, and any aces turning up this time foretell moderate good fortune and a good chance (but no certainty) of the wish coming true. A fourth deal is not permitted, and aces still left in the pack forbode some difficulties ahead for those owning them.

Three for Luck

A much larger number of people can try this. Each in turn takes the pack and while wishing, deals herself three cards face upwards. The lower the value of the three cards (taking picture cards by their numerical value, as given on page 160) the greater the luck during the next four weeks.

Add the three numbers together and the one with the lowest total will be the luckiest of those present and so on. Those in the top third (that is, the first three if nine are wishing) are sure to get their wish; for the second third it is doubtful, and the last third had better wish something different next time.

If more than five people are trying this method, use the complete pack instead of only thirty-two cards.

It is unlucky to try any method more than once for the same person on the same day.

The Magic Card Numbers

Here is a wish method using the full pack of fifty-two cards. It is for one person only each time.

The consultant shuffles the pack and cuts once with the left hand while wishing.

Take the pack from her and slowly deal the cards one at a time, face downwards. While dealing goes on, the consultant may choose any three cards she pleases, without having seen their faces. Set these cards aside and when the three are chosen place them in a row, face upwards, in the order in which they were selected.

By this method ten and picture cards stand for nought, while each other card has its own number value. Add up the total value of the cards. Thus a King, an eight and a two would add up to ten, as the King is a nought.

Whatever the final number adds up to, try if it will divide exactly by seven or by three (two lucky numbers) or by both. If by either number, there are very good prospects of the wish; if by both, it is certain and will bring general good fortune.

YOUR NAME AND YOUR NUMBER

DID you know that your name has a number—in fact, several numbers—and that these numbers are lucky to you and tell you a great deal about yourself?

Well, it's true. A modern discovery is that vibration is the basis of most things. We know of nine ordinary rates of personal vibrations and every one of us, like a radio set, tunes in to one (or more) of these nine vibrations. The sort of folk we are and the sort of lives we lead depend very largely on which of the nine we are linked with.

It's very easy to discover your number—or anyone else's. You only need a person's name and a little very simple arithmetic to work out his or her vibration. You'll find it such a convenience to have a fortune-telling method which you can do for friends who are not present or for people, perhaps, you have only met once or had a letter from.

Naturally it's easier to deal with these semi-strangers in business or social life if you know something about them by means of privately studying their names.

Every letter in the alphabet—and consequently every letter in a name—has a number value.

You'll find them all in this table, which you will very soon get to know by heart.

A	B	C	D	E	F	G	H	I	J	K	L	M
1	2	3	4	5	6	7	8	9	1	2	3	4

N	O	P	Q	R	S	T	U	V	W	X	Y	Z
5	6	7	8	9	1	2	3	4	5	6	7	8

To find your numberscope, as it is called, just print your name in block letters, using the name you are ordinarily known by, which is general the Christian name and surname without any middle names you may have. If, however, you are called by the second of two Christian names, you have and not by the first, use this second name with the surname.

Nicknames may give quite different figures. But the mere fact that some people call you by a nickname suggests that you have a second personality which you show to these people only, and which is worth studying as well as that given by your actual name. Of course, if everyone knows you by the nickname, linking it with your surname and never using your Christian name at all, you should make your numberscope from your nickname added to your surname.

Having printed out your name as suggested above, place *over* each vowel its correct number and *under* each consonant its number in the same way, taking them from the table already given. The letter Y is reckoned as a consonant except when there is no other vowel in the word, as in names like Glyn or Pym, when it is counted as a vowel. In either case, of course, its number is seven.

Each name yields three different numbers, obtained in this way.

(1) The Heart Number is gained by adding all the vowel numbers together—those placed above the name. This number represents the inner, private you, with your ideals and wishes. You know this self very well but only the most intimate of your friends see it.

(2) The Personality Number, obtained by adding the consonant numbers, placed under the name, is the outside you which all the world sees, the self you show all day and every day.

(3) The Vocation Number is the sum of the Heart and Personality Numbers, obtained by adding *all* the letter numbers of the name together. It shows the kind of work you are fitted for and to some extent the sort of career you will have.

There is one peculiarity in adding figures in numberscopes which does not apply in ordinary arithmetic. That is that only the digits from 1 to 9 inclusive are used. So

if any total comes to two figures, those two figures must be
added together, if necessary more than once, till a single
digit is obtained.

Thus a total of 15 becomes 6, because 5 and 1 are six. Or
a total of 28, when the 2 and the 8 are added, becomes 10.
But this is still a double figure, so we add again, and the final
result is 1.

Here is an instance of an actual name worked out to its
three numbers, to guide you in doing your own.

```
5      9              1    9  5      = 2 9 = 1 1 = 2
E  D  I  T  H      D  A  N  I  E  L
4     2  8         4     5        3  = 2 6 = 8
Heart Number  =  2
Personality Number  =  8.
Vocation Number  =  1.
```

Having found the three numbers of a name in this way,
consider in turn the meaning and value of each, how they
will fit in with one another and where they will disagree. The
contradictions and difficulties in a person's life arise where
two of her numbers clash, making her want to do both of two
opposite things.

For example, No. 1 wants to lead and No. 2 to follow. It is
easy to see that someone with both a 1 and a 2 will both
desire leadership and dislike it. Again, No. 6 (the homebird) clashes with No. 5 (the wanderer) and No. 9, who has
wide and international sympathies.

Here are character studies of the nine numbers.

Number One

This number corresponds with the planet Mars and the
signs of Aries and Scorpio in astrology and always shows a
leader and a person at the top.

When we say of a friend, "She always looks out for
Number One," we are unconsciously quoting astrology. One
is an intensely personal number, somebody who feels set

apart from and above others. It is not for nothing that in the Chinese army the man in command of each regiment is called the Number One.

Miss One is well aware of herself and wants everyone else to be so, too. She demands the limelight and is not unduly modest. In fact, she is inclined to be conceited, and to let you know how capable she is.

Don't try to exploit a Number One in any way. You will surely get the worst of it, for she knows very well how to take care of her own interests.

Perhaps she *is* a bit selfish, but she has heaps of splendid and lovable qualities to offset this fault. For instance, she is very self-reliant, standing firmly on her own feet. If she does not put herself out too much for others, neither does she sap their vitality by leaning on them for support.

There is nothing lazy of feebly imitative about her. She has plenty of originality and the determination to carry through her own ideas against opposition, if need be. So you may be sure that she will come to the front, unless both her other numbers are quiet ones to hold her back.

She's a born leader, somewhat bossy but very efficient. Her chief defect in positions of power is that she has no tact, but says just what she thinks. Also she wants her own way and is not always willing to work in with others. For this reason it is often best for her to run a one-man concern, or be an independent employer, rather than hold a position in a big firm. She must avoid also conceit and interfering in other people's affairs.

In appearance she is generally rather striking and dresses unusually, either ahead of fashion or definitely disregarding it.

When the Vocation Number is One, she is suited for jobs requiring leadership, originality and creative power, and will do well as a teacher, manageress, head of a department, dress designer, interior decorator or in advertising. The Civil Service favours her, too.

Her lucky colours are red and pink, lucky gems aquamarine and turquoise and her lucky day is Tuesday.

Number Two

We all know the expression "playing second fiddle," and this is an apt description of Number Two, who is modest and retiring, preferring to take a back seat.

This number corresponds with the planet Moon and the sign Cancer in astrology and always shows a subordinate or second in command. She makes a splendid "right hand man" in business or home affairs, because she is conscientious, tactful and good at detail. But she dislikes responsibility and wants some one else to make the big decisions for her.

She is timid and economical. She will not take risks, with money or anything else and so does not rise far. "Safety first" and "Peace at any price" are two of her favourite maxims. In fact, she is such a peace-lover that to avoid friction she will often give way when really in the right.

Where other people are concerned, though, her tact and ability to see both sides of a question makes her an ideal peacemaker or arbitrator. She's a gentle, motherly soul with plenty of sympathy and as she can adapt herself to any company she is always popular.

When the Vocation Number is Two, clerical or secretarial jobs, work as a receptionist or saleswoman, or in the home, are all suitable.

Number Two's lucky colours are white and silver, her lucky gems are the moonstone and pearl and her lucky day is Monday.

Number Three

This number corresponds with the planet Venus and the signs Taurus and Libra in astrology and is the number of self-expression and the artistic temperament.

Miss Three contributes some form of creative work towards the enjoyment of the world in general and becomes an actress, a musician or a writer; failing these, she is a splendid hostess, entertaining guests rather than audiences or readers.

She is full of the joy of life and anxious to share it; hers is a cheery, light-hearted temperament, very much fonder of laughter than of gloom, though she has dark moods at times. She is optimistic and easy-going.

As she likes showing off, she is certain to have one or more party tricks, and loves plenty of social life in which to display them. A jolly crowd is more to her taste than a *tête-à-tête*.

Perhaps she won't help to lighten your troubles, but she is sure to amuse you till you forget them temporarily. She's the best companion in the world for mirthful moments. You'll find her clever, a bit eccentric, loving comfort and fine clothes and disliking hard or dull work.

She should avoid biting criticisms of more stupid folk and not be so positive that she is always right and others always wrong.

A girl with Number Three as her Vocation Number is fitted for work that gives the public pleasure. She will shine as an entertainer, musician, air hostess, writer, actress, lecturer, singer, receptionist and similar jobs.

Her lucky colours are blue and violet, her lucky gems are the amethyst and turquoise and her lucky day is Friday.

Number Four

This number corresponds with the planet Uranus and the sign Aquarius in astrology and shows rather a contradictory temperament with touches of strangeness.

Generally speaking, four has a calming and steadying influence, and those whose names add up to this digit are, above all, industrious, reliable workers who will stick to their job. They can be absolutely counted on for carefulness and faithfulness to duty. You seldom or never hear a Number Four say apologetically, "I'm sorry, I forgot to do it."

She is fond of home and spends much time there. She loves her country, too, and generally takes her holidays at home rather than abroad, though this is partly conservatism! She is even-tempered, rather serious-minded, and combines a thoroughly practical outlook with a fair dose of intuition.

She is an excellent organiser and can take responsibility on these lines. She can be relied upon to keep a home or business going smoothly, and is skilled with her hands.

So far you have the picture of a quiet, reliable, unexciting person, and this is just what Miss Four is most of the time. But there is a queer, unexpected streak in her, and at least once or twice in her lifetime she will, so to speak, explode violently in some direction, causing upheaval all round her.

This is especially the case when she is young, when she may quarrel violently with her family or embark on some hectic love affair. As time goes on she settles down more and more to calmness.

She should, if Four is her Vocation Number, choose a career offering scope for her clever hands or for her undoubted organising ability.

This gives her plenty of choice. For instance, she would do well at a craft, especially one such as weaving, which requires patience and care in details rather than brilliance of ideas. She is suited also to cookery, dressmaking, hotel or restaurant posts. She might be an engineer, a machinist or a forewoman or manageress.

Her lucky colours are fawn and navy blue, her lucky gems are the emerald and zircon and her lucky day is Sunday.

Number Five

This number corresponds with the planet Mercury and the signs Gemini and Virgo in astrology, and shows, above all, versatility.

"Give me variety!" cries Miss Five, for change and excitement are the breath of life to her and monotony the thing she cannot stand.

She is a Jill of all trades and, alas, usually mistress of none, but her adaptability enables her to turn her hand quickly to anything new. So, although she seldom keeps jobs long, she never has much difficulty in finding a new one. "When one door closes, another opens," is truly said of Number Five.

You can't teach her to be punctual, however hard you try, and she is erratic and rather irresponsible. But what a host of good points she has! Witty, good company, generous, forgiving, tolerant—she's all of these, and full of impulse and good-heartedness. She's a great chatterbox.

Untidiness is one of her characteristics.

She likes not only change, but movement, and it irks her terribly to sit still all day. So when five is the Vocation Number, a career should be chosen which gives variety and movement or travel.

The stage (especially touring), commercial travelling, teaching (with the long holidays for getting about), demonstrating and advertising are all good. So is photography.

Miss Five's lucky colours are all shades of grey, her lucky gems are the olivine and sardonyx and her lucky day is Wednesday.

Number Six

This number corresponds with the planet Jupiter and the sign Sagittarius in astrology and belongs particularly to the "ministering angel" type of woman.

Miss Six is a homebird—a rather quiet soul who thinks little of having a good time, but is first and foremost when there is someone to be nursed, mothered or protected.

A girl with Six as her Heart Number is the ideal wife and mother, with her tender sympathies, her great homemaking ability and her harmonious temperament.

She is very skilled in all housewifely things and does better within her own four walls than anywhere else. But if Fate denies her marriage she will still find people to nurse and care for, or throw herself into philanthropic or educational work which helps the old, the sick and children.

Hers are clever fingers that can mend, make and contrive successfully, and she's a talent for making ends meet. Her home is well run and artistic on a small amount of money and looks more expensive than it is.

She will soothe quarrels in the family and listen sympathetically to everyone's troubles, while she plans out ways of setting things right.

Her ideal of happiness is not a crowd and noisy band, but wireless at home or one or two friends taking tea with her in the garden, of which she is very fond.

It must be admitted that she is neither original nor particularly quick in her ways, preferring well-trodden paths and to go at her own rather leisurely pace. She can be very short with well-meaning people who try to hurry her or to get her to do things out of what she considers their proper order.

She's a bit of a gossip and pays rather too much attention to her neighbours' opinion of her. But she is essentially an unselfish and kind soul who can be lived with happily.

She shines best of all at home-making, but if earning her living should choose a profession with a domesticated touch, such as that of hospital or children's nurse, doctor, housekeeper, matron in a school or saleswoman in a shop selling home furnishings.

Her lucky colours are green and mauve; her lucky stones are the diamond and topaz and her lucky day is Thursday.

Number Seven

This number corresponds with the planet Neptune and the sign Pisces (see page 79) in astrology and belongs to a rather aloof, set-apart personality. Of all the nine numbers found in names Seven is said to be the rarest and the most difficult to live up to, and, as far as my experience goes, this is undoubtedly true.

Intuition, understanding and solitude are the heritage of those whose Heart Number is seven. This hard but inspiring number is that of the mystic and the profound thinker.

Miss Seven is mostly sunny and serene, and seems a little set apart from the world, in a solitude of her own. Since meditation and the search after truth are her task in life, she cannot thrive in a crowd, or even in a family, and is often thought rather queer and unsociable. She frequently lives alone.

Faith and wisdom are hers, but she inclines to pessimism at times and will brood far too much over her mistakes owing to the very high standard she sets herself.

She is religious in the best sense of the word, refined and perhaps over-sensitive, and loves quiet and old surroundings. You are likely to find a Number Seven on the shady side of some back street, surrounded by antique furniture and a garden with a long history.

She is fond and proud of her family. She dislikes new things—even new clothes—till she has got used to them. Her brains are excellent and she loves to study human nature, so is interested in such sciences as psychology and in most occult matters.

It is to a Number Seven that people take mental and emotional troubles, feeling sure of sympathetic understanding and help and a shut mouth. Number Seven is an absolutely reliable keeper of secrets.

Her best career is one giving opportunities for meditation, and for quiet, solitary work. She should never go into large bustling businesses. She may become a gardener, musician, writer, antique dealer, or take up some form of church work.

She dresses neatly and harmoniously, but not in the very latest fashion.

Her lucky colours are green and blue, her lucky gems are the agate and carbuncle and her lucky day is Thursday.

Number Eight

This number corresponds with the planet Saturn and the sign Capricorn (see page 77) in astrology and shows a personality with the keynote of achievement.

Eight is first and foremost the number of power and those governed by this digit will never remain permanently unsuccessful or insignificant, though they often wait long for their achievements to make their mark.

Miss Eight has great courage and splendid organising abilities, and always tends to make money. In fact Eight is known as the success vibration.

This girl loves power, and in whatever sphere she is, she always works for it, organising people and circumstances to this end. She is firm, efficient and energetic—sometimes, if she is not careful, rather too firm, not to say domineering—but generally she softens her harder characteristics with sympathy, tact and goodwill.

She may not make a bigger success than other people, but it is a more outstanding one because she does it with no advantages at all, often with severe handicaps. She is the real self-made woman, for she has the rare ability to "build up with worn-out tools," as Kipling puts it.

She can take an almost impossible situation in family life or business which is falling to pieces and reorganise either on sound lines, finding a solution to every difficulty. She does this by patience, grit and calmness. You don't find a Number Eight whining or fussing, but giving orders and getting on with the job.

Her faults are a tendency to become too much of a money-grabber and to exploit those who work for her—or her own family and friends.

Miss Eight has a happy knack of looking prosperous and smart whatever she wears, for she is always well-groomed and very particular about cleanliness, shoes and gloves.

When Eight is the Vocation Number, her ideal job is some form of business organisation and control. Wherever she starts she will rise and rise until she gets the big field for her activities which satisfies her.

She is likely to end as manageress, headmistress, director or as a business "boss" of some kind. She never plays second fiddle for long. If she marries she will be the stronger partner and run things in the home, however tactfully this may be disguised.

Her lucky colours are brown and black, her lucky gems are the opal and beryl and her lucky day is Saturday.

Number Nine

This number corresponds with the Sun and the sign Leo (see page 72) and belongs to a large-minded personality.

Miss Nine realises that the world is far wider than her own family, town or even country. She is not absorbed in herself, like Number One, or in her own little circle, like Number Six, but is interested in the world at large. She reaches out sympathetically towards big movements and international interests and wants to leave the world better and happier than she found it.

There is nothing small-minded about this number. Miss Nine will not be prejudiced against a person because she is a foreigner or maybe of a different colour. Most international clubs and societies are founded and supported by Number Nine folk, who usually travel and see how other people live.

She wants to do good or help the sorrowful in a big way —not just giving a hand to those she knows, but aiding movements that affect people as a whole. She is very sympathetic, helpful and well-mannered—artistic, too, with wide interests in all the arts and sciences.

She doesn't like obscurity and wants to be noticed and flattered and admired. She's impulsive, with the generosity of the impulsive and has a great deal of charm. She often has dramatic ability.

She is rather impressive-looking—not a person you could overlook—and dresses in a somewhat distinctive, artistic style.

In fact, Number Nine is decidedly lovable and attractive, but has one or two faults to guard against. These are: too much desire to be praised and rewarded for what she does, and a tendency to make dramatic and highly emotional scenes when things don't go well with her.

When Nine is the Vocation Number, a career should be sought as an actress, painter, fashion artist, doctor, nurse or teacher.

Her lucky colours are yellow and orange, her lucky gems are the topaz and chalcedony and her lucky day is Sunday.

How to Find Your Birth Number

In addition to the three numbers, those of Heart, Personality and Vocation, which may be found in the name, as described on page 103, you can find for yourself or for any friend whose day, month and year of birth you know, a fourth very interesting number called the Birth or Lesson Number.

This is worked out in a very similar way to the first three numbers, but founded on the birth-date instead of the name. The plan is to reduce the birth-date entirely to numbers and then add them, more than once if necessary, till a single digit is reached.

To take an example, suppose your birth-date is January 7th, 1922. Written entirely in figures, this date becomes $7/1/1922$—$7 + 1 + 1 + 9 + 2 + 2 = 22$. Adding the 2 and the 2 to obtain a single digit, this results in 4, which is the Birth or Lesson Number of anyone born on January 7th, 1922.

In the same way the birthday, September 20th, 1913, gives the Lesson Number 7, and she who was born on May 14th, 1939, will have the Lesson Number 5.

If the friend for whom you are doing a numberscope is willing to tell you her birthdate, it is always worthwhile to write this down below the other three numbers obtained, for while the Heart, Personality and Vocation numbers tell of the character and career as already described, the Birth or Lesson number shows the special lesson that person must learn during her lifetime.

Behind this is the idea of reincarnation, that we come into the world again and again and in each life here must learn one of the nine lessons, these corresponding to the nine numbers.

Whether you believe in reincarnation or not, in my experience it is almost uncannily true how the Lesson Number given by your birthdate, and the task that belongs to it, seems to dog your life and give you no peace until you have mastered it.

Here are the life lessons that go with each Birth Number:

Number One. You must learn to create, not copy, to stand on your own feet, be self-reliant and lead.

Number Two. You must learn to be adaptable and friendly with all without becoming a "doormat," and cultivate tact, economy and social sense.

Number Three. Your lesson is to learn self-expression by entertaining others. You must teach yourself to write, act, sing, play, or be a good hostess.

Number Four. Work steadily and do all you can for others. "Service" should be you motto.

Number Five. Learn to take things easily, to let go and refuse to cling to old ways and outworn friendships. Take life as it comes and always accept the new things.

Number Six. Your home and family should come first. Push and help them rather than going out for a successful personal career, for your best happiness will come to you through advancing others. Give up outside work when you have children.

Number Seven. Do not fear loneliness and quiet, for you need them to develop the inner self which it is your lesson to cultivate. Learn also to be optimistic and confident.

Number Eight. Your task is to use success and power without being in any way domineering or possessive. If you are a mother, do not bind your children too closely to yourself, for they must learn to stand alone.

Number Nine. Try to reach out beyond your own small circle and express yourself in a wide kind of service, without expecting reward and praise for so doing.

While you Life Lesson is permanent throughout your life, every year has its own Lesson Number, which is secondary to the permanent Life Lesson, but important during that one year. You can find your Lesson Number for this or any other year by adding the month and date of your birth to the year in question, instead of to your year of birth.

Thus, to take an example already given, to find the Lesson Number for 1951 for the girl born on January 7th of any year, make this sum: $7 + 1 + 1 + 9 + 5 + 1 = 6$. Or for a September 20th birthday the Lesson for 1951 will be 9.

Once every nine years, of course, the yearly Lesson Number will be the same as the life Lesson Number. During that year, therefore, you will have special opportunities to master your Life Lesson, and if you refuse them they will not come again so favourably for another nine years, when they will return in a harder form.

The yearly Lesson Numbers are the same as the Life Lesson numbers already given. By working out the Lesson Number each year you are able to prophesy in a rough way the kind of year you will have. Thus:

In a Number One year, expect that things will go your way, that long-cherished wishes will come true and that you will have to lead and take responsibility.

In a Number Two year, do not be disappointed if you make little advance and have to keep in the background. This will be a quiet year, but will offer opportunities for making new friends.

In a Number Three year, you should have plenty of laughter, fun and social life, and you will be called upon to entertain others either in public or private.

In a Number Four year, expect a good bit of drudgery and steady work and not much in the way of travel or amusement.

In a Number Five year, you are likely to get freedom from money and other cares, changes in the people surrounding you and an active, jolly time.

In a Number Six year, home and family matters will occupy most of your attention. Work matters will not progress greatly and you will be much in contact with sick people.

In a Number Seven year, expect to be a good deal alone and to have little social life. You will probably hear many secrets and have to keep them.

In a Number Eight year, you will be busy, important and powerful and money matters are likely to flourish.

In a Number Nine year, you will travel or meet with foreigners at home, enlarge your boundaries and get plenty of attention from others.

It is said that if the Lesson Number is smaller than the Heart Number, the lesson will be easy to learn and the life a comfortable and happy one. But if the Lesson Number is bigger than the Heart Number, then you will have to strain every nerve to master it and your life will be much more of a struggle.

This only applies to the permanent Lesson Number, not to the one for any particular year.

Is Your Name Here?

In the preceding pages you have read how to work out the numberscope of your name in a simple but effective way. Here are some special "name readings" of thirty favourite girls' and boys' names, which I have worked out for you with additional particulars that you cannot obtain in a numberscope.

Naturally it is impossible to give anything like all the English Christian names. If I did, they would fill this entire book! But names have been chosen which are more traditional than most and so you will find that the thirty given will cover quite a number of the people you know.

They are in alphabetical order, so that you can see in a moment if any particular name is there.

Thirty Name Readings

Agnes

Meaning: The name AGNES has the fine meaning of "Pure."

Character: This child will be a hard worker and can build up things, actually or metaphorically. She is full of dreams, yet also very practical. She worries too much and has an excess of sympathy with suffering, so that she will wear herself out trying to help. She should have a good singing voice. She needs praise and appreciation to keep her happy.

Life Lessons: She must learn not to jump to conclusions and not to over work herself.

Career: She should take up some form of business and, if possible, should run her own job, not be employed. She might be a dressmaker.

Lucky Days: Tuesday and Thursday.

Lucky Numbers: 4 and 6

Lucky Motto: "All work and no play make Jack a dull boy."

Arthur

Meaning: The name ARTHUR has the manly meaning of "strong" or "high."

Character: He is anxious to be helpful and to serve others, though this trait may sometimes be obscured by his equal desire to lead and to have his own way. He is original, self-reliant, decided in his opinions and skilful with his hands. He is very honest and practical; a trifle stubborn and self-centred. You can trust him thoroughly, and rely on his love of home and family.

Life Lessons: He must improve his manners, becoming more tactful and adaptable, and he must try not to interfere in other people's affairs.

Career: He would succeed in a bank, on the railways or in a travelling job such as driver, chauffeur, courier or aircraftsman.

Lucky Days: Tuesday and Saturday.

Lucky Numbers: 1 and 4

Lucky Motto: "The grace of God is in Courtesy."

David

Meaning: The name DAVID has the charming meaning, "Beloved."

Character: A boy with this name is cheery and amusing. He is artistic and has musical, literary or acting ability. He likes to entertain people and to show off a bit. He also wants to rule and has the originality and strong will to do so. With his very definite personality and opinions he will never be overlooked, but he is sometimes too blunt for his own good. He loves beauty, peace and his own way.

Life Lessons: He must learn to be more unselfish and to take a back seat sometimes.

Career: He has technical and manual skill, so he should become an engineer, a draughtsman, a carpenter or other craftsman. He should have a post where he can organise as well as work.

Lucky Days: Tuesday and Thursday.

Lucky Numbers: 1 and 3.

Lucky Motto: "Sometimes the greatest strength lies in giving way."

Dorothy

Meaning: The name DOROTHY has the beautiful meaning, "The gift of God."

Character: Here's a very cheery person, though when she is down, which isn't often, she is very, very down! She is a good hostess and can amuse her guests with her own music or by amateur theatricals. She is self-reliant, original and sociable and finishes off well anything she undertakes. Life to her is a comedy, though on occasion she is very critical and a great grouser. Her dress is fashionable and a little showy.

Life Lessons: She must learn to be less critical over trifles and not to push herself forward too much.

Career: Something domestic will suit her best. She could do well in nursing or on the domestic side of a school or institution. She might be housekeeper, hostess or teacher.

Lucky Days: Thursday and Friday.

Lucky Numbers: 3 and 6.

Lucky Motto: ''Growling will not make the kettle boil.''

Eileen

Meaning: The name EILEEN is an Irish form of Helen and means ''A torch.''

Character: Very fond of family and home life. At the same time she has a real talent for organisation and for taking charge. Hers is a sweet and tactful nature, with very charming manners; but her tact and charm disguise a strong wish to get her own way. She loves to take care of people and mother them. She is tidy, honourable, tranquil and self-confident.

Life Lessons: She must learn not to overwork either herself or other people and to live and let live.

Career: Freedom in work is her chief need. Business is excellent if she is not tied down by restrictions. She would do well in advertising, or she might become a nurse, photographer or hairdresser.

Lucky Days: Friday and Saturday.

Lucky Numbers: 6 and 8.

Lucky Motto: "In essentials, unity; in matters doubtful, liberty; in all things, charity."

Elizabeth (or Betty)

Meaning: The name ELIZABETH (of which Betty is a short form) means "The solumn promise of God."

Character: A happy, generous, excitable, light-hearted girl! She is popular, for she can get on easily with almost anyone, being gentle and adaptable. She loves freedom, change and the open air. Contradictorily, she is both impulsive and cautious, patient and impatient. If called Betty, she will be less easy to get on with, but very helpful, and clever with her hands in many ways.

Life Lessons: She must learn to be less excitable and more responsible and to rely on herself, not others.

Career: A quiet job "on her own" will suit her best. She might be a dressmaker, a teacher of music, a journalist, or take in typewriting at home.

Lucky Days: Monday and Wednesday (for Betty, Wednesday and Saturday).

Lucky Numbers: 2 and 5 (for Betty, 4 and 5).

Lucky Motto: "God helps those who help themselves.

Ernest

Meaning: The name ERNEST has the nice meaning of "Earnest."

Character: Here is someone to whom, even when he is still a child, people will instinctively go for help and instructions. He has a strong team sense and can organise and captain his playmates, ruling by firmness, tact and charm combined. He has ideas of his own and is never content to copy. He is very just and very efficient, and has much self-confidence and generosity.

Life Lessons: He must learn not to use his power over others just for his own benefit and not to be too aggressive.

Career: He should have a job in which he can serve, help

or teach others. He is cut out for a doctor, chemist, teacher, clergyman or social worker.

Lucky Days: Tuesday and Saturday.

Lucky Numbers: 1 and 8.

Lucky Motto: ''Not failure but low aim is crime.''

Frank

Meaning: The name FRANK *has the fine meaning of* ''Free.''

Character: If you want a job done or a little kindness shown, here's just the right boy. He is always glad to be of service and so handy in many ways that he can help a lot. He is an odd mixture of selfishness and unselfishness, loving his own way, yet liking to be very good to others. His are really skilful fingers and he has plenty of ideas in his clever head. He is candid, honest and practical.

Life Lessons: He should learn to be a little more modest about his abilities and to refrain from managing other people's business as well as his own.

Career: He would make a clever salesman, demonstrator, commercial artist or schoolmaster in a small school.

Lucky Days: Sunday and Tuesday.

Lucky Numbers: 1 and 4.

Lucky Motto: ''On their own merits modest men are dumb.''

George

Meaning: The name GEORGE has the sturdy meaning of ''A husbandman.''

Characer: He is excitable, restless and intelligent, full of nervous energy; yet at times he has a repose you would not suspect, for he likes quiet to think things out. He is almost too independent—even touchy—when advice is offered him. He has much generosity, vitality and kindness. He likes travel and the sea has a special appeal for him.

Life Lessons: He must learn to be less changeable and to control his fiery temper.

Career: He should preferably be a teacher. If not, a commercial traveller, actor, electrical engineer or business man.

Lucky Days: Wednesday and Thursday.

Lucky Numbers: 5 and 7.

Lucky Motto: "Fair and softly goes far in a day."

Jean

Meaning: The name JEAN has the beautiful meaning, "Grace of the Lord."

Character: There won't be a hard struggle or bitter drudgery for this lucky maiden! In some nice way or other, brave knights will always be at hand to slay all her dragons for her! She's such a popular and lucky person, with her ready laughter and sympathy, her easy-going nature and marked charm. She has a scientific turn of mind, loves warm, rich colours and often inherits money.

Life Lessons: She must learn not to exaggerate things and not to worry over trifles.

Career: She should be a teacher or nurse or enter one of the artistic professions, becoming a musician, film actress or painter.

Lucky Days: Thursday and Friday (particularly Friday).

Lucky Numbers: 6 and 3 (particularly 6).

Lucky Motto: "Tight boots are a blessing—they make you forget all your other troubles."

Joan

Meaning: The name JOAN has the lovely meaning, "The Lord graciously gave."

Character: Here is a girl who is a thinker. She is very anxious to live a fine life and has a deep sense of religion. But because she has more vision than most she will be inclined as she gets older to "boss" other people too much. She has good brains, but she is also a real home-bird, very sympathetic and anxious to help her family, very kind and loving.

Life Lessons: She must learn to be more optimistic and to work *with* the family team, instead of always trying to lead it.

Career: She has clever hands and should use them to earn her living as a dressmaker, milliner, musician, cook or upholstress.

Lucky Days: Friday and Saturday.

Lucky Numbers: 6 and 7.

Lucky Motto: "If at first you don't succeed, try, try, try again."

John

Meaning: The name JOHN is the masculine equivalent of Joan and has the same meaning. "The Lord graciously gave."

Character: In some ways this boy is a contradiction, for he loves home and quiet home pleasures, yet is also keen on travel, activity and excitement. In family life he is unselfish, a comforter and a wonderful peace-maker. He is well-mannered and cheery, but does not concentrate enough. He both likes and dreads new things (here's the contradiction again) and is very kind to sick people. He is tactful and generally popular.

Life Lessons: He must learn to stick to one thing at a time and finish it; also not to overwork himself.

Career: He will make a good secretary or clerk, or a foreman in the building trade; failing these, he should be a butler, teacher or commercial traveller.

Lucky Days: Wednesday and Friday.

Lucky Numbers: 5 and 6.

Lucky Motto: "Concentration is the secret of success."

Joyce

Meaning: The name JOYCE has the delightful meaning, "Merry."

Character: She is sure to be popular with everyone, for

she is gentle and friendly, easy to get to know. She does not push herself forward at all, but adapts herself to others, allowing them to lead. She loves peace and will work hard to heal quarrels. She is quiet and persevering, but a little lazy and unresourceful. Tact is hers, also talent for detail.

Life Lessons: She must learn not to hide behind others when there is responsibility to be taken; also to refrain from gossip.

Career: She would be a good saleswoman or could work with her hands, at typewriting, cooking, dispensing or photography.

Lucky Days: Monday and Saturday.

Lucky Numbers: 2 and 4.

Lucky Motto: ''An ounce of help is worth a pound of pity.''

Leonard

Meaning: The name LEONARD has the splendid meaning, ''Strong as a lion.''

Character: Here's a gay, sociable, artistic personality for you! He has some kind of marked talent for amusing people—perhaps clever acting or mimicking. Or he will be able to paint or sing or play really well. He has a great deal of the joy of life and shuns the society of people who are too serious. He is good company, though a little inclined to show off. He is self-reliant, original and generally liked.

Life Lessons: He must learn that he does not always know better than anyone else and he must acquire sympathy for those in trouble.

Career: A job where he is among a lot of people should be chosen, such as hotel work, a post in a club, factory or school or the stage.

Lucky Days: Thursday and Friday.

Lucky Numbers: 3 and 6.

Lucky Motto: ''Have a heart that never hardens and temper that never tires and a touch that never hurts.''

Lilian

Meaning: The name LILIAN has the beautiful meaning, of "Purity."

Character: This girl has two different personalities at once. Most often she seems gentle and retiring, sweetly ready to keep in the background and let others shine. Yet sometimes she appears as a dominating, original and forceful personality, determined to have first place and rule others. She is sometimes very tactful, sometimes blunt and honest to the point of rudeness. A queer mixture!

Life Lessons: She must learn not to boss others and to work a little harder.

Career: Business of some sort is her best field, either office, shop or factory life.

Lucky Days: Sunday and Monday.

Lucky Numbers: 1 and 2.

Lucky Motto: "The gods sell us all good things for hard work."

Margaret

Meaning: The name MARGARET has the pretty meaning, "A pearl."

Character: A lover of her own way is this girl, for she has great independence and grit. She can use her hands skilfully, is very trustworthy and can be relied upon to finish what she begins. She likes to serve others and lend a helping hand—if she can help in her own fashion! She is tranquil and bright, as a rule, but worries more than most once she begins. She is very true and honest.

Life Lessons: She must learn to let others go their own way and to be more tactful and courteous.

Career: She would do well in a shop, as a shorthand-typist or a receptionist to a dentist or in an hotel.

Lucky Days: Thursday and Sunday.

Lucky Numbers: 4 and 7.

Lucky Motto: "Life is not so short but that there is always room for courtesy."

Marjorie

Meaning: This is a variation of the name Margaret and has the same meaning, "A pearl."

Character: She is much more often laughing than serious and takes life joyfully, making the most out of the present moment and looking forward to something new to-morrow. She is a bit erratic, but generous, persevering and fascinating. She loves clothes and spends a lot on them. She is unpunctual and dislikes responsibility, as she has such a carefree nature. At times she will lay down the law.

Life Lessons: She must learn not to hoard up rubbish and not to be quarrelsome.

Career: The stage or films would suit her well, or she might be a dancer, or go into advertising.

Lucky Days: Thursday and Friday.

Lucky Numbers: 3 and 5.

Lucky Motto: "It is the little disagreements that pave the way for the big heartaches."

Mary

Meaning: The name MARY is usually taken to mean "Bitter," but another and nicer meaning sometimes attributed to it is "The Bride."

Character: This girl has two distinct sides to her nature. One is that of a born leader, self-reliant, determined and rather selfish. The other is quiet, retiring and anxious to please. So that in practice this girl will swing from one personality to the other and so be rather difficult to understand and get on with. She is good company and an excellent hostess.

Life Lessons: She must learn how to get on well with everyone, without either domineering too much or giving in too much.

Career: Office or shop life is suited to her. So is teaching.

Lucky Days: Monday and Tuesday.

Lucky Numbers: 1 and 2.
Lucky Motto: "Live and let live."

Olive

Meaning: The name OLIVE means "Dark-skinned."

Character: She is an odd mixture of stubbornness and docility, of independence and a tendency to cling. She is careful and thorough in all she does and you can always rely on her loyalty. Her affections go deep, but she does not show them easily. She's a bit opinionated, perhaps, but very lovable, gentle and tranquil.

Life Lessons: She must learn to manage money, neither stinting it nor being wildly extravagant and she must keep on trying.

Career: She could make a success of teaching or of social work. She would also be a splendid nurse or might take up an artistic career.

Lucky Days: Monday and Saturday.

Lucky Numbers: 2 and 7.

Lucky Motto: "Money was made round so that it would roll and flat so that it would stay put."

Peggy

Meaning: The name PEGGY has the pretty meaning, "Child of light."

Character: Plenty of temperament is found with this name. She is full of the joy of life, vivacious, rather fickle, easily excited, generous and loving. She never takes her opinions from other people, but has ideas which are all her own. She likes to play a leading part and is able to do so, for she is decided and self-reliant—though she may change her decisions rather often! She loves movement and independence.

Life Lessons: She must learn to be more unselfish and to so fewer things at a time.

Career: She is cut out for teaching or any kind of nursing.

She could become a home help and do very well, or work for a doctor or dentist.

Lucky Days: Tuesday and Wednesday.

Lucky Numbers: 1 and 5.

Lucky Motto: "Unselfishness is the only real religion."

Peter

Meaning: The name PETER has the fine meaning, "A rock."

Character: A boy with real creative ability, which he will express in some form of art or service for others. Yet he is contradictory, for though he wants to help and teach, he is also in some ways a bit selfish. He has plenty of ability, originality, independence and kindness, and a very definite personality of his own. He will be noticed wherever he goes. Give him plenty of love, admiration and independence.

Life Lessons: He must learn to be considerate of others and to help them in *their* way, not his.

Career: He might go into the Army, or become a preacher, doctor, chemist, painter or inventor, or take up social service. Not suited to business or a routine job.

Lucky Days: Sunday and Tuesday.

Lucky Numbers: 1 and 9.

Lucky Motto: "Inwardness, mildness and self-renouncement do make for man's happiness.

Phyllis

Meaning: The name PHYLLIS has the pretty meaning, "A leaf."

Character: This girl is rather quiet-natured. She spends a good deal of time alone, yet wants a certain amount of social life too. She enjoys repairing mechanical things. She is gentle and apparently yielding, but has strong opinions of her own. Many people ask her advice, owing to her trustworthiness and sympathy. She has brains, but will not always bother to use them.

Life Lessons: She must look on the bright side of things and not be quite so cautious about anything new.

Career: She would do well in an antique shop, as cashier in a shop or restaurant or in a bank.

Lucky Days: Thursday and Saturday.

Lucky Numbers: 4 and 7.

Lucky Motto: "Every cloud has a silver lining."

Robert

Meaning: The name ROBERT has the attractive meaning, "Bright fame."

Character: This boy will be liked by everyone—he is so good-tempered and ready to do what people want and to help them. He is careful over details and fairly patient. He mixes well with most people, though sometimes his manners are too blunt to please. He loves peace and always tries to smooth things over if people round him quarrel, but he can stand up fiercely for his own rights on occasion. He likes a leader to follow and is inclined to hero worship. He uses his hands cleverly.

Life Lessons: He must learn to be more generous with money and not to overwork himself.

Career: The medical profession would suit him well or he might be a male nurse. If not, he should enter the building or house decorating trades, or work in a hotel.

Lucky Days: Monday and Thursday.

Lucky Numbers: 2 and 4.

Lucky Motto: "Economy is a way of spending money without getting any fun out of it."

Ronald

Meaning: The name RONALD means "Powerful judgement."

Character: He is splendid company, cheery, well-mannered, the life and soul of the party. But in his own family he has a tendency to seek solitude and to go his own way independently of others. He is decided in his opinions, a little apt to show off, very trustworthy and one who thinks things out. He is enthusiastic and does things on the impulse of the moment.

Life Lessons: He must learn to take a back seat sometimes and not to talk so much.

Career: In any profession he will come to the front. He should go into bank or estate office, or become a naturalist, an actor or clergyman.

Lucky Days: Thursday and Saturday.

Lucky Numbers: 3 and 7.

Lucky Motto: "Speech is silver but silence is golden."

Sheila

Meaning: The name SHEILA is an Irish variation of Cecilia, and means "Blind."

Character: You're sure to like her, for she's full of fun and spirits, yet at the same time unselfish, considerate and motherly, with a special kindness for very young or for sick people. She likes to be noticed and deserves to be, for she has many gifts and virtues, especially in the home circle. She is clever both at making and mending clothes and has more than one attractive party trick with which to entertain guests.

Life Lessons: She should learn to be a little more enterprising and not to despise dull but necessary jobs.

Career: Something artistic would suit her and she might work in a handicrafts shop or help at a high-class photographer's. Nursing also makes a strong appeal to her.

Lucky Days: Thursday and Friday.

Lucky Numbers: 3 and 6.

Lucky Motto: "Make hay whilst the sun shines."

Thomas

Meaning: The name THOMAS means "A twin."

Character: This boy will not care much for new things. He likes what he is used to—and this includes people. He is a home-lover, yet in his own way decidedly independent.

He enjoys movement and activity. Full of moods, he is rather difficult to understand, and he dreams many dreams. He is a very good friend indeed, loyal, devoted and sympathetic.

Life Lessons: He must learn not to be a stick-in-the-mud and not to lose heart too easily.

Career: He will do well in the building trade or in mining, or in the services.

Lucky Days: Friday and Saturday.

Lucky Numbers: 6 and 7.

Lucky Motto: "He who loses hope may then part with everything."

Vera

Meaning: The name VERA has the fine meaning, "True."

Character: This girl loves home and family and shows at her best in th family circle. She is not much interested in travel or adventure, but likes sport and manual hobbies. She is very deft-fingered at all such things. Perhaps she's a wee bit timid and inclined to stay in the same old rut, but she is so sweet-natured and helpful that no one can help loving her.

Life Lessons: She must learn not to load herself up with more than she can do, and not to take too múch notice of the neighbours' opinions.

Career: Something rather "airy" will appeal to her and she could do well with a post in the wireless or aviation world. Or she might go into the dress or jewellery trades.

Lucky Days: Thursday and Friday.

Lucky Numbers: 4 and 6.

Lucky Motto: "They say. What do they say? Let them say."

Violet

Meaning: The name VIOLET has the pretty meaning, "Modest grace."

Character: She is very dependent on praise, encouragement and admiration. She badly wants to be in the limelight, yet has not much self-confidence to get her there. She is tactful and courteous. In many ways she is strangely contradictory, for she is both generous and mean, impulsive and cautious, anxious for attention and content to remain unnoticed. She will have much popularity.

Life Lessons: She must learn to be less dramatic in everyday life and to take decisions more promptly.

Career: She could probably succeed on the stage or connected with it; or take up clerical, secretarial or factory work.

Lucky Days: Monday and Tuesday.

Lucky Numbers: 2 and 9.

Lucky Motto: "Let your yea by yea, and your nay, nay."

William

Meaning: The name WILLIAM has the fine meaning, "Helmet of resolution."

Character: He lives up to his name meaning, for he is strong-willed and resolute, born to rise to the top. Combined with his energy and talent is a simple kindness which is attractive, especially to women. He is clever at making and mending about the house, rather conventional in his ideas of behaviour, but very progressive in work and thoughts. He is domesticated and will make a good husband.

Life Lessons: He must learn not to blurt out all he thinks and to be a little quicker.

Career: Carpentry, running a "one-man" shop or gardening would all suit him, or he might enter the upholstery trade or radio and television servicing.

Lucky Days: Sunday and Friday.

Lucky Numbers: 1 and 6.

Lucky Motto: "Nobody likes the candid truth excepting the person who tells it."

Winifred

Meaning: The name WINIFRED has the pretty meaning, "White wave."

Character: She loves travel and change—monotony of any kind is her greatest bugbear. She likes people, but not for long at a time. She is adaptable and easy to get on with in most ways but has some very strong peculiarities which nothing will budge. She does not care for hard work; a life of ease with plenty of sleep is her ideal. She in interesting, impulsive and changeable, yet also conservative and very economical.

Life Lessons: She must learn to work hard and steadily and not to be stubborn.

Career: She would be good at nursing or some form of social service, as a teacher or a shop assistant.

Lucky Days: Monday and Wednesday.

Lucky Numbers: 2 and 5.

Lucky Motto: "Diligence is the mother of good fortune."

WHAT YOUR HANDWRITING REVEALS

HANDWRITING is a first-class guide to character. Although experts spend a lifetime studying its finer points in order to make detailed character readings, even a small amount of study of this part of *Book of Fortune Telling* will enable you to tell a useful amount about the personalities of your friends and any strangers who write to you. You will improve with practice, too, and find it is most useful, when you are to meet a stranger for the first time, if you can find out something about him or her beforehand. The easiest way of doing this is to glance over the handwriting of the letter which makes the appointment.

Let's start with the nib or point used, because this controls to a large extent the thickness or fineness of the writing. You may say that the modern fibre-tipped pens make all

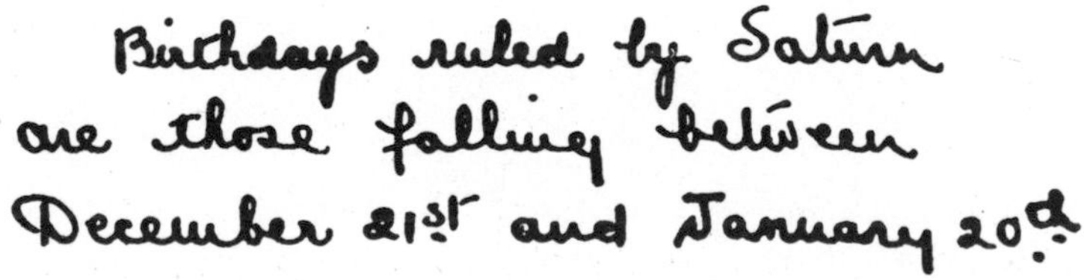

Birthdays ruled by Saturn are those falling between December 21st and January 20th

Fig. VII.
Thick large writing with letters well rounded.

writing done with them thick and of the same evenness throughout, without variation in the up and down strokes. This is quite true but it does not affect the accuracy of graphology or reading character by handwriting. It simply means that people who use fibre-tipped pens in preference to ordinary nibs have or are acquiring, the character traits which go with thick, black writing.

Thick, black, all-overishness writing, done with a fibre-tipped pen, a very soft pencil or a thick, soft nib, is seen in Fig. VII. It is a sign of an easy-going, pleasure-loving temperament, rather lazy and yet at times inclined to be abrupt and self-assertive.

Medium thickness denotes a middle course between the characteristics of thick and thin writing—someone who likes both work and pleasure, can hold her own without pushing and is reasonably diplomatic.

Fine Writing (you see an extreme example in Fig. VIII) gives an active, lively and refined person with sensitivity and

Fɪɢ. VIII.
An example of large writing.

a love of work. In Fig. VIII these traits are intensified—it is the writing of a man whose feelings are easily hurt, who is referred to by his friends as "such a gentleman" and has much tact and intuition.

Size of Writing

The next large, general point to notice is the size. Some people write a small hand, hardly to be read without a magnifying glass; others have a sprawling "fist" which gets only a few words on a page. Most handwritings, of course, come between these two, both in size and characteristics.

Large Writing (seen in Figs. VII and IX) belongs to people who are proud, generous and frank, with high ambitions and ideals. They look at things in a broad, general way and are not fond of details or particularly accurate. They have

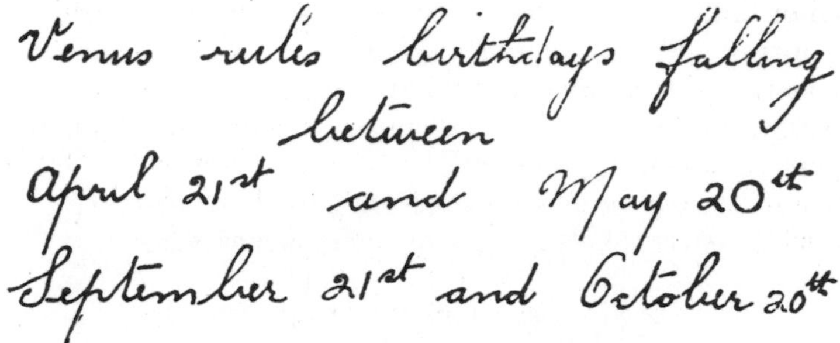

FIG. IX.

An example of large writing.

good self-confidence and like to be important; they are also kind and warm-hearted. Foresight is strongly shown and they sometimes look too far ahead and consequently miss present opportunities.

Medium-sized writing, if other indications don't contradict, shows a very well-balanced nature, which dislikes extremes and can see both sides of any questions. There are common-

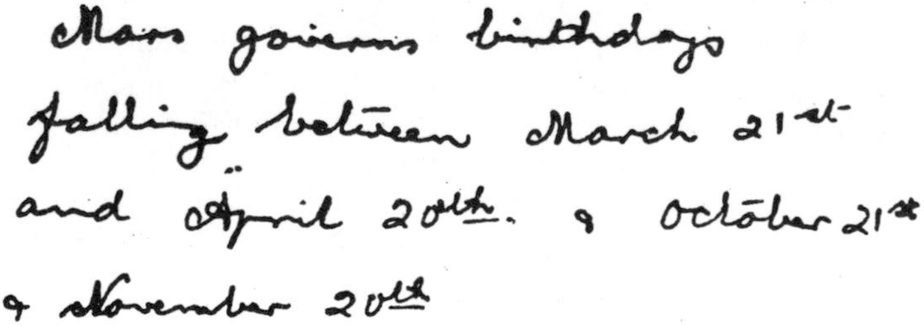

FIG. X

Broad writing, with capitals like small letters enlarged

sense and an even temper, but rather a lack of enthusiasm and energy. Fig. X shows a medium-sized hand.

Small writing belongs to a cheerful person with strong opinions, an ability to learn easily, thrifty ways with money and a reserved "shut-up" nature. There is good ability for details, but not enough looking ahead—events spring on this writer unawares because she is so absorbed in what is happening at the moment.

Very small writing, which is difficult to read unless very clear, shows either a tremendous love of detail or a small (petty) mind, or both. There may be some spitefulness, meanness in money matters and a tendency to dwell too much on trifles.

Shape of Writing

Writing varies enormously in its general shape or formation and each variation is a guide to the personality. So learn to classify at a glance the type of handwriting in any particular letter. Here are some of the most frequent.

Angular or Pointed, with a rather spiky look (Fig. VIII). This betokens a penetrating mind, firmness (which sometimes becomes obstinacy) and a quick temper. If very pointed, egoism.

Rounded (Fig. VIII) is the mark of a good-tempered and kind-hearted nature, affectionate and sympathetic. If the roundness is very naked, there would be also weakness, indolence and indecision.

Curly or Flourishly.—When there are more curls and squiggles than are necessary, especially in capital letters or at the ends of words, the writer is prone to exaggeration, has plenty of imagination and self-importance, and is rather vain and given to posing.

Narrow (that is, the letters themselves, not the strokes forming them, have a thin, rather compressed appearance). This is a sign of emotional restraint—an inability to let oneself go.

Broad (the letters themselves, as apart from the strokes that form them, being generously proportioned and rather "fat," as in Figs. VII and IX). The writer has a good opinion of herself and is a strong character, with much imagination. She has tenacity and independence.

The Slope of the Writing

More often than not, handwriting has a mildly forward slope. Sometimes this slope is exaggerated, so that one wonders if the words will fall on their faces! At other times you will see writing which is upright, with no tilt at all, or, less commonly, which has a backward slant. All these have their meanings to the careful eye.

Sloping Forward (in Fig. VIII the slant is only slight). This type of writing shows a sensitive, tender-hearted and affectionate personality, rather inclined to depend on others. The more decided the slant is, the stronger these traits are present.

Upright.—This kind of writing is particularly English—you see it well in Fig VII. People who pen their letters like this are as upright as their writing, very honest and honourable, though sometimes lacking in tact. They have more self-control than those writing slopes and more patience but are harder in their outlook.

Back Sloping. Writing which shows a slant backwards to

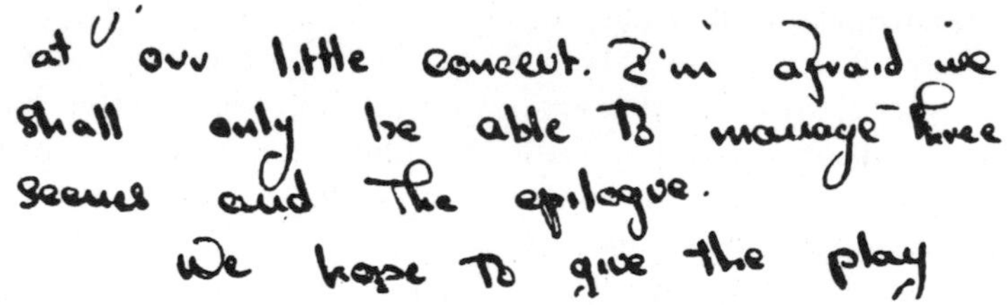

FIG. XI.

Medium-sized writing with wide spaces between the words.

the left, (in Fig. XI it is only slight) instead of the more usual forward tilt towards the right, betrays a rebellious, original obstinate nature, which *must* be different from others. There are often emotional difficulties, with feelings hidden so that you wonder if there are any in this self-contained nature! They're there, all right, but circumstances have suppressed them. There is also a tendency to look back to the past and harbour old grievances.

All Ways. Occasionally you'll meet with writing that doesn't seem able to make up its mind! One word will slope forward, another back, a third be more or less upright; or there may be a few lines of one type, then a sudden abrupt change to another and back again. Here you have a person who is very nervy and unsettled, changeable, torn by indecision, trying to face all ways at once.

The Slope of the Lines

When reading character from something written on unlined paper, notice the slope of lines. Do they tend to tilt upwards towards the right-hand margin, to keep level all along or to descend?

Ascending writing (Fig. XII) indicates optimism, cheerfulness and ambition, with plenty of energy and drive and warm feelings.

Level lines betoken a truthful and accurate person, not much subject to moods and with a strong sense of duty. (See Fig. VIII).

Descending Lines. (Fig. XIII). Sometimes this type of writing merely shows tiredness or being temporarily rundown. You can deduce this if the same person usually writes either level or with an upward slant. If the downward lines are habitual, either ill-health is habitual, too, or there is a pessimistic trend, with lack of self-confidence and a sentimental day-dreaming tendency.

Notice, also, both in the words themselves and in the lines of words, whether the writing becomes smaller towards the end of a word or line. Or larger.

Diminishing writing, where words or lines trail off small and sometimes almost to nothing, show a hasty, impatient,

Fig. XII.

Writing and autograph of Louis Couperus, famous Dutch novelist.

energetic person, always trying to do twice as much as there is time for! The intelligence is quick and shrewd.

Increasing writing, in which the ends of words or lines are larger than the beginnings, betrays frankness, a feeling of leisure, disinclination to hurry and thoroughness.

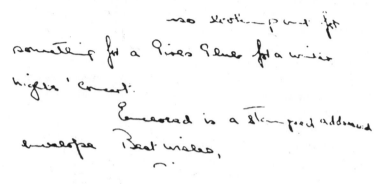

FIG. XIII.

An example of writing showing tiredness and ill-health

So much for handwriting is general. Now let's consider the way the letters are formed, the punctuation and other more detailed signs.

The Details of Handwriting

Capital Letters reveal much. Plain, well-formed capital letters, like those in Fig. VII show energy, will-power and a feeling for beauty. When the capital letter is simply a small one enlarged (see the V of Venus and the A of April in Fig. IX) you will have a simple, clear-headed nature. Very flourishy and scrolly capitals indicate some affection and vanity, with perhaps a desire to be more important than one actually is.

Large letters which are formed in an unusual way, like the L in Louis and London (Fig. XII) and the T's in Fig. VIII are the mark of imagination and originality—the person who does things a little differently from other people and has inventive ideas.

Capitals which are large or high in proportion to the rest of the writing show someone who is ambitious, proud and anxious to be prominent, generally rather an egotist. If the capitals hardly stand out from the rest of the writing, there is not enough self-confidence and too much timidity and modesty. Capitals of medium size compared with the small letters are best, showing a reasonable balance between egotism and self-importance on the one hand and the door-mat type on the other.

Signatures. As these always have two or more large letters in them, much of what has just been said about capitals applies to signatures as well. You may have an idea that all outstanding and famous people have important-looking signatures with lines and curlicues under them; but this is very far from being always true. Many well-known and brilliant people sign their names in a very simple way, while some of the large, noticeable signatures you see belong to people who *want* to be in the limelight but are really quite insignificant. The autograph which inspires confidence in both the ability and character of its owner is usually clear, with a certain look of power and energy about it and deci-sively written. It may or may not have a line under it but it will *not* be fussy.

When there is no line, the nature is kind and simple—there is no putting on airs. A full stop or dot after the signature is a sign of prudence, reserve and some pessimism. Should there be several dots with a line under as well the signer is over-prudent—suspicious and distrustful, in fact.

The same person's signature may vary at different times. Here is the moody, temperamental man or woman, perhaps very charming in some ways, but erratic and difficult to get on with because there is so much variability.

Barring of the T. Will-power is shown in several ways in graphology, for example by an angular type of writing, with thick downstrokes to the long-tailed letters. But its chief sign is in the letter T (both capital and small) and the way in which its bar is made.

Notice the striking flyaway bars to both small and capital t's in Fig. VIII, with their fine, strongly upward strokes. Here is an impulsive, ardent nature, inclined in a fit of enthusiasm to take on more than he can easily carry out. He is also decidedly artistic. The opposite kind of bar, short and thick and crushed down on the letter, betokens a rather obstinate person with very strong opinions and plenty of energy.

When the bar is long but curved upwards instead of straight, it shows refinement and artistic ability. A long bar ending in a hook formation shows a person who is not easily deflected from any purpose she has in mind. Sometimes a short, thick bar is so straight that it looks as though done with a ruler rather than merely a pen—then again there is the obstinacy of the short, thick bar mentioned above and also a slow, orderly nature.

Whenever the crossing stroke is high up it is a mark of ambition. Whenever it is low down you have a quiet, meek nature resigned to whatever Fate may bring. If the t bar does not cross at all but is to the right of the letter, as in Fig. X, energy, initiative and ability to organise and take control are indicated.

Sometimes it is wholly on the left of the upright t stroke. People who write it in this way are timid, afraid of responsibility and cannot make quick decisions. If the crossing slopes downwards read it as for downward-sloping writing as a whole.

If the bar of a final "t" joins up with the next word, you have a lively, cheerful person with a good sequence of ideas.

Endings of Words. Probably a majority of people end their words as soon as the last letter is fully formed. You can read from this that they are fairly cautious, like to get value for money and, often, that they are in a hurry to get on to the next thing they have to do. But when the last strokes of last letters are drawn out, make wide spaces between the words, the writer is particularly kind and generous. When there is a final curve which is thrown backward over the word, as sometimes happens, you can deduce enthusiasm, impetuosity and a warm heart.

Long-tailed Letters. Letters with loops going below the line are often revealing, particularly g's and y's.

Are they long and slightly sloping, with the final stroke joining up unbrokenly and gracefully to the next letter, as in Fig. VIII? Then the writer is sensitive, imaginative and fluent in speech or writing. If so long that they run into the letters of the line below, the nature is over-sensitive, with so much imagination that it leads to undue worry. If the loops are small or imperfectly formed, especially at the ends of words, you must read either great economy or, if the writing otherwise does not indicate thrift, a person who is always in a hurry.

Letters unusually formed (see the upward f loop in Fig. XI) show originality and independence.

Punctuation

Most people put in full stops, even if they are careless about punctuation otherwise. So if you see the full stop omitted entirely, as in Fig. IX, there is a person who is not very strong-willed and rather lazy and lacking in energy. A large black stop, on the other hand, shows a pleasure-loving, materialistic writer. Dots and dashes employed rather at random instead of commas and full stops are the mark of someone who is romantic, enthusiastic and rather helter-skelter. When there are frequent exclamation marks, especially if they are long compared with the size of the writing, you can deduce plenty of imagination and a tendency to exaggerate. If the mark is very sloping, there is much tenderness.

When all punctuation is neatly and painstakingly put in,

the writer is methodical, patient and businesslike. If the rest of the writing agrees, there may be literary ability.

A Brief Graphology Delineation

To wind up, here is a short reading of the inscription in one of his books written by Louis Couperus, a well-known Dutch novelist. It is usually better, if possible, to read character from a specimen which has several lines of writing in it but much can be told even from the few words given here (Fig. XII).

The medium-sized writing—except for the signature which was naturally large, because his autograph had been asked for—shows a well-balanced nature which can see all sides of a question. In type it is a compromise between the rounded and the angular, showing kindness and sympathy but also a penetrating mind. The slight forward slope of the words betokens a sensitive, affectionate and somewhat clinging temperament.

Notice the very marked upward slant of the lines and the good artistic arrangement and balance of the whole inscription, giving a very ambitious, hopeful, warm-hearted and cheerful nature, with strong artistic ability, good taste and good planning capacities. The capitcal C shows clear-headedness and the L's imagination and originality. Their size again underlines his ambition and feeling of being Somebody. Artistic powers, coupled with refinement, come to the fore once more in the curved-upward bar of the t in "most".

The letters in the words being often separated denote intuition and insight into the minds of others. The books of this author show these traits to a marked extent. From the unlooped downstrokes of the f, y and p you can guess Mr. Couperus was rather cautious and thrifty of both money and effort.

The brief specimen does not give much clue to punctuation but what there is is normal. The Roman figures in the date again emphasize the outstanding originality; and the rather flyaway bar above them betrays some inclination to impulse, in spite of the general good balance and repeats the tendency to warm-heartedness.

You will find it interesting practice to see what other character traits you can discover for yourself in the handwriting of this famous novelist.

Remember when reading handwriting to concentrate on the few most outstanding characteristics first. Details are important, too, in rounding out the picture but where there are contradictory traits give most weight to a general rather than to a small sign. Very often, of course, both the opposing points may be true, for we are all a mass of contradictions; but nearly always one of the two traits has a good deal more prominence than the other. You should assess it accordingly.

"BUMPS" AND FACE FORTUNES

HAVE you noticed that even people who declare loudly that they have no belief whatever in fortune telling or character reading invariably practise one kind of it themselves? I mean by that, there isn't a man or woman anywhere who doesn't judge people quite a lot by their faces.

Perhaps they have never heard of physiognomy, as the science of face reading is called, and wouldn't understand what the word meant if they did! But they practise it all the same, quite without realising it. For these same sceptics who scoff at fortune-telling methods will often say to you, "I never have trusted Mr. Jones—his eyes are too close together".

Or, "You can tell Mary is weak. Look what a receding chin she's got." Pure physiognomy!

Face reading is actually one of the most convenient kinds of character reading, because it can be practised just anywhere where there are faces! No need to get the consent of the subject, to look at her hand, a specimen of her writing or ask her birth-date! All you have to know about the kind of person she is is written on her face for you to read, if you know how to do so.

This knowledge is well worth while, for besides being a fascinating hobby, it gives you an immediate and useful insight into the character of any person you meet. This helps you to deal with that person in the best way and to avoid hurting or misjudging her.

Allied to face-reading or physiognomy is phrenology, the art of telling the character and talents by the shape of the head or "bumps", as it is popularly called.

Face Fortunes

By studying the *proportions* of a face, you will be able to judge of the predominant set of qualities that belongs to its owner. Just as there are the three worlds of palmistry (see page 27) which shows a person's general outlook, so in physiognomy the face can be divided into three parts in a very similar way.

The first thing is to see if these three parts are all about equal; if not, which is longer than the others and by how much. If you are definitely telling a face fortune, it's a good plan to measure the three divisions and so be quite accurate; but when this is not possible, you must judge by eye. You will, with practice, get very used to doing this and seldom make a mistake.

The three divisions in a face are: (1) the forehead; (2) the entire length of the nose: (3) from the base of the nose to the point of the chin, comprising the upper lip, mouth and chin. In each case, of course, the measurement, whether real or in the mind's eye, is taken downwards.

In a perfectly proportioned (which will also be a beautiful) face, these three divisions will be equal in length, and will give an extremely well balanced nature—which does nothing in excess and has no strong peculiarities, what we might call a perfectly normal person. In all departments of life—work, love, marriage, social affairs and so on—she will do reasonably well without being a genius at anything. In fact, a thoroughly satisfactory woman, but perhaps not a thrilling one!

A face that is fairly even balanced, but, for example, has the nose section shortest, with the other two divisions almost equal, gives a more distinctive personality.

The forehead longest shows the "brainy" person, whose intellect rules. She will think for herself and will also be mentally alive and quick. She will have foresight and the ability to teach others.

The nose longest indicates that the practical and energetic sides of the nature are the most important. There will be both physical strength and good abilities, with an active, businesslike, forcible nature and a broad outlook.

The mouth and chin area longest betoken a determined person with plenty of endurance. While this is broadly true, however, there are other factors besides length needed to make a strong chin and more about these will be found on page 222.

Now that you have settled the general type to which your subject belongs, by the "three worlds" classification, try to see the face in profile, for this again will give you a set of three distinct natures.

The convex profile is one which has a general outward curve, caused by a jutting-out nose and a forehead and chin set definitely back than the nostrils. Not only are they further back, but the forehead slopes back from bottom to top and the lips and chin slope back from top to bottom.

This person is predominantly quick—in thought, in action, in feeling, in temper. She has plenty of nervous energy and often a good share of nerves. She is impulsive, rushes enthusiastically into a new plan but tires of it if it demands long concentration or endurance. She is amusing company, does things in spurts, often changes her opinion and is very adaptable.

The concave profile is the exact opposite of the convex. When seen in silhouette, the features make an inward curve, owing to a forehead and chin which project and rather a small nose. The nose, of course, breaks the curve to some extent, but you will recognise the concave profile if the forehead slopes inward as it goes down and the mouth slopes outwards to the point of the chin.

With this silhouette you have a slow, silent, patient person. She does nothing in a hurry but is thorough and painstaking. She has no versatility like the convex type, but makes a good specialist. She is a dreamer and thinker with little energy, so is often rather lazy and absent-minded. She has plenty of determination and is tactful but often narrow and obstinate.

Concave profiles are not nearly as common in this country as convex ones, being more a southern type.

The *plane profile* is far from plain in the other sense of the word, being usually the best-looking of the three! Here the silhouette is more or less straight, the forehead being practically vertical, the chin and lips also and the nose only projecting a moderate amount.

These people correspond to those in whom the three divisions of the face are equal in length and have the same sort of balanced, all-round, never-going-to-extremes sort of nature.

Sometimes the convex and concave types may be combined in one profile. For instance, the forehead and nose may be convex and the mouth and chin concave or the other way round. In these cases you must read their characters also as being a blend of the two types, not so extreme as either the convex or concave when in a pure form.

Having made these general observations to determine the type of person you are dealing with, now you can fill in the details by noticing each feature in turn.

The Forehead

As already mentioned, the brow is the index to brain power and the amount of interest in mental things. The physiognomist divides foreheads into several different classes, according to their shape, and each is accompanied by certain traits.

The high forehead denotes roughly what we mean when we talk of a "highbrow". It shows its owner to be intellectual, fond of books and reading, anxious to improve her mind and to acquire knowledge. She probably has an excellent memory. She is also religious, high-minded and honourable and her word is her bond.

High foreheads may be narrow or broad. If narrow, the owner is learned, but not original or independent. She thinks over what she learns, but does not add anything to it. She is reserved and unpractical and keeps in the background.

A forehead broad and high is excellent to have, for it gives the best abilities, combining the intellectual and the practical, the imitative and the inventive, in just the right proportions.

The low forehead belongs to a simpler, less ambitious and more unthinking person, who accepts the world as it is and does not try to puzzle things out. Often the memory is not very good and she is more impulsive than her friend with a high forehead—in fact pretty much what we mean when we speak of a "lowbrow."

The broad forehead shows good abilities, though less memory than with the "highbrow" type. The brains are not so much of a thinking and bookish order as constructive and reasoning. This girl is persevering, money-making and can get things done—the type of the successful business woman.

The narrow forehead shows more or less of the narrow outlook, with a timid, conservative disposition. Such people will often have old-fashioned, prejudiced views which nothing will induce them to change. They are not musical or good at languages and they have not very good judgement because their prejudices sway them. A narrow forehead is improved if it is also high, as described above.

The square forehead is moderately high in proportion to its breadth and the same width at the bottom as at the top. It is not a very common shape of brow, but it is a good one, for it shows the same characteristics as the square type of hand (see page 17), that is, trustworthiness, complete honesty and good judgement combined with energy and an eminently practical outlook. The owner of this forehead has good constructive ability, whether for making a dress or writing a story (if imagination is added) and is also inventive and able to handle big things.

The Eyes

Someone called eyes "the windows of the soul," and this is an apt description, for the eyes are a good guide to the feelings, general behaviour and temperament of each one of us.

Don't consider only the colour but also the size, shape, nearness to the nose and the amount of sparkle. As regards size, remember that there are really no such things as large and small eyes, for all eyes are much the same size. The difference lies in the fact that what we call large eyes are widely opened ones, while those which are partly closed appear small.

Large eyes are observant (especially if round) and eager rather than deeply thoughtful. They show a person who takes people rather at their own valuation, believes what she reads and is therefore somewhat easy to exploit. In artistic matters she is imitative rather than original. If the eyes protrude at all, they belong to a chatterbox.

Medium eyes are the commonest of all and show an average nice person, without the pronounced faults of either a large-eyed or the small-eyed. Common sense is a leading trait of medium eyes.

Small eyes denote shrewdness and concentration. Think how people tend to close their eyes partly when they are absorbed in something or doing a bit of calculating! Because the concentration is greater, these folk see fewer things than those with large eyes, but take them in better. The memory is less good, but reasoning powers, independence and judgement are all superior.

If the eyes are over-small, however, be on the look-out for a sly and suspicious nature with a turn for trickery and an inclination to avarice. When small eyes are of the piercing "gimlet" type, they show undue curiosity, quick temper and spitefulness.

Wide-apart eyes (those with more than the width of an eye between them) show a reliable, loving and generous person, but one who is almost too trusting and so get deceived.

Eyes close together (less than the width of an eye separating them) denote a suspicious, unbelieving, calculating and prudent nature.

How much vitality and sparkle have the eyes you are noticing? A very wise old aunt of mine used to say that she judged people's brains more by the brightness or otherwise of their eyes than by the shape and size of the forehead, and I think there is a lot of truth in that. Bright, keen eyes show that their owner is alert and will make the most of the abilities denoted by her forehead. In this way she may go further and seem more brilliant than the apparently cleverer person who, with dull, lack-lustre eyes, fails to take full advantage of her brains.

It is noticeable that in most illnesses the eyes go dull, but in fewer, when the mind is usually strung up and very active, they are extra bright and glittering.

The colour of the eyes is important, too, though much rubbish has been set down about it by unthinking people. Here is an old French rhyme, evidently written by someone who had an unreasonable prejudice against brunettes:

> "Blue eyes go to the skies,
> Grey eyes to Paradise,
> Green eyes to Hell are bound,
> In purgatory black are found."

And here is another, a Scottish one, which implies that there are no good eyes of any colour—except perhaps blue!

> "Grey-eyed, greedy;
> Brown-eyed, needy;
> Black-eyed, never blin' (blink)
> Till it shames a' its kin."

However, take courage, brunettes, for in verse of this kind I'm afraid easy rhymes are often more considered than accurate statements! Actually the dark-eyed compare

very favourably with blondes, as you will see by the following lists of traits for different coloured eyes.

Blue eyes show good self-control, optimism, energy, viva-
city, good judgement and shrewdness. Their owners concentrate well, can reason, are original and practical. Their
memories are not too good.

Grey eyes (also those which are *pale* blue) belong to the
person who is systematic, self-controlled, matter-of-fact,
businesslike and rather cold and hard. These folks are
usually successful.

Green of grey-green eyes are the mark of good brains, many
talents and plenty of energy and enterprise. This lady is
temperamental and uncertain-tempered and may be inclined to deceit.

Hazel eyes belong to a kind, gentle, affectionate nature,
with something childlike about it even in middle age. Unless
the owner's hair is auburn, giving energy and drive to the
personality, this will not be a very strong character.

Brown eyes mark the emotional person, with great intensity
of affection and much capacity also for hatred. She is good
at detail, very artistic, demonstrative and sympathetic, but
has not great self control, showing her moods rather easily.

Black eyes belong to the south and are very uncommon in
England. They are like brown eyes, but more so, carrying
both the virtues and faults of the brown-eyed to extremes.
They are often jealous, but are very faithful to those they
love.

You sometimes here people say, "He must be deceitful
because he can't look at you without blinking and
wavering." Don't believe this, for it is founded on a
mistake.

The ability to look steadfastly at a person or thing (to
stare, really) depends not so much on character as on the
kind of sight you have. It is a matter of being able to
focus at a short distance. Short-sighted people do this easily
and so gain a reputation for honesty and truthfulness; while
those with long sight, who can stare intently at an

object a long way off and see all its details, may be quite
unable to keep their eyes fixed on someone at the other side
of the table.

So do not judge honesty by a person's gaze, but rather by
the various characteristics of the eyes which I have given
above.

Eyebrows

These usually "match" the eyes in a general way, but
have a few special points of their own serving as guides to
character.

Thin eyebrows show a calm, rather slow and silent person.

Thick, heavy eyebrows are the mark of an intense, nature,
with passion, devotion, jealousy and a tendency to get
obsessed by people or ideas.

Course, bushy eyebrows indicate uncommon abilities, but
they are often largely unused and merely make their owner
peppery.

Fine, flat eyebrows denote a strong-willed, optimistic person
with much perseverance.

Medium eyebrows, neither very thin, thick nor anything
else, show a medium, well-balanced person.

The direction and curve of the eyebrows is also revealing.

Straight eyebrows are those of a magnetic, vital nature.

Eyebrows curving downwards from the nose betoken great
impatience and impulsiveness.

Eyebrows curving upwards from the nose go with a temperament which loves mystery, intrigue and complicated
detective stories.

Arched eyebrows indicate a dreamy person who takes things
a good deal on trust instead of investigating for herself.

The Nose

"When I want good headwork, I always choose a man, if
otherwise suitable, with a long nose." So Napoleon is

reported to have said and he was a shrewd judge of men.
The nose shows not so much the brains a person has, but the
"headwork" he or she possesses in the sense of force of
character, energy and culture.

We can divide noses, according to shape, into several
types, such as the Greek, the Roman, the aquiline, the
hooked and the snub or *retroussé*. Also, of course, the average
nose, giving the usual "ordinary" (in the best sense) type of
nature.

The Roman nose, large and with an arched bridge, shows a
quick, active, powerful person, who can both do and
command and has much physical and mental strength. She
is determined and brave, a woman of action. But she is
impatient, restless and too much of a worrier. The longer the
nose the more assertive the nature, while breadth in this type
of nose generally gives strength of character. When high and
thin, this is sometimes called the aristocratic nose, as it is
common among those of high social standing.

The Greek nose is handsome and makes a straight line with
the forehead. It is not very common among English people.
It often accompanies a plane profile (see page 212) giving a
harmonious, moderate disposition, with courtesy and
adaptability. Such a person is artistic and cultivated, with
beautiful taste and a strong sense of justice. He is self-
controlled and wonderfully even-tempered.

The aquiline nose is arched in one continuous curve all down
its length, and is usually rather large and thin, like an
eagle's beak—differing thus from the Roman nose, which
has only the bridge arched. It gives somewhat the same
characteristics as the Roman nose, but with more refinement and peaceableness. Such a person seems born to
command, and this is also very largely an aristocratic
nose.

The hooked nose is large, well arched and broad, with a
characteristic downward and outward curve at the tip which
gives it rather an angular appearance. It belongs particularly
to the keen business woman, who is ambitious,

money-making, shrewd and calculating. She has much tact and observation, so that she can sum people up and therefore know how to persuade them to do what she wants. If this nose is short there is a sense of humour, but when it is long the less pleasant money-making characteristics predominate, giving more of an acquisitive temperament. At home the possessor of this nose is very devoted to her family and generous to them.

The retroussé or snub nose is depressed rather than arched, this depression being caused by an upturned tip. It is nearly always a small, short nose, more common to women than men. It indicates a cheerful, sunny-natured, sociable person, sometimes rather restless and inquisitive, and usually too impulsive. Tact is present, and also a certain amount of shyness, which may be hidden under a rather pert or abrupt manner. Miss Retroussé is vivacious and good-natured, and she is amazingly patient and persistent in sticking to a troublesome job till it is done.

The Mouth and Lips

Take great pains to be accurate in your judgement of mouths, for, with the eyes, they are the most expressive features in the face and give valuable clues to personality. The lips individually and the mouth as a whole, often have separate characteristics, but they are so closely linked in other ways that I am putting them under one heading here.

A small mouth of the rosebud type was considered a beauty asset in a woman, but I am afraid it is not a character asset, for it shows small-mindedness. There are culture and refinement, but these are carried to extremes and become affectation. The memory is excellent. When a small mouth is pursed up, expect to find a very orderly person, who is severe, economical and selfish.

A large mouth, while not pretty, is a good possession, for it belongs to a large-minded, tolerant and generous person.

The health is good; there is plenty of common sense and energy. This subject enjoys talking, and is good-natured and sociable.

Notice the set of the mouth and lips in the face—whether the corners turn up, turn down or remain level.

A turned-up mouth shows optimism and often accompanies a short, snub nose. Its owner has a happy nature which expects the best to happen. She likes company and laughs a good deal; she is cheerful and pleasant to deal with. But as she does not take anything very seriously, do not expect her to be a profound thinker or to solve complicated problems.

A turned-down mouth indicates exactly opposite characteristics—a pessimistic, melancholy nature, which sees the difficult side of everything and anticipates the worst. "Blessed is she that expecteth nothing, for she shall not be disappointed" is her gloomy motto. Often this attitude is partly caused by indifferent health. At the same time the pessimistic person, enjoying serious things, can deal with them more efficiently than the snub-nosed optimist.

A straight mouth, especially if the lips are moderately full, is almost ideal, for is shows a nice balance between gloom and frivolity, in addition to an even temper, kindness and a reasonable amount of firmness, refinement and ability to get on well with others.

When the lips protrude the digestion is often poor, and the nature impulsive, emotional and full of moods. Such a person has little patience and tends to do everything too fast. When she is faced with a long, slow job she is apt to show up badly. She is a chatterbox, and rather quarrelsome and aggressive, but quick, kind and sympathetic. Protruding lips usually go with a convex profile (see page 211).

When the lips, which are mostly thin, *recede,* you have a quiet, rather pessimistic nature, with reserved and conservative ideas. She is rather retiring, likes to be alone and is very trustworthy. Her self-control is good, but she views new ideas with gloom and distrust. Generally this mouth is set in a concave profile (see page 211).

When the mouth is plane (neither protruding nor receding) its owner is reliable and considerate, with much kindness and reasonableness.

Full, thick lips are not a very favourable sign, for they show a lack of self control and consequent greediness, coarseness or sensuality. Such people do not concentrate well, they are too indulgent with themselves and consequently do not make a great success. They have little enterprise and a lack of firmness in dealing with others.

Lips of only medium thickness, on the other hand, are excellent, provided the lips are held firmly and do not fall slackly open. Here's a good friend, courteous, kind, easy-going and sympathetic, with good taste and an appreciation of good food without greediness. She shows affection and unselfishness.

Thin, compressed lips belong to the cold, unapproachable person. She is hardworking, shrewd and determined and can control others, but alienates people by her reserve, carefulness over money and aloofness. Her abilities are much more noticeable than her charm.

Study also each lip separately.

The upper lip short betokens a great desire to be praised and approved of, with a good deal of vanity. Such people are full of animation and make pleasant companions.

The upper lip long belongs to an ambitious person with a strong individuality. She is obstinate and persistent and loves her work for its own sake, whether she is praised for it or not.

The lower lip short generally goes with a short chin and indicates weakness—a person with little reliability or self-control and often with poor health. A projecting chin will counteract these unfavourable traits.

The lower lip long bespeaks determination and faithfulness. Here's a kind, resolute and dependable person who will make an excellent friend and a good employee.

The Chin

The chin shows individuality. Have you noticed that animals never have chins? They are made more or less all to one pattern, however much we may flatter ourselves that our pet Fido or Pussy is entirely different from any other dog or cat! Animals are slaves to people and cannot act independently. The same is true of people—fortunately few—in whom the chin is almost completely lacking.

Chins may be protruding, receding or average. Remember that the average chin is *slightly receding,* so that for a chin to be labelled as receding or weak it must fall away very definitely, not just a little. You will make some bad mistakes and hurt many feelings if you dub as weak and stupid the owner of every chin which retreats slightly from the lips.

A definitely receding chin shows that its owner has grown up under circumstances where little or no call has been made on her endurance, self-control and power to make decisions. This is often the case with an only child who has been over-protected and indulged by fond parents. Such a person grows up with no more determination and character than a baby and it remains to be seen whether a harder environment will bring these out. If it fails to do so there will be weakness, "softness" and a temperament very easy to influence or order about.

Broadness of chin shows strength, so if a receding chin is broad this takes away a great deal of its weakness.

An average chin is in a straight line with the lips, when seen in profile, or falls away only slightly. With the slight falling away you have an average person who is a little quicker, more haphazard, impulsive and lacking in endurance than is usual. The straight or plane chin shows the moderate, well-balanced person associated with the plane profile (see page 212).

A protruding chin sticks out more or less in the profile and its owner's characteristics and determination "stick-out" in the same degree. She is not merely resolute, but often extremely stubborn. She is very slow and deliberate, thinks many times before she acts, but is also sure and has great endurance.

Broad chins, as already mentioned, bespeak strength, both physical and mental, especially if the jaws are square. Their owners are also very conscientious.

Narrow chins show more fragile health and less energy and will power. Narrow-chinned people seldom lead, as they have not the necessary initiative and "fight."

What of the shape of the chin in outline when seen from the front? There are several different shapes, giving varying characteristics.

Square: Obstinate, reliable, independent.

Pointed: Discontented, not very strong, quick perceptions.

Oval: Artistic, charming, kind, capable.

Double: Self-indulgent, good-natured, rather uncontrolled.

Dimpled: Ardent, artistic, fond of the opposite sex, self-willed.

Finally, consider the chin and jaw in proportion to the upper part of the face. They should not be of greater width than the forehead, because, if they are, there is too much domineering and inconsiderateness in the temperament. On the other hand, if the jaw is considerably narrower than the brow, its owner is either swayed and imposed upon. Both the same width is the ideal.

The Ears

When studying faces, people often forget to take the ears into account, yet they will enlighten you on some useful points if you remember to notice them.

Size is important—of course in relation to the size of the head.

Large ears betoken a rather go-ahead person, with a keen sense of values.

Medium ears show open-mindedness and fairness.

Small ears belong to rather cautious, conservative people.

Some ears lie snuggling close against the head. Others stick out from it noticeably.

Ears lying flat to the head show a considerable amount of caution.

Ears projecting show dash and originality.

The size if the lobe of the ear shows how much the person "warms up" to others. The larger the lobe the more friendly and responsive the nature, while small-lobed people warm up only to a chosen few.

If the tops of the ears are pointed—"faun" ears, as they are often called—you have a witty, amusing person who is full of clever backchat.

"Bumps" and What They Tell

The science of phrenology, or character by the shape of your head, divides the head into a great number of sections, and, as practised by the expert, is very skilled and difficult. However, you do not need to have studied the subject profoundly in order to be able to tell enough to interest yourself and your friends.

Instead of the elaborate classification of the experienced phrenologist, try using the simple Seven-Group system given below. Naturally it has not the same detailed accuracy as the professional method, but you will be delighted to find what a good general idea it will give you of the character of anyone whose head you examine by this plan.

To learn this easy system make yourself a simple chart—in this way.

Trace a head outline from any good-sized magazine illustration or other picture showing a head in profile. If it is a woman's head, disregard any "bumps" caused by curls in the hair and so on and in your tracing give the natural outline of a close-cropped head.

Rule a horizontal line across the traced head from eyebrow level in front straight across; it will end at the back somewhat below the crown of the head, behind the upper part of the ear. Rule another line parallel with it half way between it and the top of the head, then divide each line downwards into three sections of even width. Thus you have divided the whole top of the head above the face into six approximately equal sections, though the curve of the head will make some of the top three smaller than the others and the backmost one in the lower row probably larger than the remainder.

Number these sections 1 to 6, make No. 1 the top one nearest the front, working along the top row to 2 and 3, then starting the front one in the second row as No. 4 and working backwards to Nos. 5 and 6. The irregular space behind the ear, below No. 6, should be labelled No. 7

Thus you have your seven groups. Each section covers the space allotted by phrenologists to a group of allied qualities, and we are simplifying the job by taking only the groups, without splitting them up into their numerous sub-sections.

Memorise thoroughly the traits contained in each of the seven groups. Here they are:

Group One (front section, upper row) is the Sympathetic Group, including all the qualities of sympathy, understanding of others, and ability to work and play with others in association.

Group Two (middle section, upper row), is the Religious or Devotional Group. Under this heading comes such qualities as reverence, faith, hope, veneration and idealism.

Group Three (back section, upper row) is the Governing Group and from this you judge the ability to lead and control others and the amount of determination, self-confidence, desire for approval, efficiency and other qualities which make a person able to be a "boss" rather than an underling.

Group Four (front section, lower row) is the Intellectual

Group and gives a key to the kind of brains. It includes such traits as memory, sense of time and comparison and constructive ability.

Group Five (middle section, lower row) is the Self-Preservation Group, by which you can judge how much the subject will safeguard her own interests. This group includes ability to acquire money, caution, power of keeping secrets and the capacity to destroy or to carry out. If too strong it denotes the self-seeking person whose motto is, "Take care of Number One."

Group Six (back section, lower row) is the Social Group, dealing with relationships with other people, such as friendship, capacity for marriage on its companionable side and love of home.

Group Seven (the lowest section behind the ear) is the Vitality Group, covering love of life, ability to protect oneself, sex and parental love and nervous energy.

Now you have learnt the positions of the various groups and what each means and want to read someone's "bumps." Put your subject in front of you, hatless, so that you see her exactly in profile, and notice which of the sections—you mentally see these divisions on her head—is normal in size, which is extra large or bumpy and which is extra small or flat. You judge accordingly whether the qualities covered by a particular section are normal, very strong or rather weak.

If a side view leaves you in doubt, feel the head so that you can judge of the amount of "bump," or view it from the back in order to see the middle sections in profile, or from the front to estimate the front groups more exactly.

A little practice is needed, of course, to know what is average and what strong or weak, but this soon comes once you start studying head outlines. Now that so many people go hatless you can practise silent bump reading in trains and buses.

Let us take a sample reading. Suppose you study a head and assess the sections as follows: Groups One, Four and

Five, normal; Groups Two and Seven, weak; Groups Three and Six, strong.

Here is the character description you might give for such a head.

"You have good abilities and a good memory, with an average sense of time and fair constructive power. You are sympathetic and kind and can keep secrets faithfully. You understand others and get on well with them, but at the same time you look after your own interests and want to make money and succeed. You would do better if you had more vitality and lived more intensely.

"You probably will not marry or marriage will at any rate not be very important to you, as you have little liking for sex or for children and do not care much for home life. Yet marriage will give you companionship. You are rather a pessimist and have not a pronounced religious sense.

"Where you are mainly interested is in ruling and leading, both in business and in social life. You want very much to be liked, to have plenty of friends and to be sociable; though you do not care much for home in itself, yet you value it as a centre in which to entertain people. Your self-confidence, efficiency and good social qualities will make you shine among your friends and wherever you have an opportunity to control others, but be careful that you do not domineer over them."

DREAMS AND DESTINY

FROM the earliest times dreams and their meanings have fascinated people and been closely studied. The Bible is full of dreams which had a prophetic meaning and came true in at least a symbolic way and the ancients paid close attention to the visions of their prophets about what was going to take place.

Most of us dream to a greater or less extent every night but nine out of ten dreams vanish from memory the instant we wake. Don't try to recall them—if they go so quickly they are not important or significant. The tenth, perhaps, is a vivid dream which stays in your mind and still seems like a real experience long after you are up and going about the day's work. This is sort of dream which you should try to interpret by the list of meanings given in the following pages.

When using this key to dream topics, pick out the most important or striking subject first, as that will give you the main meaning. Afterwards you can look up the lesser bits and try to get a definite significance into the whole.

The Meaning of Dreams

ABROAD. To dream of being in a foreign country or going there denotes a pleasant journey at an early date, which to a spinster will result in marriage.

ABSENCE. If absent friends come to you in sleep, they will be returning, probably at short notice.

ACCIDENT. Occurring to the dreamer, a happy surprise, often a success is indicated. When happening to another, some danger is predicted.

ADMIRATION. If you are the subject to be admired it

shows that you are soon to be in a congenial atmosphere where you will be much appreciated.

ALTAR. An early wedding is indicated for you, if unmarried; if already wed, the marriage of a close friend.

AEROPLANE. A wealthy marriage is in store for you.

ARMY. A fighting army shows a change in your life with access of wealth.

ASHES. A usual indication of mourning, not necessarily for a close friend.

BABY. A happy baby foretells prosperity; a crying one, disappointment.

BAGGAGE. To dream of the conveyance of baggage means unexpected news of a worrying nature.

BANNS. To hear of banns being read is a good sign. It signifies happiness for you in the immediate future.

BANQUET. A sure sign of social advancement and financial benefit.

BATHING. To dream of bathing and swimming in deep water shows achievement very satisfying to yourself. If the water is too shallow, a sense of frustration is present.

BED. If a friend is seen in bed, an illness is indicated, but if it is your own bed it denotes a speedy marriage. To buy or make a bed means a change of residence.

BIRDS. A sign of good luck. If a flock is seen it means a journey abroad. To see birds shot shows that bad news is on the way.

BIRTH. If in your own house it will bring good fortune, if in another's, bad news will follow.

BLOOD. Serious illness or accident is indicated.

BOAT. A happy omen. You are about to start a new enterprise with great success.

BURN. A house on fire signifies loss of personal property.

CAT. An unpleasant sign indicating false news and deceitfulness.

CLIMBING. A sign of prosperity in business and good luck in the future.

CLOCK. Many good investments will come your way.

COFFIN. This brings news of the marriage of a near relative or close friend.

CUP. A full cup spells opportunities in the near future, but an empty one means trifling worries.

DANCING. A happy and fortunate event to come.

DANGER. A warning to look into your business affairs and your state of health.

DARKNESS. To have lost your way in the dark means perplexities which are worrying you unduly.

DEATH. An omen of marriage. To talk to dead people means a hopeful future.

DELUGE. A warning sign. Give up any enterprise which you are contemplating at the moment.

EATING. Others eating is a sign of good fortune. To be eating yourself indicates quarrels and separations.

EMBRACE. A close embrace for yourself shows the end of unhappiness; if of two friends, it will bring bad luck to one of them.

ENTERTAINMENT. Successful entertainment denotes slight illness in the family; unsuccessful, a death is foretold.

FAINTING. The fainting of another means loss of money. Yourself fainting indicates quarrels and disgrace.

FALL. This is usually an unfavourable sign and shows disappointment.

FLOWERS. Growing flowers seen in a garden are a lucky dream. If withered, slight illness is shown.

FLYING. You will be disappointed in your ambitions of the moment.

FUNERAL. This means a wedding or other important festivity.

GAMES. The playing of games indicates a great deal of physical activity to be undertaken shortly by you.

GHOSTS. A disappointment of one dear to you is in store, or slight sickness of a near relative.

GIFT. To receive one indicates a spell of bad luck in business, but to give one means new enterprises.

GOLD. If held in your hands, selfish ambitions must be

checked. If in someone else's hands, you will gain financially.

GRASS. Wide stretches of grass signify the birth of a child.

HAIR. To dream that you are bald means great riches, but to see a woman with long, beautiful hair means an accident.

HAPPINESS. Great happiness in a dream spells uncertainty in love, and should be taken as a warning that affairs may not turn out as well as you expect.

ILLNESS. Illness of yourself means that a journey will shortly be taken, but illness of another suggests the curtailing of a pleasant holiday for oneself.

JEWELS. A very favourable sign, bringing plenty of good luck.

KEY. The loss of keys foretells great vexation, but to find a key shows: to the unmarried, acquisition of property, and to the married, a child at an early date.

KING. To be in the presence of royalty indicates aspirations to social success, followed by promotion.

KISS. A great deal of kissing means you will receive a present quite soon.

LADDER. A sign of warning. You will be apt to incur debts and lose your friends.

LETTER. The receipt of a letter indicates good news and happiness in love; writing one, a successful enterprise will be undertaken.

MARRIAGE. To attend a wedding as a guest denotes good fortune coming; to be present at your own, an early divorce for you.

MIRROR. An unlucky subject to dream about. Quarrels will follow, and many hard words be said.

MONEY. The finding of money means a birth; losing it, a bad disappointment in love.

MOON. To dream of the moon is invariably a good omen, indicating happiness in all love affairs.

MOURNING. Mourning worn by others shows that a

wedding is shortly to be expected, but if on yourself, good fortune in money will come your way.

MUSIC. Sorrow is coming to the dreamer from far off.

NAKED. To dream of appearing naked or insufficiently clad in public is a warning of trouble ahead, which will result in a good deal of worry.

NUMBERS. Sheets of figures show worry in affairs of the heart, and a little scandal.

OAR. The loss of an oar while rowing signifies death in your own family.

OCEAN. If you are on the water, it is a sign that you are being talked about maliciously. If watching the water, you are contemplating a journey ahead.

PAIN. An unexpected sum of money will come to you. If you have a son, he will win a great distinction.

PHOTOGRAPH. One's own photograph being taken is a sign that an accident may befall you. To be given a friend's, bad feeling will arise between you.

PRISON. To be in prison denotes an offer of marriage in a short time.

PURSE. The loss of your purse means money worries. To dream of one being given to you, an unexpected adventure.

QUARREL. Unwelcome news awaits you, and a visit from an unexpected friend.

RAILWAY ACCIDENT. A sign of ill luck ahead. A friend will deceive you, and you will lose money.

RING. To be given a ring shows a broken promise, but to lose one indicates good news about business prospects.

SHIPWRECK. Misfortune is ahead of you. You will travel, but not happily.

SINGING. If you are singing yourself, unhappiness is in store for you, but if hearing others sing, you will have good fortune.

SNOW. To watch falling snow indicates that an important letter will arrive for you shortly.

STAIRS. To go up stairs shows that your ambitions are

being realised; but to come down them means scandal, leading to dismissal from business.

STRANGERS. To dream of moving among strangers denotes an early change of scene, bringing good luck.

SWIMMING. An unexpected death is foretold. When swimming as if in danger, financial trouble is at hand.

TEARS. To cry means that great joy and unexpected happiness will be yours.

TELEGRAM. The receipt of one yourself predicts a new friendship, with very important results.

TWINS. To talk with twins is a sign of special prosperity.

UMBRELLA. The loss of your own means an unlooked-for present from your beloved.

UNDERTAKER. To a married woman this indicates the birth of a child; to a spinster, usually success in love.

VOYAGE. You will shortly hear news from a friend abroad, and will be lucky in your immediate enterprises.

WALKING. To take a long and tiring walk means that you will hear serious news of a dear friend.

WASHING. The washing of clothes denotes a speedy change of abode; the washing of oneself, a threatened danger to a member of one's family.

WATER. To dream of drinking water is a sign of good fortune for your lover or husband.

YELLING. Prolonged screaming by oneself shows great fear of treachery from a friend; listening to yells, an omen of coming joy.

ZOO. To dream of animals in captivity warns of enemies who are in danger to you.

A Modern Method of Interpreting Dreams

As I have said, in ancient days and especially in Eastern countries the interpretations of dreams was considered very important. Then, as time went on people troubled far less about the meaning of these sleep visions and began to think it was "all rubbish", in many cases.

In the last few years, however, scientific men have started to study the meanings of dreams from a new angle—that of the modern science of psychology—and have found them often of immense value, not for reading the future, as in the old system given above, but to throw light upon the inner workings of the human mind.

During sleep, our reasoning and commonsense faculties are at rest. The subconscious mind, which does not reason and is quite instinctive, holds sway and it is this subconscious mind which produces our dreams.

Dreams *do* mean something on these modern lines, especially what I might call regular dreams—those you have not once, but at freqent intervals. Other dreams worth noting and trying to interpret are "once only" ones which make such an impression on you that you can remember them twenty-four hours afterwards.

These aren't numerous, for most dreams, as you know, are entirely forgotten half an hour after waking.

According to psychology, most dreams are very individual things. They have not a set meaning, but must be interpreted differently for each person dreaming them. However there are a few dreams which seem to be common to almost everyone; that is, there is hardly a person anywhere who has not dreamed some of them sometime or other.

These very common dreams have been found to have a definite meaning which hardly ever varies, whoever's sleep they may appear in. Therefore, as far as these sleep visions are concerned, if you dream one of them you can feel fairly certain as to its meanings.

Such dreams, when interpreted, generally fall into one of two general classes, which are:

1. Dreams which fulfil a wish that remains ungratified in waking life or which compensate for some defect.

For instance, someone who is hard-up dreams that she has her hands full of gold or a cripple dreams of winning a race. These dreams do not mean that such unlikely joys will actually come to pass, but only that those are the things the dreamer wishes for, but has never been able to attain, either because they are really impossible or because a great enough effort has not been made.

For instance, very likely the hard-up girl could be better off if she put more energy into her work. The cripple cannot hope, of course, to outrun normal people, but she may win some other race—passing an examination or getting promotion in her work—if she will try hard enough for it.

Such dreams thus often indicate that the dreamer is not doing her utmost to get what she wants. So if your sleep visions are of this type, ask yourself if there is anything you can do to make them come true. There usually is!

2. Dreams in which a muddle is made owing to the dreamer's own fault. These will often tend to "put you off" some new step you were contemplating, by making you feel that it will end in disaster. This does not mean that that step will really be disastrous at all, but merely that you "funk" it, and should bring a little more courage and efficiency to bear on it.

These dreams are worrying and disagreeable, and are more common than the "wish" type.

Here are the most frequent of the "standard" dreams, with their accepted psychological interpretations. You will find it interesting to compare these modern meanings with the ancient traditional ones given on pages 228 to 233.

Baby. Desire for motherhood, or merely for someone weaker than yourself whom you can control. If this dream occurs frequently, probably you are too much dominated yourself by others and seek compensation; or you have too great a desire for power over other people.

Examinations. People long past the usual examination age may have such a dream. For examination, read some problem or difficulty which is occurring in your life. If the dream examination worries you or you feel you have failed, you are funking your problem and not facing up to it properly. If you dream that you pass the examination, you are reassuring yourself that all will be well. Should the examination be one which even in your dreams you know you have passed some time ago, then the problem is similar to a previous one which you solved successfully and you can master it on the same lines.

Falling. This very common and unpleasant nightmare takes many forms, but always the dreamer is falling from a height or through space, and either the falling itself or the landing at the bottom is very unpleasant. Sometimes the fall is caused by a push from behind when standing on a high place.

This is the dream of a too-ambitious person, who always wants to be first, cleverest or most loved—an impossible ambition, for no one can be *always* on top. Eldest children, who are first the only one and made the centre of attention and then have to share the honours with the next baby, often get this "I must be first" unconscious ambition and are very liable to falling dreams. Such dreams will disappear if the dreamer can cure herself of always wanting the limelight.

Flying. This shows a good form of ambition, the person who wants to rise high, but does not demand the first place as a right. Instead, she will work for it courageously.

Heroine. I give this name to the dream in which the dreamer does something wonderful and is the heroine of the occasion. As a rule she acts with great calm and efficiency in an emergency and others obey her admiringly, or she effects a dashing rescue of somebody from a fire or other danger.

This dream fulfils in a very satisfactory way a great wish to be admired and heroic. It is so much easier to dream oneself a heroine than actually to be one! If you often get this dream, guide your desire to help and be admired into humbler channels. There are so many simple everyday ways of keeping cool and taking care of others. Make use of them, instead of waiting for the dramatic moment which may never come.

High Place. A fear of looking down from or falling

over high places such as cliffs or the gallery of a theatre should be interpreted in the same way as falling dreams.

Missing Train, Ship, Coach, etc. This is a very frequent "muddle" dream belonging to Class 2. You are going on an important journey or for your holiday and you miss the train—or fear you will do so—for some reason any sensible person would have provided against. For instance, you can't find your passport or have filled your suit-case so full that it's impossible to close it!

This is a "funk" dream. It is *not* a warning to abandon whatever new step you are taking. On the contrary, pluck up your courage and remember the many new steps you have taken in the past which have turned out successfully.

Mountain Climbing. Here again, as with the "heroine," an easy dream is substituted for a difficult achievement. If you dream you are climbing mountains, you are leading too easy a life, have got slack and so are making up for it in your sleep. What troublesome thing in real life are you shirking? Climb *that* "mountain" and the dream will vanish.

Naked. Many people dream of finding themselves in the streets or some other public place in their birthday suit, to their extreme embarrassment. This dream is a sign of some fear connected with sex or marriage. Try to dig it out and overcome it. It may be due to ignorance or wrong teaching in childhood and greater knowledge of the subject will often cure it.

Paralysed. Most of us know the dream in which we are suddenly paralysed and unable to move in the face of some sudden danger or when our legs without warning give way under us. The interpretation and remedy are much the same as for the train dream given above.

Racing and Running, or any great hurrying in a dream show a very strong desire in the unconscious mind of the dreamer to catch up with, or beat, someone who, she feels, is outdistancing her in real life in some way. The second child in a family, trying perpetually to be as big and important as the first older one, or the younger of any two children in a family who are close together in age, is very apt to have this dream. The remedy is to train yourself simply to do your best, without bothering whether someone else with more advantages does better or not. In other words, you are overdoing competition.

Water. Water prominent in a dream, whether in the form of the sea, a river, a lake or floods, shows some emotional difficulty. Such a dream often occurs if the dreamer is anxious over a love affair—or is worried because love seems to pass her by. Try to discover and remedy any trait in yourself which makes you unattractive to the other sex.

CRYSTAL GAZING

WHILE some types of fortune telling, such as cards and teacup reading, may be done with good results by any sensitive person who can learn a list of meanings and use a little judgment in combining them, reading the future in the crystal is really a special gift.

You may have this gift. No one can say whether you have or not until you have given it a good trial to see what results you get. If the gift is dormant in you, practice and self-training will bring it out and strengthen it. But crystal-gazing is rather like an ear for music—it can be trained if it is there, but if it is missing it can never be acquired, however hard you try.

Only a few people have the ability to see visions in the crystal. Those few, by practising, can often get really wonderful results.

As I have said, only by experiment can you be sure whether you can become a crystal gazer or not, for it is never possible to say beforehand exactly who has the gift. But it has been found from general experience the most crystal seers belong in one of two groups that the bulk of crystal readers are recruited. So if you correspond with either, at least we can say that you are a likely subject to take up the crystal with success.

See if you answer to either of the following descriptions.

The Two Types of Seers

The positive seer type is muscularly well developed, active and nervous of mind and body and rather excitable. She has somewhat large, marked features, prominent bony brows, a dark complexion and a very intent gaze. This type searches the crystal, and, as it were, draws the images out of it by her own force of character—hence the term "positive seer."

The passive seer type is quite different—plump and indolent, with a pale skin, eyes usually blue and fine hair that is quite straight and rather colourless. Her hands are small, plump and always feel rather cold. She has little animation and her voice is thin and high. This seer makes no effort when looking at the crystal, but simply renders her mind a blank, so that it can catch any images that come from the crystal and transmit them in words to her sitter.

Every crystal gazer falling into one of these groups must use the method which is suited to her personality. A positive seer who tries to remain passive will not meet with success, while a passive gazer will get no result if she tries the searching and concentrated plan that suits her more energetic sister.

A proper crystal is necessary and unfortunately a good one is not very cheap. There are Eastern seers who get wonderful results by using a mirror or even a pool of water, but these methods are not for the beginner.

How to Practise Crystal Gazing

There is a definite technique for seeing visions in the crystal sphere, and you must obey certain simple rules before you can even hope for success.

(1) Sit with your back to the light, in a room which, without being at all dark, is what we call shady. You should be able to see to read in it, but there must not be bright light anywhere, either daylight or artificial. In the day-time a north room is best.

(2) The crystal should either be held in the palm of your hand, resting in your lap, or should be put on a table, with the stand sold with it under it. In this case it is a good plan to cover the table with a dull black (or black velvet) cover, as this will cut off reflections from the crystal and help you to concentrate.

(3) The other people in the room must sit at least an arm's length away from the seer—further than that is better. If they ask her questions during the sitting, they should use an expressionless, monotonous voice, all on one note, as this will not startle her or distract her attention from the crystal.

(4) Apart from any necessary questions or anything the seer may describe, there must be total silence during a sitting, which at first should not last longer than a quarter of an hour, as it is very tiring to be a beginner. When developing the seeing power, it is a great help to sit every day in the same place at the same hour, so that a regular habit is established. If possible, the same people should always be there.

(5) Only two should be present besides the seer, and these should be folk who are sympathetic towards crystal gazing, towards the seer and to each other, so that there is no disharmony in the atmosphere.

(6) The seer must look steadily into the crystal all through the sitting, ignoring her surroundings and trying to let her mind wander as it will. Do not concentrate; do the exact opposite, opening your mind to whatever chooses to come in. Forget yourself and all your affairs. These things are not easy to accomplish, but to the right type of person they become simple with practice.

(7) It is quite likely that at the first sittings you will get no results at all. But if you are a natural-born seer, one day the moment will come when you see that the crystal is no longer as clear as a mirror, but clouding over and becoming milky in appearance. The milkiness will change to other clouded colours, each darker than the last, and finally turn black. Then comes the thrilling moment when the blackness dissolves like a curtain which is pulled aside and you see a living picture in the crystal—a picture your intuition will enable you to interpret to your sitters.

Remember when you get to the stage of seeing visions that these may be of two kinds—events which are usually going to happen, which appear to you vividly in every detail or symbolic pictures which have to be interpreted. In the second case the actual picture does not matter; it is its *meaning* which you must seek and translate. If sitters have asked for information on definite questions, the answers will most often come in this way.

It is impossible to give a list of symbols and their meanings, as in dream interpretation, for with the crystal so much depends upon the individual seer. The meaning is generally grasped by her own psychic sense. However, one may say in a general way that a symbol must be interpreted according to its nature and the uses to which it is put.

Thus a ship which travels denotes voyages and intercourse between people at a distance. The sun, brightly shining, means prosperity and honour; the crescent moon, which is soon to become bigger, stands therefore for increase of success or improvement of some kind.

The crystal is, after all, only the medium which focuses your attention and so puts you into touch with the unseen world. What you see there you must bring back in your own fashion to those who are sitting with you, translating the symbols into languages which they will understand and not relying on any cut-and-dried list of meanings.

DIVINING BY SAND

SAND divining, like crystal gazing, is not based on a set of rules, but on the psychic and magnetic faculties which are hidden, to a greater or less extent, in practically all of us. Many sensitive and intuitive women have the power, if they only realised it and practised accordingly, of divining something of the future in a tray of sand.

This kind of fortune-telling is practised with marvellously accurate results in the East, but is almost a novelty in England. Your friends will be very intrigued if you are able to do it for them.

The equipment could hardly be simpler. All you need is a little silver sand of the child's sand-pit sort (or sea-shore sand, if you live on the coast), with a tin or wooden tray and a long pencil. If the sand seems at all damp, put it in the oven or a warm place until dry and crisp, then fill your tray two or three inches deep with it.

Seat yourself before the tray with the pencil in your hand and your wrist resting on the rim of the tray, in position to write. Then get someone to blindfold you. The object of this is to help you to concentrate completely and to shut out things that might influence your mind and prevent the magnetism working.

Tell the friend whose future you are trying to divine to sit opposite you, perfectly quiet, for three minutes by the clock. She must concentrate her mind upon any subject she specially desires you to tell her about.

Fix your thoughts on the same thing yourself (she must tell you what it is, of course), holding the pencil quite loosely. Probably nothing will happen for some time, and you may get impatient. But if you have any occult faculty (and there are few people who haven't some at least) presently you will feel a desire to move the pencil in the sand.

Let it wander just as it pleases, and don't try to guide it in any way, but still concentrate on the chosen subject. When your hands stop moving, take the bandage from your eyes and look at the sand in the tray.

You may find that you have formed words or letters, or perhaps the marks you have made build themselves up into some sort of picture that can be interpreted. Very often you will only get initials and not words, such as "y" for yes, "n" for no, or "p" for perhaps. If you have asked a question regarding when something will happen, the initial for the day or month of its occurence may appear, or the first letter of a name, should the question have concerned a person.

For instance, if your sitter has asked, "Who shall I marry?" any initial you make in the sand will be that of her future husband.

While a small y, n and p bear the meanings given above, the same letters in capitals are probably the initials of names.

Generally speaking, the interpretation of the sand-marks must be left to your own intuition, but there are a few besides those already given that commonly occur and have fixed meanings which do not vary.

One long, deep line. A journey.

One short, deep line. An unexpected visitor.

A small circle. A marriage.

A large circle. A misfortune.

A cross. An obstacle to be overcome.

A cross made diagonally, like kisses in letters. A love affair, which will be happy if the cross is well made and distinct.

A triangle. Success in work.

Time is shown by the position of the marks on the sand. The width of the tray measures a year, counting from the left-hand rim. A quarter across would mean three months ahead, nearly to the right-hand rim eleven months and so on.

Never try sand divining for more than three, or at most five minutes at a stretch; if you feel no impulse to move the pencil in that time, try again another day. It may take a week of daily attempts before you get anything you can understand.

When a small group of friends are together, it is interesting to give each in turn three minutes blindfolded at the sand tray, and to see who gets the clearest result. After each person has tried, smooth over the sand completely, by shaking the tray, before the next has her turn.

DICE DECISIONS

"HE shook them up once, he shook them up twice. And staked all his luck on a throw of the dice." says an old verse, and really he might have done worse, for if you cannot make up your mind between two plans it is not a bad idea to let the dice decide for you. Nor is this such pure chance it seems, for your subconscious mind, which often sees further ahead than the conscious, is likely to step in and settle the matter by casting (without your realising it) so that the right solution comes up.

Dice decisions are simple and quick. Even if you have nothing definite to settle, a throw of the dice will give you an idea of what to expect in the near future. It is considered unlucky to try the dice on a Monday or Wednesday, but any other day is propitious.

You will need three dice. With your left hand put them in their box. Then draw a circle with chalk on a table or board and throw the dice out on to this circle or as near it as possible. Count up the total of the numbers exposed and read according to the following list.

Three. A pleasant surprise.

Four. An unpleasant surprise.

Five. You meet a stranger who will become your friend.

Six. You will lose something you value.

Seven. Scandal will touch you.

Eight. You will be justly blamed for something that is past.

Nine. A wedding near at hand.

Ten. A christening will prove momentous to you.

Eleven. Death of someone you know.

Twelve. A letter of acceptance will soon arrive.

Thirteen. You will sigh and shed tears.

Fourteen. A new admirer.

Fifteen. Take care, keep out of trouble which threatens.

Sixteen. A happy journey.

Seventeen. Profitable business on, or from across, the water.

Eighteen. Some great good is coming to you.

Dice prophecies are said always to come true within nine days.

The above meanings only apply to such dice as fall inside the chalk circle. If any roll outside, their number must not be included and the rolling outside foretells a quarrel or an estrangement if the dice roll on to the floor. If one should fall on the top of another, you will receive a present which is not altogether to your advantage and might be best refused.

DEDUCTIONS FROM DOMINOES

FOR many, many centuries people have consulted the dominoes when wishing to know something of the future, and have been able to deduce their fortunes according to the numbers turned up.

Here is a specially simple way of using dominoes, which does not need the meaning of each one to be remembered. It is therefore a good method to start off with.

The Western System

Two people (but not more) can try their future at once by this system. Remove all dominoes with any blanks on them and spread the others out face downwards on the table.

The two people now draw a domino each alternately with the left hand, placing it face upwards until each has three dominoes. Then the fortunes are interpreted according to the following rules:

Sixes. All sixes are fortunate and bring good luck of a general kind or in connection with any wish held in the mind while drawing the dominoes.

Fives. These refer to the work or career.

Fours. Money matters.

Threes. Love affairs.

Twos. Friends and social affairs.

Ones. Journeys and travel.

You will find it quite easy to combine two numbers and draw your deductions accordingly. Thus, if the six-five is drawn, you would read it as meaning good fortune in connection with work, while six-two would prophesy good luck coming from a friend. Again, three-one would foretell a journey to do with a love affair or resulting in a love affair. And so on all through.

In addition to these straightforward combined interpretations, the "double" dominoes have special meanings which must be remembered. These are:

Double-six. —The wedding of the person drawing this domino; or if already married, very special good fortune arising out of a wedding.

Double-five. —A new job or promotion to a new kind of work with the same firm.

Double-four. —Unexpected money coming in a dramatic way.

Double-three. —A new and important love affair.

Double-two. —New friends and an enjoyable time with them.

Double-one. —A happy journey or holiday to a place never visited before.

You will see that "something new" is the keynote of all the double dominoes.

In addition, there are two dominoes which are definitely unlucky. These are:

Four-two, which indicates a disappointment, in addition to its general meaning: and *three-one,* foretelling bad news of a temporary kind.

The Eastern System

This is a little more complicated. It uses the whole domino set and gives a different meaning to each piece.

To use this method, set the dominoes out face downwards and shuffle them well without seeing their faces. Draw one with the left hand and it will give the leading event in your life during the next week. It is unlucky to draw again within that period.

Here are the domino meanings.

Double-blank. —Life will be uneventful and dull.

Double-one. —While out of doors you will make an advantageous discovery.

Two-one. —Before long you will mortgage or pawn a piece of property.

Double-two. —The jealousy of another clouds your life.

Two-blank. —Vexatious delay, but it will soon be over.

Three-blank. —An illegitimate child.

Three-one. —You will make an important discovery.

Three-two. —Avoid any gambling or chance matters, as you will lose in such.

Double-three. —An unexpected wedding will annoy you.

Four-blank. —You will receive an angry letter.

Four-one. —Debts will worry you.

Four-two. —Your fortunes will mend quite suddenly.

Four-three. —You will meet again a former suitor.

Double-four. —A merry party some way from home.

Five-blank. —A funeral you attend, but not in your own family.

Five-one. —A love affair.

Five-two. —An outing on the water.

Five-three. —An improvement in your work.

Five-four. —A speculation turns out well.

Double-five. —You will move and benefit thereby.

Six-blank. —Beware of scandal spread by a supposed friend.

Six-one. —You meet and help an old friend.

Six-two. —You receive a gift of clothing.

Six-three. —A visit to a theatre or cinema.

Six-four. —You will play a part in a lawsuit.

Six-five. —The birth of a child will change your life.

Double-six. —A good sum of money comes to you.

YOUR FORTUNE IN THE FIRE

ON winter evenings, when you sit gazing half dreamily into the glowing heart of the fire and watching the vague shapes made as the coals burn and fall, try to see these indefinite pictures more clearly and to interpret them as symbols of what is coming to you in the near future.

Any number of people can read their own fortunes in the same fire, for it is a curious thing that the same formations of coal will present different pictures to different people. This is partly because every seat round the hearth gives a slightly different view of the fire, but more because each person's intuition and magnetism will enable her to pick out of the innumerable images just those which fit her own case.

This is almost the only kind of fortune-telling which another person cannot do for you. You *must* do it for yourself.

It may happen that however long you gaze into the fire, you can see nothing clearly, but only vague shapes that convey no meaning to you. When this occurs, you may know that your life is in a state of flux at the moment and the future too vague to be seen. This is not necessarily unfavourable, but only shows that changes are taking place which, so to speak, muddle the picture.

Try again in a few days and you will probably get clearer results.

Do not do this fire-gazing for more than five minutes on any one occasion. If during these five minutes a piece of coal should jump out of the fire near your feet, you may be sure of great good luck for twelve months to come.

Naturally you must choose a time when the fire is burning brightly and flames are leaping. Little or nothing can be discovered from a fire which is dying or banked up with slack to last a long time. If you *must* see your fortune at a moment when the fire is dull and quiet, throw salt on it. This will revive it temporarily and give you some vivid pictures.

What you see should be interpreted according to the alphabetical list of meanings given for Teacup Reading on page 270.

THE FIVE PHYSICAL TYPES

IT has recently been discovered that there is a scientific connection between the kind of person you look and the kind of person you are..

By a new system people are classified into five biological types, according to which part of their physical make-up is most noticeable—bony framework, digestion, muscular system, circulation or brain development. Each physical type has a corresponding temperament that goes with it. So that you have only to take a good look at a person to form a working idea of what she is like.

Study the five types and you will be able to gauge pretty accurately the character of anyone you come across—not to mention your boy friend, your best girl friend and yourself!

The Reliable (Bony) Type

Let's start with the class in which well-developed bones are the most noticeable physical feature. These are the people who have no difficulty in keeping slim—not to say thin—and who have long (but not narrow) faces, with pronounced cheek and jaw bones. Look also for long, thin necks, square chins and shoulders and thick hair.

Most of these folk are very tall, but there is a less frequent bony type only of medium height.

We call these people the Reliable type, because reliability is the keynote of her character. If a Reliable undertakes to do something, you need worry no more about it; she will not muddle or forget it. But don't try to rush her over it, for Reliables are essentially deliberate, conscientious and careful. They can't be hurried.

They are careful with money and easily save, as they

have no expensive tastes. They care little for dress, preferring old things which are comfortable. Their favourite
amusements are very active ones. For instance, when you
have toiled, panting, to the top of a mountain, there you will
find a Reliable or two, full of pep and not in the least out of
breath!

They hike and cycle, also, but are too awkward to be good
dancers.. Physically they are very strong and Spartan.

Reliables are not very good mixers or rulers, as they
are rather clumsy and tactless. But, on the other hand,
they are too independent to make the best subordinates, and
so should choose jobs which they can run in their own
way.

Active, outdoor work suits them best. They also make
careful business women.

In the main they are unemotional and love few people.
But to those few they are entirely devoted and "faithful unto
death" exactly describes their type of affection. As they
dislike change and new ideas they grow set rather young in
life, but they are splendidly high-minded and self-controlled.

Each of the five types has its corresponding hand. That of
the Reliable is long and bony, with prominent finger joints.

The Prosperous (Digestive) Type

The second type is in many ways a complete contrast to
Miss Reliable, for in this case the digestive system is the
strongest and most vital part of the physical make-up, giving
a temperament which is accurately described as the
Prosperous type.

You may know a Prosperous person by her plump figure
without much waist, her round and cheery face, with
dimples in cheeks or chin, her short, plump neck and limbs,
small head and full lips.

Prosperous she certainly is, but life isn't all honey even for
this lucky girl. She is such an easy-going, comfortable

creature, for instance, that she has a constant struggle (if she bothers about it) to keep an even reasonably slim silhouette! However, she laughs rather than cries over her troubles, for she's of the optimistic class.

The Prosperous have two main characteristics—they enjoy and they acquire. The love life and put zest into living, but they do not wear themselves out in the process.

They are feather-bed folk, demanding comfort, four good meals a day of the best food, plenty of sleep, leisure and fun. They hate the strenuous activities of the Reliables, and enjoy amusements which can be carried out sitting down, such as motoring, reading and playing bridge.

You seldom find a girl of this type making her own dresses or washing up after family meals. She is so jolly, generous and good-tempered that she can always persuade some devoted mother or friend to "fag" for her. It must be admitted that she is rather lazy physically, though she has a mind which is generally keen and leads her to success.

All the things the Prosperous loves cost money, consequently she concentrates on obtaining it. Even if she comes from a poor home, she will soon rise and be able to afford better things. She is an excellent organizer, and with jokes, smiles and liberal pay she "jollies" her subordinates into doing all the work.

One good thing about her is that she never worries.

She can always get the best out of people without that. This makes her good at jobs where she comes into contact with crowds, and has to handle complaints or persuade folk into things. Generally she prefers business with a social element in it.

Miss Prosperous is usually rather pretty—if plump—and her easy cheerfulness attracts men. So she tends to marry young, usually someone rather successful. She makes a good wife and a mother who spoils her children.

You will know her hand by its plump softness, denoting love of ease. It is rather a small hand, with the mounts (see page 29) well developed.

The Enthusiastic (Circulatory) Type

"Keen as mustard!"

How exactly that description fits some of the people we know! And nearly always they'll be found to belong to the third of the types—the Enthusiasts.

The strongest physical points of such folk are good breathing capacity and a very sound blood stream pumped by an energetic heart. These health traits naturally produce the impulsive, eager and emotional temperament that goes with the enthusiastic type.

The good blood supply gives a well-coloured skin. No really pallid person belongs to the Enthusiastic class. If you are identifying this type, look for a rosy complexion, rather a long face, head high rather than broad, and a short body with long limbs. Height will be medium, hair probably fair, light brown or red, eyes blue or grey.

The Enthusiasts, with so much pretty colour and features that are generally clear-cut, are distinctly a good-looking class, and include many famous stage and screen beauties.

As you may imagine, acting, with its colour, change and movement, makes a ready appeal to these folk.

They loathe monotony and crave for a varied and interesting life full of emotional experiences. They are always changing jobs and residences—not to mention opinions! They are quick, and adaptable to fresh surroundings and work.

One must admit that they are fickle, unreliable and rather shallow. But their tolerant sympathy and bright, amusing personalities make them popular. They *must* have admiration and approval and lay themselves out to win it.

They have the artistic temperament, but their hatred of drudgery often prevents them from developing their talents. They love the beautiful. They read widely and think acutely and humorously, but not with any depth.

You'll find them generous, extravagant and happy-go-lucky.

Good professions for them are the stage, dancing, singing (they almost always have good voices) or travelling jobs of some kind. The steadier Enthusiasts make good confidential secretaries but ordinary business does not suit them at all.

The Enthusiastic hand, like its owner, has an eager, restless appearance. Look for short, tapering fingers (impulse and intuition), the fine skin and many tiny lines of a sensitive nature and a thumb with a rather flattened tip, denoting love of approval.

The Athletic (Muscular) Type

There are some people whose muscular system is the strongest part of their physique. This give them unusual vigour, endurance and accuracy—all points very favourable to games. And games these folk love, so they are well called the Athletic type.

In appearance they are a little under the usual height, but squarely built, with broad shoulders. They have real oval faces, short necks, thick hair and are usually more dark than fair.

"Always on the go!" might be their slogan. They detest idleness and dreaming. Action is their ideal, and they work as hard as they play, provided the work is something that needs physical energy.

Athletic folk are essentially practical, and they, more than any of the other types, make the wheels of life turn efficiently.

An Athletic girl prefers comfortable sports clothes which give perfect freedom. She puts fashion second. She is not fussy about food. Let it be plain and plentiful and she won't worry about flowers on the table.

She is very strong and shines at all games and sports which need steady, continued effort, such as gymnasium activities, cycling, swimming and rowing.

She has good self-esteem, and is apt to despise lazy or

inefficient people. She does not suffer fools gladly. She is conscientious and dependable, quick-tempered and rather domineering, with a strong will of her own.

Under a self-controlled exterior this girl is deeply emotional and sentimental and loves music. She lives in the present, though, and has little reverence for old customs and bygone days.

She is simply splendid at putting things to rights—and sometimes gets dubbed Meddlesome Matty for her pains!

The best work for her is something requiring physical activity, skill with the hands or both combined. She makes a good gardener, doctor (particularly surgeon), cook, dressmaker, games mistress or demonstrator.

You can't mistake the Athletic hand. Its palm is square, with short, square-tipped fingers. The palm has a hard and energetic feel.

The Imaginative (Brainy) Type

Do you know a Janey-Head-in-Air—mostly up in the clouds, vague, dreamy, lonely and rather delicate? Such a girl belongs to the fifth physical type, in which the brain and the nervous system are predominant.

To identify this Imaginative type, look for a slightly built, rather small physique, fine skin and delicately cut features. The head is unusually large and the face has a wide and high forehead, tapering down to a pointed chin. The shoulders are narrow and sloping, giving a somewhat helpless look.

The Imaginative folk actually *are* the most helpless and lonely of all types. They live so much in their own inner world of dreams, ideals and thoughts, which few people understand, and are never quite able to hold their own in the bustle of everyday life. They can't do heavy physical work of any kind, though they can stand a nervous strain better than any other type.

They are always a little afraid, both of practical matters

and of people in general, and so spend much time alone, thinking or reading.

Theirs is the world of ideas, and sport and manual occupations make no appeal to them. They have very little money sense, and are the folk who are easily "taken in and done for."

An Imaginative girl should have the best possible education, as she has the type of mind to benefit from it, and on her own lines shows good concentration and perseverance. Her tastes are highbrow. The pictures bore her, but she enjoys rather gloomy plays which contain ideas and clever conversation.

Her sense of humour is not strong.

In dealing with an Imaginative girl, one must appeal to her mind, her ideals and her very sensitive appreciation of beauty. The people and things surrounding her should be as harmonious as possible, or she will soon become irritable and unable to concentrate.

She is a hopeless failure in business, except where she may be able to plan for the future on new and original lines, leaving someone else to carry out her really fine ideas. She must have a thoroughly congenial job, even if it is badly paid, and as she is timid and a poor fighter, she works best where she is somewhat protected and has a regular income.

Imaginative kinds of writing or art work, research work, the teaching of philosophy or consultative posts should suit her best.

Her hand is long, narrow and thin. It is usually fine-skinned and sensitive-looking, with rather pointed fingers which show the delicacy and refinement of this particular type.

Mixed Types

When you begin to sort your friends into the five different types already described, you will soon find a good many who do not fit exactly into any one of them, but seem to combine the points of two, or even three.

Such mixed types as these are very numerous, and it is just as well they are, for a pure type, being specialized, is bound to be rather ill-balanced, whereas the mixture people are less extreme in character and more all-round in their talents. With a little practice you will soon learn to identify these blends almost at sight.

First, a few general rules to guide you.

People with ruddy complexions are always some Enthusiastic combination. So are practically all *natural* blondes and redheads. Really fat people, especially if young, are sure to have a strain of Prosperous in them. All very tall folk belong, at least in part, to the Reliable type.

And so we get such often-met-with people as the following:

Reliable-Prosperous. Large bones well-covered, a broad, firm face, tallness and a dark skin mark this type. She is slow and methodical, rather set and stolid and a strict disciplinarian. She is likely to choose teaching for her profession. This is not one of the best mixed types.

Reliable-Enthusiastic. This mixture gives a tall and angular figure, though there is also a small slender type. The skin is ruddy and the colouring fair. Here is an excellent blend, combining the quick energy of the Enthusiastic with the trustworthy qualities of the Reliable. She is practical, gets on well with people and is thorough, though rather slow. She makes a good business woman or an excellent housewife.

Reliable-Athletic. Dark and tall, with a rather oblong face, is this girl. She has endurance and willingness to try the unknown. She will strike out some new line at home or emigrate. She is strong-willed, courageous, original and dogged.

Reliable-Imaginative. This mixture gives a tall, rather bony build and a narrow-jawed head well developed at the brows, with large features and mainly dark colouring. She is careful and thorough, excelling in detailed work and figures, clever, persevering, but not quick. She should do well in any work concerned with statistics and requiring detail and finish.

Prosperous-Enthusiastic. This blend gives plumpness combined with firmness and without the puffy look of the pure Prosperous type. The face is longer, too, and so are the fingers and there are rosy colour and blue eyes. A genial, fairly quick and active personality this, appreciating comfort and beauty, but not a slave to it. She is more settled and less artistic and erratic than the true Enthusiastic type.

Prosperous-Athletic. She is rather short and plump, but not flabby, with a round face and square shoulders. She is very strong and active, but prefers planning a job to doing it. She would make a good head of a department, as she can organise well and is fairly popular and diplomatic.

Prosperous-Imaginative. In appearance this is a refined and more intelligent edition of the Prosperous, with the broad Imaginative forehead. She is under medium height. She excels at organising or dealing with money in any form. So she does well as a cashier, book-keeper, bank clerk or almost any financial post.

Enthusiastic-Athletic. Rosy complexion, light brown or golden hair, usually blue eyes. Face fairly long, often oval and rather short, sturdy build. This mixture has plenty of energy and initiative, thinks and acts quickly and is usually well liked. She is capable and alert, fond of games and generally an excellent dancer. The stage or a profession with a certain amount of movement and excitement will suit her best.

Enthusiastic-Imaginative. A blonde type, with a clever head, wide forehead, pointed chin and a delicate, refined face with pink colour. Her hands and feet are small, her figure on the slender side. She thinks very quickly and will always rise to an emergency. She is rather changeable and fond of excitement, but will work hard at occupations that appeal to her, such as the artistic, literary and musical professions.

Athletic-Imaginative. This blend gives a person who is short and rather squarely built, with a bulging Imaginative head, slender neck and dark or medium colouring. This is perhaps the best all-round combination of types, as she can both think and act. Business, home-making and nursing all suit her. She has perseverance, endurance and brains.

There is an almost infinite variety of people who combine three and even four of the types. But you will find that if you get the two main groups identified first, you will have the keynote to the character. Then you can modify your reading a little to fit the extra type or types more slightly represented.

KNIFE PROPHECIES

LET'S start by saying that this form of fortune-telling is not intended to be taken seriously! It is just an entertaining game for an informal little party or to amuse yourselves *en famille* on a wet holiday. Such games often "break the ice" when people are assembled who don't know each other well or are of very different ages and tastes, and a lot of good fun results.

You will need an ordinary table-knife and either a large circle of white cardboard, or better still, a round salver. Mark round the edge of the cardboard or on slips of gummed paper pasted round the rim of the salver, various *short* prophesies of a fairly cheerful kind.

If you haven't time to prepare a salver beforehand, a good plan is to take everybody into your confidence and let each write one prophesy according to his or her fancy on a gummed strip of paper. Then they can be affixed at even distances round the salver in a few minutes.

Here are some suitable prophecies:

> "Your love will prosper."
> "Splendid news coming."
> "Laughter after tears."
> "Beware of false friends."
> "A letter from abroad."
> "A new admirer."
> "Success in business."
> "Wedding bells."
> "An unexpected visit."

With these suggestions to guide you, you will easily think of others.

When the salver is prepared, place the knife in the middle of it.

Each person in turn twirls the knife by its centre three times and notes the prophecies at which the blade stops. Women must twirl with the right hand, but men use the left. If at any of the twirls the blade stops at a space between two prophecies, the indication is that at least part of the immediate future will be uneventful.

However, as this is rather dull, it can be avoided if you write enough prophecies to touch each other all round the salver rim.

SENSE FROM SCRIBBLES

WHEN you sit, pencil in hand, waiting to take a telephone message, in the intervals of a lecture of which you are taking notes or between whiles at a class you are attending, you must have noticed how you scribble and draw. Not deliberately, but while your mind is elsewhere, your unoccupied hand quite naturally uses the pencil you are holding to produce all sorts of odd little pictures or meaningless patterns.

Or go round a room after a board meeting has been held and look at the pads in front of each place. On half of them at least you will probably find idle scribblings of this sort, done almost unconsciously during a speech or discussion.

Meaningless as these seem, they are not so really. An American handwriting expert recently became interested in these doodles, as they are called, and started to puzzle them out in the light of graphology. He discovered that such idle drawings, if rightly interpreted, give up some of the secrets of the unconscious mind and provide valuable clues to personality and hidden wishes.

If you begin to collect your own or someone else's doodles, made over a period of weeks or months, you will find that certain shapes or types of drawing recur over and over again in one person's scribbling, and thus become an index to his or her state of mind.

For instance, a fondness for drawing triangular shapes (Fig. XIV top left) betrays good abilities of a very thoughtful kind. If a nobody draws triangles when not thinking about it, you may be sure that nobody has the capacity and ambition to become somebody (with a capital S) one day! If she adds squares and oblongs to her scribblings she would make an excellent business woman, especially if she blocks in or otherwise shades these shapes to give them more solidity.

Those who always draw faces show that they are more interested in people than in things. They often like to

Fig. XIV.

Doodle drawn by a thoughtful, businesslike, motherly woman.

dabble in writing, but without triangles added to their facial drawings will probably never work seriously at this. S forms, much repeated, also show literary ambitions.

Doodles which contain many curved lines or shapes (see Fig. XV) indicate an emotional, impressionable temperament, those whose moods vary widely and who are enthusiastic. You will find, if you have the opportunity to observe them, that such persons as actors and musicians make much-curved scribbles.

Some people draw simple flowers, such as the daisy and simple leaves more than anything else. These show a tender-hearted, motherly and protective nature, with a natural love

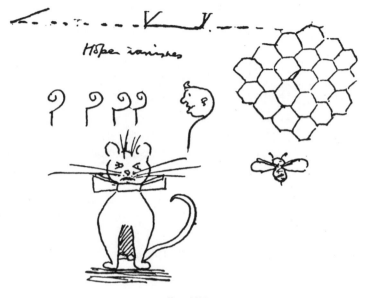

Fig. XV.

This doodle shows too many contradictory aims and interests.

for children, animals and even such growing things as plants. If trees are frequently drawn as well, their artist has a talent for educational work and will be attracted to teaching in some form.

If the scribblings are always unpleasant and rather sinister, taking the form of horribly distorted faces, monsters, deaths' heads and so on, the mind which created them is in a rather morbid and nervous condition. This is probably owing to difficult circumstances in the daily life or to uncongenial companionship. When the cause is remedied the scribbles will become much more pleasant.

Sometimes words are formed and their meaning will give a good clue to what is filling the writer's mind. Not so long ago I saw a page of scribblings which consisted of built-up angular formations rather like pyramids, with many attempts beside them of the word "Success" printed in capitals. But each time the spelling was muddled, such

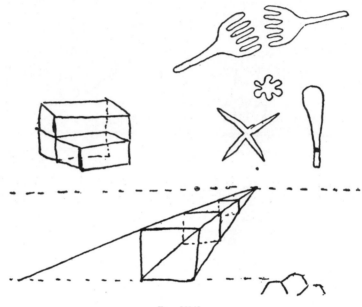

FIG. XVI.

These scribbles show scientific and mathematical ability.

as "SSCCSSS" and similar variations. These scribbles were made by a man who had an intense ambition to succeed in an executive capacity and to control others (the tri-angles), but at the same time feared he would never achieve his ideal. Hence the spoilt attempts at the word "Success."

Sometimes scribbles will combine curves, squares, tri-angles and various other shapes with more or less contra-dictory meanings. In such a case the mind is undecided and its owner is trying for several different things at once. She does not concentrate enough and is likely to fall between two or more stools. (See Fig. XVI.)

It is very interesting to study doodles, and try to evolve other meanings for yourself. Opportunities are many, for besides the sources of scribbling already mentioned, think how often you find things scrawled up on a whitewashed wall, on the margins of a magazine, all round a public telephone and even on the table cloth at a restaurant. By the way, if you find figures dotted about in the last case it doesn't necessarily mean that the customer doubted the correctness of her bill and totted it up this way! You may judge instead that such a person is constantly troubled about ways and means and that the subconscious mind is largely occupied with the general problem of making a little money behave like a lot!

TEACUP FORTUNES

FORTUNE TELLING from the tea leaves left in one's cup is a very old practice, dating back, probably, as long as tea has been known in this country. It is a very interesting method when a few friends are having tea together and want to know a little about the immediate future.

Tea cup reading is not difficult. It requires a certain amount of imagination to see the shapes into which the tea leaves collect, as these shapes are often far from exact. But given this imagination, a little intuition and a good knowledge of human nature, this form of fortune telling can be practised with great success.

When tea cup reading is intended, if possible the tea should be drunk from the plainest utility cups available, as a patterned cup, especially where the design is a dark floral one, makes it more difficult to see how the tea leaves lie.

What to do with Your Cup

The person who has agreed to have her fortune read should swill it round with the dregs of the tea in it so as to scatter the leaves well over the cup. She should hold her cup in her right hand and pour the tea away gently, then turn the cup upside down in her saucer for a moment or two, ready for the fortune-teller. Men who want their fortunes told should swill the dregs of tea round in a clockwise direction, and women in an anti-clockwise direction.

You should begin your reading at the top of the cup and read round and downwards.

The chief signs of good luck are triangles, horseshoes, rings or circles, flowers and trees, animals, crowns, and the figure 7.

The best of all lucky signs is the three-leaved clover. If the leaves have formed themselves into this shape near the top of the cup it means that you will have a bright and happy future. If it is in the middle of the cup your good fortune is coming to you, but it may be delayed for a year or two; and if it is at the bottom of the cup you will be happy and prosperous in your old age.

Girls always want to know if they are likely to get married and when. There is one old way of telling when as follows:

Balance your teaspoon on the edge of the cup. The spoon should be perfectly dry. Then drop tea into the balanced spoon, a drop at a time until the spoon is upset. The number of drops will tell you the number of years you have to wait before you will be married.

Large clear rings or circles formed by tea leaves are indications of a happy marriage. If there is a letter close to the ring it means that an unengaged girl will not have to wait long before announcing her engagement. A double ring means a hasty marriage which may or may not be happy, depending upon the readings from the other parts of the cup. If the ring is at the bottom of the cup it is a sign that lovers will be separated. A bell is another sign of a wedding, and if there are two or more entwined it will be a very happy one and not long delayed.

The following gives the meanings of the shapes most likely to be formed by the tea leaves.

ANCHOR. Usually denotes a voyage leading to happiness. For a girl going on a holiday cruise it means that she will meet the man she will marry.

ARCH. You will travel in the near future. An arch is one of the wedding signs and means that you will shortly be married if you are engaged, or you will soon meet your future husband.

BALLOON OR AEROPLANE. There is prosperity ahead of

you. If the balloon or aeroplane is near the rim you will receive a legacy in the near future. If in the middle of the cup, fortune will come to you in middle life, and if at the bottom of the cup you will have a prosperous old age.

BELLS. These are signs of a happy marriage. If they are connected by a rope of tea leaves you may look forward to receiving good news which you have been expecting.

BIRDS. A bird with its wings extended is a sign that good news is coming to you or that you will get a very pleasant surprise in the near future. If the bird is surrounded by a circle or square of tea leaves, you will receive a proposal. When a number of them are clustered together you will go on a successful journey and increase your prospects.

BOOKS. Books signify that you are in need of advice and help. If the book lies close to a stick it is an indication that you will marry a writer, a lawyer or a clergyman.

BOTTLE. A bottle shape close to a stick is a sign that you will fall in love with either a doctor, a chemist or a publican. If surrounded by dots you should take it as a warning not to neglect your everyday affairs for cocktail parties and dances, as you may find it difficult to resist them.

BUTTERFLY. This is a warning sign to a girl that her love is liable to prove fickle.

CHAIN. If you see a chain in the tea-cup you should put all your energies into the work you have in hand to make it successful. Should the chain be broken, look out for some hidden enemy who will try to bring you unhappiness.

CLOCK. You will shortly be asked to meet a person who will have a very great influence on you.

CRESCENT. You will be lucky in money affairs or some fresh interest will come into your life leading to greater happiness.

CROSS. You may expect shortly to hear bad news. If it is near the rim of the cup it will soon pass away. If near the bottom you may go through a long period of anxiety. Someone near and dear to you may have a long illness.

CROWN. You will have great honours coming to you.

DART OR ARROW. You will shortly have a proposal of marriage. Both indicate a happy love affair.

DICE OR CARDS. You will lose money if you gamble. These are unlucky signs and you will be wise not to be tempted into any form of speculation.

ENVELOPE. Good news will be coming to you.

FISH. The sign of the fish means that you will receive good news from abroad. If the fish are surrounded by dots they are a sign that you will emigrate; if close to a stick, that a sailor will propose to you.

FLAG. This is one of the very lucky signs. It is the bringer of good news or good fortune.

FOOT OR SHOE. You will have good news, but it will not come for some time.

GATE. There are difficult times ahead of you, but if you are patient you will surmount all your problems and pass through the gate to success and happiness.

HAMMER. A sign that no matter how difficult things may seem you will triumph over them and obtain your heart's desire.

HARP. Another of the really lucky signs. You will be fortunate in love and marriage and will never be poor.

HAT. If a man's hat in the teacup of a woman, this signifies some misfortune. If a woman's hat, that she will be lucky in the next thing she does.

HATCHET OR AXE. Beware if you see this sign. It means there is danger ahead, either in a love affair or business, and you should be very careful what you say or do. Never let your anger get the better of you, or it may lead to disaster.

HEART. One of the lucky marriage and love signs. If close to a ring or circle you will be married very soon. If a crown is close by you will gain honour through your marriage. If a number of small leaves are close to the heart you will marry riches. Two hearts together and small leaves means a lover's quarrel.

HORN. This is a sign of prosperity.

KEY. A key indicates that you will shortly have a new home, though not necessarily by marriage. It also denotes that something which has been puzzling you will soon be cleared up.

KNIFE. An unlucky sign. It indicates a quarrel between lovers or friends.

LADDER. If on the side of the cup, your fortunes will steadily rise. If at the bottom, you may suffer some financial misfortune.

MAN. The figure of a man, if well defined, indicates a visitor who is dark; when not very clear that he is a fair man. If one arm is apparently outstretched, he will bring you a present.

MOUNTAINS. If the formation of the tea leaves look like a range of mountains you may expect difficult times ahead.

RING OR CIRCLE. One of the lucky marriage signs. (See also HEART.) Usually a ring denotes marriage. If there is an initial letter close by it will indicate to a girl the name of her future hushand.

ROAD. Two parallel lines of tea leaves forming a road are a sign of a change in circumstances, usually for the better. If the lines are straight, fortune will come quickly. If wavy there may be difficulties in the way before it is finally reached.

ROCK. A single large rock shape shows a period of great anxiety and difficulty; a number of small rocks that you will meet small troubles, but you will quickly surmount them.

ROOF. If the leaves have the appearance of the roof of a house you will shortly leave home, probably to be married. If you are already married, it signifies a period of great happiness.

SCALES. A scale or balance indicates that you have mis-judged your friend or lover and that you should revise your judgement if you do not want to be unfair.

SHIP. A ship is a sign of good luck from a journey, usually one undertaken for business reasons.

STICKS. Leaves which resemble sticks indicate persons. They are important symbols to look for. Near a ring or heart they indicate marriage. Look to see if they are short, stout, dark or fair according to the size and thickness of the sticks. A small plump stick usually denotes a woman friend, a tall straight one, a man friend. If two sticks cross one another it is an indication that they are enemies. When leaves are clustered round a stick it indicates someone bringing bad news. If there are a large number of dots or tiny leaves close by, the person will bring you prosperity.

TREES. Trees if well defined are a sign of good health, but when vague, of illness. A group of trees foretells that a long-felt wish will soon be fulfilled. If dots are near the trees you will have to travel to obtain your wishes. If a stick (indicating a person) is near, your wish will come true when you meet him or her.

WEB. A sign which looks like a spider's web is a warning that misfortune may come to you through ignoring the advice of your dearest friend.

WOMAN. A woman is indicated by a short stick-shaped leaf. It usually means that you will be fortunate in your love affairs. Two crossing one another is a sign of jealousy and a warning to be careful in your relations with your women friends, especially where men are concerned.

When reading signs from the tea leaves remember that the more definite the signs are the more quickly, as a rule, will things happen. Vague outlines are an indication that what is read from them may not happen, and in any case these events are not likely to come true in the very near future.

Let your intuition take charge, as it were. Practice will help you immensely to see shapes which, at the beginning, look a hopeless muddle. The more you practise the quicker and more sure you will become at reading the teacups.

YOU CAN BE LUCKY

SINCE the beginning of time people have fervently believed that certain things were lucky and certain things unlucky. In these modern days we are much more sceptical. Yet there is this in luck beliefs—that good fortune is so very largely a state of mind, an outlook on life, that if you believe yourself to be lucky you are going a long way towards actually being so.

A mascot, colour or date really is a luck-bringer in the sense that if you think it will bring you good fortune you will inevitably have an optimistic outlook. You will smile at the world and the world will therefore smile back. You will look out for opportunities you would miss on an "unlucky" occasion. You will make the most of benefits and minimise any mischances.

A luck-bringer of any kind will also be likely to remind you, when things are not going well, of that fickle goddess called Luck; and, thinking of her, it is very likely that your pessimistic mood will lighten and the day turn out not so bad after all!

There is an additional point connected with your fortunate flower, jewel or colour that anything which helps you to look your best or sheds beauty around you is likely to make you cheerful and inclined for good fortune. And what we expect we usually get!

Sayings about Luck

Here are a few of the many, many proverbs and quotations concerning Mistress Luck. If you want to attract her to you, it is a wise plan to choose the saying you like best, write or paint it on a card or embroider it on a piece of linen, frame it and hand it over your bed.

Or, instead of a frame, suspend it from a ribbon of your lucky colour. (For lucky colours see pages 166 to 175).

"Behind bad luck comes good luck."

"Oppose a good countenance to bad weather."

"There is a tide in the affairs of men, which, taken at the flood, leads on to fortune."

"Luck is another name for optimism."

"Lucky at cards, unlucky in love."

"Fortune is full of fresh varietie; constant in nothing but inconstancie."

"Good luck deceives people, bad luck teaches."

"Let not one look of fortune cast you down; she were not fortune if she did not frown."

"When ill-luck falls asleep, let nobody wake her."

"Fortune makes a fool of the man whom she favours overmuch."

"What said Pluck, 'The greater knave, the greater luck!' "

"Luck is a mighty queer thing. All you know about it for certain is that it's bound to change."

"Lucky men need no advice."

"There's luck in odd numbers."

"Take good luck with modesty and bad luck with courage."

"A chip of change weigheth more than a pound of wit."

"Luck is mostly pluck."

"The worse luck now, the better another time."

"We should talk less about luck and do more to deserve it."

"Some people are born with silver spoons in their mouths and some with wooden ladles."

"Fortune can take nothing from us but what she gave us."

"When one door closes another opens."

"Luck has always two faces and as many minds."

"No one can have all the luck."

"Luck is the handmaid of self-confidence and serves her right well."

"Luck is infatuated with the efficient."

"Fortune may have yet a better success in reserve for you, and they who lose to-day may win to-morrow."

THE LUCK OF PRECIOUS STONES

SINCE the beginning of the world women have been irresistibly drawn to jewels. When we wear lovely gems we feel that we look our prettiest and most prosperous. It's not just an idea, either—for jewels, as everyone knows, really do bring luck.

Not every jewel to every woman, of course. Good fortune is always more individual and specialised than that. As explained on page 90, there are twelve signs of the Zodiac, corresponding with the twelve months of the year and each sign has a special gem associated with it bestowing on those who wear it a particular kind of luck.

Generally speaking, too, the colour of the Zodiac stone is one which is extra becoming to the type of woman born under the corresponding sign. So that, from all points of view, there is no better way of choosing your particular gem than by the month in which you were born.

The stone and the special luck which it brings are given in the traditional rhymes set out below. Remember, however, that the Zodiacal months don't correspond exactly with the calendar months, but run from about the 21st to the 20th. Beside each month, in brackets, you will find the period it covers. There is often an overlap of a few days at the time the signs change and if your birthday, comes between the 20th and 24th of any month you may find that either the stone for the period just ending or that for the period just beginning may be more favourable to you, even should the date not be correct within a day or two.

In this case adopt as yours the jewel of the two for which you have decided preference and feel happiest wearing.

Note also regarding lucky gems that the good fortune

they bring is greatest if they are worn touching the skin. For this reason your Birth Stone should be mounted as a pendant, bracelet or ring rather than as a brooch or clip. If your engagement ring contains your Birth Month Stone, your marriage should be specially blessed by Fate.

Each Month's Birth Stone

January (December 21st to January 20th).

> By her who in this month was born
> No gem save Garnets should be worn.
> They will ensure her constancy,
> True friendship and fidelity.

February (January 21st to February 20th).

> The February-born shall find
> Sincerity and peace of mind,
> Freedom from passion and from care
> If they the Amethyst will wear.

March (February 21st to March 20th).

> Who on this world of ours their eyes
> In March first open, shall be wise,
> In days of peril strong and brave,
> And wear a Bloodstone to their grave.

April (March 21st to April 20th).

> She who from April dates her years,
> Diamonds shall wear, lest bitter tears
> For vain repentance flow. This stone
> Emblem of innocence is known.

May (April 21st to May 20th).

> Who first beholds the light of day
> In spring's sweet, flowery month of May,
> And wears an Emerald, all her life,
> Shall be a loved and loving wife.

June (May 21st to June 20th).

> Who comes with summer to this earth,
> And owes to June her hour of birth,
> With ring of Agate on her hand
> Can health, wealth and long life command.

July (June 21st to July 20th).
>The glowing Ruby shall adorn
>Those who in warm July are born.
>Then will they be exempt and free
>From love's doubt and anxiety.

August (July 21st to August 20th).
>Wear a Sardonyx or for thee
>No conjugal felicity.
>The August-born without this stone
>'Tis said, must live unloved alone.

September (August 21st to September 20th).
>A maiden born when autumn leaves
>Are rustling in September's breeze,
>A Sapphire on her brow should bind.
>'Twill cure diseases of the mind.

October (September 21st to October 20th).
>October's child is born for woe,
>And life's vicissitudes must know;
>But lay an Opal on her breast
>And Hope will lull those woes to rest.

November (October 21st to November 20th).
>Who first comes to this world below
>In drear November's fog and snow,
>Should prize the Topaz's amber hue,
>Emblem of friends and lovers true.

December (November 21st to December 20th).
>If cold December gave you birth,
>The month of snow and ice and mirth,
>Place on your hand a Turquoise blue,
>Success will bless whate'er you do.

What the Birth Stones Look Like

In case you are not sure of the colour and appearances of the twelve Birth Stones, here is a brief description of each, with some additional luck points about them. They are in alphabetical order for quick reference.

Agate (or *Scotch Pebble*). A semi-precious stone with bands or ribbons of colour, usually brown, dark red or yellow, but sometimes blue or green. It is specially lucky not only to the June-born, but to farmers, foresters, gardeners and florists. It brings good fortune in making and keeping friends.

Amethyst. A kind of quartz with beautiful clear purple, voilet or mauve colouring. In Greek the meaning of the word is "to ward off drunkenness," and it is therefore a good gift to anyone who is fond of drink. It is specially lucky to lovers, as it is linked with St. Valentine, their patron saint, and it brings faithfulness in love to those who wear it, with freedom from anger and jealousy.

Bloodstone. A semi-precious stone which is dark green with red spots like small bloodstains. Its name may be due to this or to the fact that in olden times it was believed to stop bleeding. In consequence many soldiers carried it to staunch their wounds. It is not a pretty stone for a girl to wear, but it is a mascot for warding off illness and accidents. It also brings courage to its wearer.

Diamond. A precious stone which is a pure form of carbon, the colour of water and very sparkling. It is luckiest when worn on the left side. It symbolises strength, virtue, bravery and insight and will bring these find attributes to those who wear it. The Hebrews long ago believed that it lost its sparkle if touched or worn by a traitor's hand.

Emerald. A precious stone of the beryl type, but distinguished from the beryl by its beautiful green colour. The Romans believed it to be good for the eyes and their cruel Emperor, Nero, wore emerald eyeglasses. Legend says that if given by one lover to another it will pale and grow dull when love fades between them.

Garnet. A semi-precious stone, usually red and looking like an inferior ruby, but sometimes brown, yellow, black or green. When cut into a round or oval shape it is called a carbuncle. It brings a healthy and cheery disposition and wards off inflammatory diseases.

Opal. A very lovely precious stone of cloudy white, but flashing with rainbow hues as it catches the light. This gem is considered unlucky as an engagement ring unless worn by the October-born, as it is said that with a wearer of any other month the marriage will never take place. For those whose birth stone it is it gives second sight, hope and faith. As with the emerald, legend says that it loses its brilliance if worn by an unfaithful lover.

Ruby. This is the most precious of all jewels. It is the same in composition, except for its colouring matter, as the sapphire and has a similar clear brilliance. We think of it as deep glowing red, but it may range between pink and almost violet. It brings good fortune in friendship and banishes grief.

Sapphire. A precious stone which at its best is a clear cornflower blue. Like blue colour in general (the Venus colour), this gem is specially lucky to lovers and engaged couples, bringing peaceful, optimistic happiness.

Sardonyx. A variety of onyx which has white and dark red or white and dark brown markings in bands or layers. It brings married happiness and preserves against the bites of snakes.

Topaz. A more or less transparent precious stone which is usually clear yellow, but sometimes yellowish white, blue or even pink, though the last colour is generally artificially produced. The ancients believed that it warded off chest and rheumatic trouble and asthma, and brought fidelity in friendship and love.

Turqoise. A waxy, translucent or opaque precious stone of a blue to blue-green colour. Its colouring and lustre vary with the feelings of the wearer, and it is said to fade when she is nearing death. It protect from danger or misfortune.

BRIDAL LUCK

NOTHING in life is more ringed round with superstitions than a wedding. There is hardly anything a bride can do on her marriage day which some old saying does not call lucky or unlucky. This is only natural when one considers the great glamour of a wedding and how vitally getting married affects the whole life of a girl.

Both in rhyme and in prose many a warning is uttered to the bride.

Suppose we take the rhymes first. What month shall she choose for her marriage morn?

The Best Marriage Month

Married in January's frost and rime,
Widowed you'll be before your time;
Married in February's sleety weather,
Life you'll tread in tune together;
Married when March winds shrill and roar,
Your home will be on a foreign shore.
Married 'neath April's changeful skies,
A chequered path before you lies.
Married when bees on May-blooms flit,
Strangers around your board will sit;
Married in queen-rose month of June,
Life will be one long honeymoon.
Married in July's flowery blaze,
Bitter-sweet mem'ries in after-days.
Married in August's heat and drowse,
Lover and friend in your chosen spouse.
Married in gold September's glow,
Smooth and serene your life will flow.
Married when leaves in October thin,
Toil and hardship for you begin.
Married in veils of November mist,
Fortune your wedding ring has kissed.
When December's snows fall thick and fast,
Marry and wedded love will last.

Or you may find this version truer of the weddings you know among your family and friends.

Marry when the year is new,
Always loving, kind and true.
When February birds do mate
You may wed nor dread your fate.
If you wed when March winds blow
Joy and sorrow both you'll know.
Marry in April if you can—
Joy for maiden and for man.
Marry in the month of May,
You will surely rue the day.
Marry when June roses blow
Over land and sea you'll go.
They who in July do wed,
Must labour always for their bread.
Whoever wed in August be
Many a change are sure to see.
Marry in September's shine,
Your living will be rich and fine.
If in October you do marry,
Love will come, but riches tarry.
If you wed in bleak November,
Only joy yours to remember.
When December snows fall fast,
Marry, and true love will last.

Luck of the Wedding Day

Monday for health,
Tuesday for wealth,
Wednesday the best day of all;
Thursday for losses,
Friday for crosses,
Saturday no luck will befall.

Other Wedding Day Superstitions

To be fortunate a bride must wear on her bridal day:

"Something old and something new,
Something borrowed and something blue."

On her wedding eve she can ensure good luck and a rise in the world by mounting first on a chair and from there on to a table.

All the pins worn by the bride on her wedding day are considered to be mascots for those who can steal them without her knowledge.

All the pins worn by the bride on her wedding day are considered to be mascots for those who can steal them without her knowledge.

On no account must a bride try on her wedding ring beforehand. This superstition is so widespread that all jewellers selling rings keep dummy circles by which the fit can be tested.

If on her wedding morning the songs of birds awakens her or swallows fly past her window at dawn, this is a very good omen.

She must not read or hear the marriage service, either on the wedding day itself or the day beforehand, until she hears it during the ceremony.

She must not look at herself in the glass once she is fully dressed for her wedding. It by accident she does so, the bad luck will be averted if she makes some small addition to her clothes, by adding a piece of jewellery, putting another hairpin in her hair or something similar.

If a cat in the house sneezes on the wedding day, the best of happiness will attend the bridal pair; it is also lucky to see a lamb or a dove on the way to the church.

After the wedding the bridesmaids should draw lots for the bride's bouquet, or she should throw it to them from upstairs. The maid drawing the lucky lot or catching the flowers will be the first of the group to marry, usually within twelve months.

Any guest who can steal a kiss from the bride after the ceremony before the bridegroom does so will have good luck all through the year.

Once started on the wedding journey, even if only a few steps, the bride should never look back or return, even though something important has been forgotten.

Good luck is assured if the bridegroom carries his new-made wife over the threshold of their first home together.

THE LUCK AND MEANINGS OF CHRISTIAN NAMES

PARENTS often think they choose their children's names, but even they will admit that their choice is far from being absolutely free. Sometimes a name seems to choose the child, as when both parents agree from the first, even before the baby's birth, upon the name, though it may not be a family one or even one they particularly like. It just seems to fit that child and *insists* on being selected!

This feeling that the Christian name is specially appropriate to its owner comes out in the great interest most people take in the meaning of their name. It is due to their unspoken belief that the meaning fits them and gives a key to their personality, and in nine cases out of ten this will be found to be true. So no apology is needed for including a list of names and their meanings in this book.

Meanings of Christian Names

The language from which the name came is given in brackets after each name, the following abbreviations being used: C., Celtic; F., French; G., German; Gr., Greek; H., Hebrew; L., Latin. Where no bracketed abbreviation follows the name, it is of English origin.

AARON (H.) : High mountain.
ABEL (H.) : Breath, fleeting vapour.
ABIGAIL (H.) : A father's joy.
ABNER (H.) : Father of light.
ABRAHAM (H.) : Father of a multitude.
ABRAM (H., if not a contraction of Abraham) : Father of height.
ADA (G.) : Rich gift.
ADAM (H.) : Man.
ADELA (G.) : Noble.
ADELAIDE (G.) : Nobility.

ADELINA, ADELINE (G.) : Noble maiden.

ADRIAN (L.): One who came from Adria (a place).

ADRIENNE (F.): Feminine form of ADRIAN, with the same meaning.

AGATHA (Gr.): Good.

AGNES. See page 179.

AILEEN (Gr.): Light.

ALAN: Cheerful.

ALBERT (G.): Nobly bright.

ALEXANDER, ALEXANDRA (Gr.): Helper of men.

ALFRED: Wise councellor.

ALGERNON: Whiskered.

ALICE, ALICIA: Noble.

ALICK, ALEC: Shortened forms of ALEXANDER.

ALINE (G.): Noble.

ALISON: Famous fighter.

ALMA (C.): All-good; (L.) kindly. A name coming from two different languages and consequently with two different meanings.

AMABEL. See AMY.

AMBROSE (Gr.): Immortal.

AMELIA (Gr.): Flattering.

AMY (L.): Beloved.

ANASTASIA (Gr.): She who will rise again.

ANDREW (Gr.): A man.

ANGELA, ANGELICA (Gr.): Messenger from God.

ANGUS (C.): Excellent virtue.

ANNE, ANNA, ANNIE (H.): Grace.

ANTHONY (L.): Strength.

ARCHIBALD (G.): Holy prince.

ARNOLD: Power of the eagle.

ARTHUR: See page 179.

AUDREY (G.): Noble counsellor.

AUGUSTUS (L.): Venerable.

BARBARA (Gr.): A stranger.

BARNABAS (H.): Son of consolation.

BARRY (C.): Good marksman.

BASIL (Gr.): King.

BEATRICE, BEATRIX (L.): Blessed.

BENJAMIN (H.): Son of my right hand.

BERTHA (C.): Shining one.

BESSIE, BETH, BETTY. See ELIZABETH.

BLANCHE (G.): White, fair.

BOB. See ROBERT.

BRENDA (G.): Sword.
BRIAN (C.): Strong.
BRIDGET (C.): Strength.
CAROLINE, CAROL. See CHARLOTTE.
CECIL, CECILIA: Blind.
CELIA (L.): Heaven.
CHARLES: A man.
CHARLOTTE: Feminine form of CHARLES.
CHRISTABEL (Gr.): Fair follower of Christ.
CHRISTINE (Gr.): Christian.
CHRISTOPHER (Gr.): Christ-bearer.
CICELY: A variation of CECILIA, with the same meaning.
CLARA (L.): Famous.
CLARENCE (L.): Bright.
CLAUD, CLAUDIA (L.): Lame.
COLIN (L.): Dove.
CONSTANCE, CONNIE (L.): Firm.
CORA (Gr.): Maiden.
CUTHBERT (G.): Well-known splendour.
CYRIL (Gr.): Lordly.
DAISY: Pearl.
DANIEL (H.): God the Judge.
DAVID. See page 180.
DEREK, DERRICK: People's ruler.
DIANA (L.): Goddess.
DONALD (C.): Proud chief.
DORA: See DOROTHEA.
DOROTHEA, DOROTHY (Gr.): Gift of God.
DOUGLAS (C.): Dark grey.
DULCIE (L.): Sweet.
EDGAR (G.): Happy spear.
EDITH: Rich gift.
EDNA: Perfect happiness, rich gift.
EDWARD: Rich guard.
EFFIE (Gr.): Pleasant-spoken.
EILEEN (C.): See page 181.
ELEANOR, ELEANORA (Gr.): A torch.
ELIZABETH (H.): The solemn promise of God.
ELLA: Elf-friend.
ELLEN. A variation of HELEN, with the same meaning.
ELSIE: A variation of ELIZABETH, with the same meaning.
EMILY (Gr.): Flattering.
ENID (C.): Spotless purity.
ERIC: Ever king.

ERNEST. See page 182.

ESTHER, ESTELLE (Assyrian): A star.

ETHEL: Noble.

EUNICE (Gr.): Good victory.

EVA, EVE (H.): Life.

EVELYN (C.): Pleasant.

FANNY. See FRANCES.

FELICITY (L.): Happiness.

FERDINAND (G.): Adventurous life.

FERGUS (C.): Strong-armed.

FLORA, FLORENCE (L.): Flowering.

FRANCES, FRANCIS, FRANK: Free.

FREDERICK (G.): Peace ruler.

FREDA. See WINIFRED.

GABRIEL (H.): Hero of God.

GEOFFREY: God's peace.

GEORGE, See page 183.

GERALD (G.): Firm spear.

GERTRUDE (G.): Spear-maiden.

GILBERT (G.): Bright pledge.

GILES (Gr.): Shield-bearer.

GLADYS: A Welsh form of CLAUDIA, with the same meaning.

GRACE (L.): Thanksgiving.

GWENDOLEN (C.): White-browed.

HANNAH (H.): Grace.

HAROLD (H.): Powerful warrier.

HARRIET: Home ruler.

HARRY. See HENRY.

HELEN (Gr.) A torch.

HENRY: Home ruler.

HERBERT (G.): Bright warrier.

HESTER: A variation of ESTHER, with the same meaning.

HILARY (L.): Cheerful.

HILDA (G.): Battle-maid.

HONOR (L.): Honour.

HUBERT (G.): Bright mind.

HUGH: Mind.

IAN (C.): Scottish form of JOHN, with the same meaning.

IDA (G.): Rich gift.

IMOGEN: Last-born.

IRENE (Gr.): Messenger of peace.

ISAAC (H.): Laughter.

ISABEL, BELLE (H.): God hath sworn.

IVOR: Archer.

JACK. See JOHN.

JAMES (H.): Supplanter.

JANE, JANET (H.): Grace of the Lord.

JASPER (Persian): Master of the treasure.

JEAN. See page 184.

JENNIFER (C.): White wave.

JEREMY (H.): Exalted by the Lord.

JESSICA, JESSIE: Variations of JANE, with the same
     meaning.

JOAN. See page 184.

JOHN. See page 185.

JONATHAN (H.): The Lord's gift.

JOSEPH, JOSEPHINE (H.): Increase.

JOY, JOYCE; See page 185.

JULIA (L.): Soft-haired.

KATHERINE, KATE (Gr.): Pure.

KATHLEEN: The Irish form of KATHERINE, with the same
     meaning.

LANCE: a servant.

LAURA, LAURENCE (L.): Laurel.

LENA (Gr.): Light.

LEONARD. See page 186.

LESLEY, LESLIE. See under Surnames.

LETTICE, LETTY (L.): Gladness.

LILIAN. See page 187.

LIONEL: Little lion.

LILY (L.): Purity.

LOUISA (C.): Like a lion.

LUCY (L.): Born at dawn.

MABEL (C.): Mirth.

MARGARET. See page 187.

MARJORIE (Persian). See page 188.

MARTHA (H.): Becoming bitter.

MARTIN (L.): Disciplinarian.

MARY (H.): See page 188.

MAUD (G.): Mighty battle-maid.

MAURICE (L.): Moorish.

MICHAEL (H.): He who is like the Lord.

MILDRED (G.): Gently strict.

MINNIE (G.): Love.

MIRIAM: (H.): Bitter.

MONICA (L.): Adviser.

MURIEL, MYRA (Gr.): Perfumed.

NANCY (H.): Grace.

Nessie, Nesta (L.): Pure.
Nicholas (Gr.): Victory of the people.
Noel: (L.): Christmas.
Nora, Norah (L.): Honour.
Norman. See under Surnames.
Olive. See page 189.
Oscar. (C.): Bounding warrior.
Owen (C.): Lamb.
Pamela: All sweetness.
Patrick, Patricia (L.): Noble.
Paul, Paula, Pauline (L.): Small.
Peggy. See page 189.
Penelope (Gr.): Weaver.
Peter. See page 190.
Philip (Gr.): Lover of horses.
Phoebe (Gr.): Shining.
Phyllis (Gr.). See page 190.
Priscilla (L.): Ancient.
Queenie: A queen.
Rachel (H.): Gentleness.
Raymond (G.): Wise protection.
Reginald (G.): Powerful judgment.
Richard, Dick (G.): Stern king.
Robert. See page 191.
Roger (G.): Spear of fame.
Roland (G.): Fame of the land.
Ronald. See page 191.
Rosalind (L.): Like a rose.
Rose, Rosa (L.): A rose.
Rupert: Bright fame.
Samuel (H.): Asked of God.
Sara, Susan, Sadie, Sally (H.): My princess.
Sheila, Sheelagh (L.): Blind.
Simon (H.): Obedient.
Sophia, Sophie (Gr.): Wisdom.
Stella (L.): A star.
Stephen (Gr.): A crown.
Susan (H.): Graceful white lily.
Sybil (Gr.): Wise.
Sylvia (L.): Leafy, woody.
Terence (L.): Tender.
Theodore, Theodora (Gr.): Gift of God.
Theresa: The reaper.
Thomas. See page 192.

TIMOTHY (L.): Fear God.
TONY: See ANTHONY.
UNA (C.): Born in famine.
URSULA(L.): Little bear.
VALENTINE (L.): Healthy.
VERA (L.). See page 193.
VERONICA: (L. and Gr.): Ideal saint.
VICTOR, VICTORIA (L.): Conqueror.
VIOLET. See page 193.
VIRGINIA (L.): Flourishing.
VIVIAN. (L.): Lively.
WALTER (G.): Powerful warrior.
WILFRED (G.): Resolute peace.
WILLIAM. See page 194.
WINIFRED (C.): See page 195.
YVONNE (G.): Archer.
ZACHARIAH (H.): Rememberance of the Lord.
ZOE (Gr.): Life.

SOMETHING ABOUT SURNAMES

AS I have said on page 287, Christian names are chosen for children and usually seem to fit their personalities very well. If a name just does not team up with its owner, somehow it is never used, and that person is known by a nickname instead, so the fitting process applies even here.

Surnames are rather different. No one, not even your parents, selects your surname for you. It is the label which has been attached to your family for centuries and represents that family as a whole, not any one member of it as the Christian name does. When a numberscope is done for anyone (see page 163) the numbers which are derived from the surname represent the *family* characteristics which he inherits or has acquired by his upbringing in the family home, while the numbers of the first name denote the personal and individual character. The complete name is the combination of the two—inheritance and individual traits—which makes up the unique personality.

Christian names are bestowed. Surnames have grown up through the centuries, gradually and imperceptibly. In ancient days a person had one name only—that which his parents had given him. This worked very well as long as communities were very small, little more than family groups. But people began to live close together for safety or convenience, and then it was impossible to be sure that in a given village there would only be one John or Edward or Mary.

As soon as there were several people with the same Christian name, some way had to be found of distinguishing one John or Mary from another. One plan was to mention also their father's name; another was to tack on some personal characteristic of height or walk or colouring.

Another, again, was to add the trade the man followed or the place where he lived. A very large number of our British surnames come from one of those four sources.

Descriptive Surnames

One John might be tall and another short. One Mary might have chestnut hair and another might be the possessor of dark skin. Edward might be lame or walk in a distinctive way or possess unusual strength. And so began surnames like Long (tall), Small, Little, Ambler, Beggie (which also means "little"), Bigg, Benedict (good speaker), Dark, Black (also meaning "dark"), Fairchild, Aird (tall), Alder (elder), Allan or Allen (fair, handsome), Armstrong (strong-armed), Askew (crooked, deformed), Bain (active), Ball (chestnut-haired), Blacklock or Blake-lock (black-haired), Stout, Courage, Good, Short, Sharp and Young.

Some surnames you would hardly think of as descriptive ones, because they come from old words not commonly used now, are Cullen (handsome, fair), Curtis or Curtice (courteous), Duffy (dark), Fairfax (fair-haired), Finnigan (fair-skinned), Howell (sprightly) and Hore (grey-haired), Glass (pale), Garry (changeable) and Bay (chestnut-haired).

Son of . . . Surnames

In the same English village, perhaps, John had a son named James. So had Richard, David and Philip. That was easy. To distinguish the four boys with the same Christian name, you called them respectively John's son, Richard's son, David's son and Philip's son, so that they soon became known as James Johnson, James Richardson, James Davidson (or Davison) and James Philipson. The "son" part was often abbreviated to a mere "s," so that Johnson became Johns or Jones, Richardson Richards, Davidson Davies or Davis and Philipson was also called Philips.

Probably all surnames ending in "son" and a great many that end with an "s" have this origin. One can think of Robertson, Roberts, Anderson (son of Andrew), Nixon (son of Nicholas), Peters, Edwards, Walters, Harrison (Harry's son), Jackson, Addison (Addy's son), Ellison (Alice's son), Stevenson and Stephens or Stevens, Jameson, Dickson or Dixon and many another.

There are other beginnings or endings to surnames which also mean "son of". In Scotland the innumerable Macs or Mcs were originally the sons of Donald, Andrew, Alister, Gregory (McGregor), Kenneth or Kenzie (MacKenzie) and all the rest.

The Irish equivalent is O', which accounts for names like O'Neill, Odell, O'Grady, O'Donovan, O'Sullivan and many others. The Welsh form of "son of" is Ap (sometimes shortened to "p"), and so we get names like Pritchard (Ap Richard) and Probert (Ap Robert). Upjohn was probably Ap John to begin with. When the Normans came over at the Conquest they brought Fitz, their prefix meaning "son of" and this account for such surnames as Fitzgerald, Fitzhugh, Fitzherbert, Fitzjohn, Fitzpatrick and Fitzroy.

Trade Surnames

The number of these is simply enormous and many of them are very frequently met with, too. The three commonest English surnames are Smith, Taylor and Brown, and of these the first two are trade names, while Brown is descriptive. The seven commonest trade names are Smith, Taylor, Clark, Wright, Walker, Turner and Cooper.

Smith is the most popular name of all because in olden times a Smith was not merely a blacksmith—though every village had one or more of these in the days before cars—but *any* worker in metal. Thus there were shoesmiths (another form of Blacksmith), arrowsmiths, locksmiths, bladesmiths, knifesmiths and so on, and many of them soon got their last name abbreviated to Smith. Goff is the old

Cornish dialect word for a smith and Gow is the Scottish form, so owners of both these names join the great army of smiths. Wrights usually made things of wood, so there were Arkwrights, who made arks or bins, Wainwrights, who made wains or wagons, Tellwrights (tilemakers) and so on. Taylors, of course, made clothes, Clarks wrote books or letters, Turners were lathe-workers and Coopers made casks.

Other trade names are Butcher, Baker, Butler, Footman, Chamberlain (the officer who used to manage a royal household), Bailey or Baillie (a landowner's bailiff), Steward, Tyle (tilemaker), Hillier, Hellier or Thacker (all thatchers), Capper or Capman (makers of caps), Horner (horn-maker) and Chapman (a dealer or trader).

Patch or Patchett was the jester or clown who was in the retinue of every king or great noble to keep him amused with wisecracks and songs. He was so called from his variegated attire or motley. Do you remember how Jack Point, the jester on *The Yeoman of the Guard,* calls himself "A wandering ministrel I, a thing of shreds and patches"?

Chandler dealt in candles and oil, Naylor made nails, Brewer brewed beer, Spicer traded in spices and Mercer in textiles, Plowman ploughed. Fuller—think of fuller's earth!—cleaned and thickened cloth, Dyer dyed it, Reeve was a magistrate, Broster was a broiderer or embroiderer, Hamper made hanaps or goblets and Caird was a (Scottish) tinker. Other obvious trade surnames, to give only a few among many, are Carpenter, Paynter, Farmer, Shepherd, Foreman, Cook, Carter and Tanner.

Place Surnames

Surnames which came from adding to a man's Christian name the place where he lived are legion. It was so easy to distinguish on John from another by say John from the Wood or John near the Church, and, of course, they were quickly shortened to John Wood and John Church.

Others will leap to your mind—Brook, Bywaters, Coombe (a steep, short valley), Beach, Field, Meadows, Dale, Rivers, Ash, Ford (place where a river could be crossed without a bridge), Elms, Willows, Underwood.

There are also names giving the direction in which people lived, like North, East, West, Northfield, Southcott, Southwell, Southern, Western, Westwood and Eastwood. We don't always recognise the place surname because they may use old, forgotten words. For example, "lea" or "ley" means field, which accounts for names like Lee, Lea, Leigh and Woodley. "Holt" and "shaw" are both words for a copse, hence Holt, Holthouse, Northolt, Shaw and Birkenshaw. From "croft" (a small field or piece of land near a house) come Croft, Bancroft, Cockcroft and similar names. "Hurst" means wood, "royd" a clearing, "ton" a farm, "bury" a town or borough, "cot" a cottage, while "al" or "ald" is a form of old and "ast" is a word for east. You will find surnames incorporating these old words in the list given on page 301.

Religious Names

A fifth class of surnames, not so numerous as the four types already described, but still quite common, are those derived from religion. The time when surnames began to be used was betwen 1066, when William the Conqueror landed at Hastings and 1400, and during these centuries, the Church was a leading power and influence. So it is not surprising that religion played a notable part in people's names.

I have suggested Church as a place surname, but in other cases it may have been a religious one. Then people were frequently called after saints. Stennett and Stimpson came from St. Stephen, names beginning with "Sil" or "Sel," like Silvester, were a form of Cecilia, a famous saint and, Jarvis was once Gervase. Saint Christopher gave rise to names like Christie and Kitson (Kit being short for

Christopher) and Anness or Anniss is a corruption of Agnes. Clemens, Clemence, Clements and Clementson derived from Clement, Catt and Catlin from Catherine, Martin from Martin—all familiar saints to the people of those times. The name of the Archangel Michael was, in olden days, often pronounced to rhyme with "trial," and from it came a whole group of surnames—Miall, Myall, Michael, Mitchell, Myhill, Mayall, Mighill, Miles and Miggles.

Surnames derived from a religious festival include Christmas, Yule, Nowell, Easter and Nation (abbreviated from Incarnation).

Flower Surnames

English people so love flowers and gardening that it's not surprising to find many flower surnames. What more natural and pretty than for a man who spent all his leisure growing a particular blossom to be called after it, or something that connects with flower culture? And so we get surnames like Bloom, Blossom, Bramble, Cutbush (there's a London nursery gardener with this apt name), Daisy, Flower, Flowerdew, Hawthorn, Lillie (or Lilley), Primrose, Rose and Tulip (yes, really!). Many of these, of course, are feminine Christian names as well.

Robert Herrick, a poet of three hundred years ago, was a great flower lover and wrote a charming little verse, *Upon One Lillie, who Marryed with a Maid Call'd Rose:*

> "What times of sweetnesse this faire day foreshows,
> Whenas the Lilly marries with the Rose!
> What next is lookt for? but we all sho'd see
> To spring from these a sweet Posterity."

Among the Jews there are a great many flower names, and there is a reason for this. At the end of the seventeenth century, when the Jews were much persecuted, ordinances were made in several parts of Europe that Jews might not use the ordinary surnames of the countries they lived in, but must invent distinctive ones for themselves from the words for colours, metals or natural objects such as flowers, trees and mountains.

Thus many flower and tree surnames arose, such as Lilien (lilie), Lilienfield (field of lilies), Applebaum (apple tree), Kirschbaum (cherry tree), Lindberg (lime tree mountain), Rosen (roses), Rosenberg (rose mountain), Rosenkranz (wreath of roses), Rosenthal (valley of roses) and Tannenbaum (pine tree).

The Word "Surname." It is interesting to know that your surname is your sire-name, that is, the name you got from your sires, ancestors or family.

SOME SURNAMES AND THEIR MEANINGS

IT is impossible to give here the many thousands of surnames found in Britain, but below is a list which includes a large number often met with. "Son" names which can be easily understood from what is said in "Son of . . ." (page 295) are omitted. For names which are both Christian and surnames, such as Harry, Evelyn and Joyce, consult "The Meanings of Christian Names" on page 287.

ABBOT, an abbot.

ACKMAN, AIKMAN, sharp director.

ACLAND, ACKLAND, dweller at the oak-land.

ACREMAN, field-worker, husbandman.

ACROYD, ACKROYD, dweller at the oak clearing.

ADAIR, dweller at the ford by the oaks.

ADAM, red earth.

ADDISON, Addy's son.

ADLAM, ADLEM, noble protector.

AGAR, AGER, dread army.

AGATE, dweller at the gate.

AGNEW, lamb.

AGUILER, needle-maker.

AIRD, tall, noble.

AKED, dweller at the oak-hill.

AKEHURST, dweller at the oak-wood.

AKRIGG, dweller at the oak-ridge.

ALBANY, white.

ALBRIGHT, ALLBRIGHT, bright, glorious.

ALCOTT, dweller at the old cottage.

ALDER, elder.

ALDERSMITH, the smith by the elder tree.

ALDHOUSE, ALDOUS, ALDIS, dweller at the old house.

ALDRICH, ALDRIDGE, old ruler.

ALDWORTH, dweller at the old farm.

ALFORD, dweller at the old ford.

ALLAN, ALLEN, bright, fair, handsome.

ALLARD, all-strong.

ALLENBY, dweller at Allen's farm.

ALLISON, Alice's son.

AMBLER, slow walker.

AMES, Amy's son.

AMNER, alms-giver.

ANCELL, servant.

ANDERSON, Andrew's son.

ANNESS, ANNISS. See page 299.

ANNING, Anna's son.

ANTHONY, ANTONY, descending from Hercules.

ANTROBUS, amid the woods.

APLIN, APPLIN, lion's son.

APPLEBAUM. See page 300.

APPLETHWAITE, dweller at the apple clearing.

APPENRODTH, APPENROTH, red apple.

APPLEYARD, dweller at the orchard.

ARBUTHNOT, river mouth.

ARKWRIGHT, a bin-maker.

ARMITAGE, ARMYTAGE, dweller at the hermitage.

ARMSTRONG, strong-armed.

ASCROFT, ASHCROFT, dweller at the east croft (small field).

ASH, ASHE, dweller at the ash tree.

ASKEW, crooked, deformed.

ATHERTON, dweller at the spring farm.

ATTENBOROUGH, dweller at the stronghold.

ATWELL, dweller at the well.

AUCKLAND, dweller at the temple land.

AUSTEN, majestic.

AUSTIN, prosperity, honour.

AVERY, elf-ruler.

BACH, BACK, brook.

BACKHOUSE, dweller at a bake-house.

BACON, swineherd.

BADDELEY, BADLEY, dweller at the bad (poor) field.

BAILEY, BAILLIE, a bailiff.

BAIN, active, alert.

BAIRD, a bard, ministrel.

BAKER, a bread-maker.

BALDWIN, a bold friend.

BALLISTER, cross-bowman.

BALL, chestnut-haired.

BANISTER, basket-maker.

BANK, dweller at the embankment.

BANNERMAN, standard-bearer.

BANNISTER, cross-bowman.
BARBER, BARBOUR, hairdresser.
BARCLAY, BERKELEY, dweller at the birch-field.
BARKER, bark-stripper, tanner.
BARR, dweller at gateway or barrier.
BARRATT, BARRETT, bear-counsel.
BARTLETT, bright, glorious.
BARTON, dweller at the barley grange.
BASS, BASSETT, low, short.
BATCHELOR, young knight.
BATEMAN, boatman.
BAXTER, BACKSTER, baker.
BAY, Chestnut-haired.
BAYLISS, a bailiff.
BEACH, dweller on the seashore.
BEALE, BEALL, fair, handsome.
BEAMISH, dweller at the tree-place.
BEAUCHAMP, BEECHAM, dweller at the fair field.
BEAUMONT, dweller at the fair mount.
BECKETT, BECKITT, little mouth.
BEECH, dweller by the beech tree.
BEGBIE, dweller at the big farm.
BEGGIE, little.
BELCHER, pretty face.
BELL, fair, handsome.
BELLAMY, fair friend.
BENEDICT, good speaker, well-spoken.
BENN, dweller at a peak.
BENDIX, Benedict's son.
BENHAM, dweller at the bean-land.
BENNETT, good speaker.
BERG, mountain.
BESANT, one from Byzantium.
BEST, beast, animal.
BETTERIDGE, powerful in battle.
BEVAN, BEAVAN, BEVIN, son of Evan.
BEVERIDGE, dweller at the beaver marsh.
BEVERLEY, dweller at the beaver lake.
BIBBY, BEEBY, dweller at the bee-farm.
BIDGOOD, battle-god.
BIGG, (E.), big, tall.
BINNIE, dweller at the little hill.
BIRD, birdlike.
BISHOP, a bishop.

BLACK, BLACKLOCK, dark-haired.

BLAIR, dweller on a plain.

BLAKE, BLAKELOCK, black, dark, black-haired.

BLOSSOM, a gardener.

BLUNT, blond, fair.

BOND, husbandman, farmer.

BOOTH, dweller at a hut.

BOYD, yellow-haired.

BRADLEY, dweller at the broad field.

BRAMBLE, dweller at the bramble-patch.

BRANDON, dweller at the beacon hill.

BRETT, briton.

BREWER, a maker of beer.

BRICE, BRYCE, quick.

BRIGGS, son of the bridge-dweller.

BROADBENT, dweller at the broad common.

BROOKS, dweller at a streamlet.

BROSTER, an embroiderer.

BROWN(E), of dark, reddish complexion.

BURGESS, a citizen.

BURROWS, BURROUGHES, dweller at a stronghold.

BURTON, dweller at the byre, stronghold or hill.

BUSH, dweller at a bush or thicket.

BUTCHER, a dealer in meat.

BUTLER, bottler, bottle-keeper.

BYWATERS, dweller by the rivers.

CADE, battle.

CALLAGHAN, warrior.

CALVERT, a calf-herd.

CAMPBELL, a fair field.

CANNON, a canon.

CAPMAN, CAPPER, a maker of caps.

CARMICHAEL, Michael's stronghold.

CARPENTER, a worker in wood.

CARR, dweller at a marsh.

CARROLL, a champion.

CATLIN, CATT. See page 299.

CHADWICK, dweller at Chad's place.

CHAMBERLAIN. See page 297.

CHANDLER, a dealer in candles.

CHAPMAN, a dealer or trader.

CHRISTIE. See page 298.

CHRISTMAS. See page 299.

CHURCH, dweller by the church.

CLARE, famous.

CLARK(E), clerk, writer, educated man.

CLAYTON, dweller at the clayey place.

CLEMANCE, CLEMENS, CLEMENTS, CLEMENTSON, Clement's son.
    See also page 299.

CLIFTON, dweller at the cliff farm.

COATES, dweller at the cottages or pens.

COBORN, COBURN, dweller at the woodcock stream.

COCKCROFT, dweller at the small cocks' field.

COHEN, COEN, COHN, a priest.

COLE, victorious people.

COLLINS, COLLYNS, Colin's son.

COMPTON, dweller at the combe (valley) estate.

CONNOR, counsel-help.

CONWAY, hound of the plain.

COOMBE, dweller in a steep valley.

COOPER, a cask-maker.

COPE, COPP, dweller on the hill-top.

CORDER, a rope-maker.

COURAGE, bravery, valiance.

CRADDOCK, CRADICK, full of love.

CREASE, CREESE, loving, fond.

CREW(E), dweller at the cattle-pen.

CRIPPS, CRISP(E), curly-haired.

CROFT, dweller at the small field.

CROSBIE, CROSBY, dweller by the Cross.

CROUCH, dweller by a crucifix.

CULLAN, CULLEN, COLQUHOUN, handsome, fair.

CURTICE, CURTIS, CURTOIS, courteous.

CUTLAR, CUTLER, a knife-maker.

DAISY. See Christian Names, page 289.

DALE, dweller at the dale (valley).

DALLAS, dweller at the waterfall field.

DALRYMPLE, dweller at the crooked pool field.

DALTON, dweller at the dale farm.

DANCE, Dan's son.

DANVERS, native of Antwerp.

DARCY, DARSEY, dark, swarthy.

DARK, swarthy, dark-haired.

DASHWOOD, dweller at the badger wood.

DAVENPORT, dweller at the river gate.

DAVIDSON, DAVISON, DAVIES, DAVIS, David's son.

DEVENISH, from Devon.

DAW, beloved.

Day, dairy servant.

Deacon, Deakin, a deacon.

Dean(e), dweller in a hollow.

Dell, dweller in a small valley.

Devlin, boisterous.

Dibden, Dibdin, dweller in a deep valley.

Dickson, Dixon, Dick's son.

Dott, little.

Dove, a dove.

Drayton, dweller at the dry-built farmstead.

Drinkwater, teetotaller.

Duffy, dark.

Dunlop, dweller at the bend of the hill.

Dunne, dark-skinned.

Dyall, worshipper of God.

Dyer, a dyer of cloth.

Eade, prosperity, happiness.

Eames, uncle's son, cousin.

Earl, nobleman, chief.

Earnshaw. dweller at the eagle wood.

East, one from the east.

Easter, born at Easter.

Eastwood, dweller by the east wood.

Eaton, dweller at the riverside farm.

Edge, dweller at a hill-ridge.

Edwards, Edward's son.

Eliot(t), God the Lord.

Ellis, Elias's son.

Elms, dweller by the elm trees.

Emery, famous.

Emmett, Emmott, ant-like, busy.

Endicott, dweller at the end cottage.

English, Englishman.

Erskine, dweller at the high cleft.

Everard, brave as a boar.

Evered, Everett, Everitt, boar-counsel.

Evan, Ewan, Ewing, well-born.

Eyre, heir.

Fair(e), blond, handsome.

Fairchild, pretty or blond child.

Fairfax, fair-haired.

Falconer, Faulkner, falcon-keeper.

Faber, a metal-worker.

Fane, joyful, glad.

FARMER, a farmer.
FARRAR, FERRIER, a farrier.
FAY, dweller by the beech tree.
FELLOWES, partner, companion.
FELTON, dweller at the farm on the plain.
FENWICK, dweller at the place on the fen.
FIELD, dweller at a field.
FIELDING, dweller at the meadow on the plain.
FINNEGAN, FINNIGAN, fair-skinned.
FISHER, fisherman.
FITZ names. See page 296.
FLAXMAN, flax-spinner or flax merchant.
FLETCHER, arrow maker, featherer.
FLINT, dweller at the stream.
FLOWER, FLOWERDEW. See page 299.
FOOT(E), dweller at the hill-foot.
FOOTMAN, a man-servant.
FORD. See page 298.
FOSS, dweller at a waterfall.
FOWLER, bird-catcher, gamekeeper.
FRANCIS, Frenchman.
FRANKLIN, free man, freeholder.
FRENCH, one from France.
FROBISHER, furbisher or cleaner (or armour).
FRY(E), free.
FULLER, a cleaner of cloth.
GAITSKELL, dweller at the goat's ravine.
GALE, gay, lively.
GALLACHER, GALLAGHER, eager help.
GARDNER, gardener.
GARRARD, GARRATT, GARRETT, spear-brave.
GARRICK, spear-ruler.
GARTH, dweller at the yard.
GAY(E), merry, blithe.
GEARY, changeable.
GEDDES, fellers of trees.
GENTRY, gentleness, noble birth.
GIBBS, Gilbert's son.
GILCHRIST, disciple of Christ.
GILDERSLEEVE, gilded sleeve.
GILES, downy-bearded.
GILL, dweller at a ravine.
GLADSTONE, GLEDSTONE, dweller at the kite rocks.
GLASS, pale or livid of complexion.

GLYN(NE), dweller in a glen.
GODDARD, GODDART, God-firm.
GOFF, a smith.
GOLIGHTLY, light-footed.
GOOD(E), virtuous, good.
GORDON, dweller at the three-cornered land.
GOSWELL, dweller at the goose well.
GOULD, gold.
GOW, a smith.
GOWER, dweller at a croft.
GRAHAM(E), dweller at the grey enclosure.
GRANT, big.
GRANVILLE, dweller at the big estate.
GRAVES, GREAVE, dweller at a grove.
GREG, GREGG, GREGORY, a watchman.
GREY, grey-haired.
GRIFFIN, ruddy, rosy.
GRISEWOOD, dweller at the swine-wood.
GROGAN, a warrior
GROSVENOR, a great hunter.
GROOM, a tender of horses.
GROVE(s), dweller at a small wood.
GULLIVER, wolf-army.
GUNN, war, battle.
GUSTER, a taster.
HACKER, a woodcutter.
HADFIELD, dweller at the heath ford.
HAGUE, HAIGH, dweller at the hedged farm.
HALDANE, HALDEN, half-Dane.
HALE, dweller on a slope.
HALL, dweller at or near a hall (big house).
HALLIDAY, born on a holy-day.
HAMMOND, chief protector.
HAMPER, a goblet-maker.
HAND, an employee, labourer.
HARDCASTLE, dweller at the herd enclosure.
HARDING(E), brave, firm, hard.
HARKER, army spear.
HARPER, HARPUR, harp player.
HARRIES, HARRIS, HARRISON, Harry's son.
HARRAP, HARROP, HARRUP, dweller at the hare valley.
HART(E), hart-like.
HARVEY, army.

HASLETT, HAZLITT, HASSALL, HASSELL, dweller by the hazel-tree.

HATTON, dweller at the heath farm.

HAVELOCK, sea-battle.

HAWKER, huckster, pedlar.

HAWTHORN, dweller by the thorn tree. See also page 299.

HAY, dweller at a hedge.

HAYWARD, HEYWOOD, dweller at the hedged enclosure.

HEALING, dweller at the corner meadow.

HEATH, dweller on the heath.

HEBDEN, dweller at the dog-rose tree valley.

HEDGER, hedge-maker or hedge-trimmer.

HELLIER, HELLYER, HILLIER, a roofer, thatcher.

HENLEY, HENLY, dweller at the high field.

HEPBURN, HEPPELL, HEPPLE. As HEBDEN.

HERRICK, army-ruler.

HESKETH, dweller at the hassack (grass) heath.

HEWIT(T), soul thought.

HIBBERD, HIBBERT, high-bright.

HICK, HIGGIN, little Richard, Dick.

HILARY, HILLERY, cheerful, gay.

HILL, dweller on a hill.

HILLIER, a thatcher.

HIND(E), a peasant, servant.

HITCHCOCK, little Richard.

HOBB, a rustic, a hobgoblin.

HODGE, a rustic, countryman.

HOLBROOK, dweller on a river island or lowland.

HOLT, dweller at a wood or wooded hill.

HOLTHOUSE, dweller at the house by the wood.

HONEYMAN, a beekeeper.

HOOD, a hood.

HOOKER, a hook-maker.

HOPE, dweller in a valley.

HOPKIN, HOPKINS, little rustic.

HORE, grey-haired.

HORN(E), an old person.

HORNBLOWER, a trumpeter.

HORNER, a horn maker.

HORSLEY, dweller at the horse field.

HOSIER, a stocking maker or dealer.

HOWARD, high or chief warden.

HOWELL, sprightly.

Hoy, Hoey, dweller at a bluff or hill.

Huckster, a woman pedlar.

Hudd, a hood.

Hunt, a hunter, huntsman.

Huntley, dweller at hunter's field.

Hurst, dweller at a wood.

Huson, Hugh's son.

Hutton, dweller at a farm.

Hyde, dweller at a field ridge.

Iddon, capable.

Ide, prosperity, happiness.

Ifield, dweller at the yew-field.

Ile(s), dweller at the island.

Illingworth, from Illingworth (Yorkshire).

Ince, dweller at the big house.

Ing(e), dweller at the meadow.

Ingersoll, dweller at Ingar's hall.

Ingle, favourite, darling.

Intram, Ing's raven.

Inman, an innkeeper.

Iremonger, Irons, an ironmonger.

Ironside, brave soldier.

Irvin(g), dweller by the white river.

Ismay, a girl.

Ireland, person from Ireland.

Iven, ivy-girl.

Ivemey, ivy-girl.

Jack(e), little John.

Jackson, Jack's son.

Jacoby, a supplanter.

Jaggar, Jagger, a pedlar, carter.

Jameson, Jamieson, James's son.

Jardine, dweller at a gardin.

Jarrold, Jerrold, firm spear.

Jarvis. See page 298.

Jeaffreson, Jefferson, Geoffrey's son.

Jekyll, generous judge.

Jellicoe, handsome, pleasing.

Jennings, little John's son or Jenny's son.

Jerningham, eager warrior.

Jerome, holy name.

Jessop, increase.

Jevan, Jevon, young.

Johnson, Johnston(e), John's son.

JONES, John's or Joan's son.

JORDAN, descender, goer down.

JURY, dweller at Jewry, (Jews' quarters).

KAHN, a priest.

KAISER, KAIZER, KAYSER, an emperor.

KAPLAN, a chaplain.

KAY, see MACKAY.

KAYE, fire, ardour.

KEARNEY, a soldier.

KEARTON, dweller at the marsh enclosure.

KEATING, sagacious.

KEBLE, famously bold.

KEELER, worker on a keel (or ship).

KEEN(E), sharp, bold, comely.

KEIR, dark-skinned.

KEITH, dweller at a wood.

KELLAWAY, dweller at the marshy way.

KELLY, warrior.

KELVIN, dweller by the narrow river.

KEMP(E), champion, soldier.

KENDALL, dweller in the bright dale.

KENNEDY, ugly chief.

KENT, white, bright.

KER(R), dweller at a fort.

KERSLAKE, dweller at the cress stream.

KIBBLE, famously bold.

KILNER, a kiln worker,

KINGHAM, dweller on the king's estate.

KINGLEY, dweller at the king's field.

KINGSTON, dweller at the king's house.

KINNAIRD, dweller at the high hill.

KIPLIN(G), dweller at the waterfall's edge.

KIRK(E), dweller by the church.

KIRSCHBAUM. See page 300.

KITCHENER, KITCHINER, kitchen officer.

KITSON. See page 298.

KNOLL, KNOLLYS, dweller at a round hillock.

KNOTT, dweller at a rocky hill-top.

KYNASTON(E), dweller at the king's stone.

LACY, one from Lassy (France).

LADD, lad, servant.

LAIDLAW. dweller at the tumulus (burial mound).

LAKE, dweller by the water.

LAMBERT, land-bright.

LAMBORN, LAMBOURNE, LAMBURN, dweller by the lamb stream.

LANE, dweller in a lane.

LANG, long, tall.

LARCHER, the archer.

LASCELL(ES), LASSELL, dweller by the hermit's cell.

LATCHFORD, dweller by the pool ford.

LATIMER, a worker in latten (a mixed metal), or Latiner (interpreter).

LAUDERDALE, dweller in the valley of the deep river.

LAURENCE, LAURANCE, LAWRENCE, laurel tree.

LAW(E), dweller at the hill or mound.

LAYCOCK, dweller at the water by the oak.

LEA, dweller at the field.

LEADER, a carrier.

LEAF(E), beloved, dear.

LEAPER, LEADMAN, basket-maker.

LEE, LEIGH. As LEA.

LEECH, LEACH, a physician.

LENNOX, dweller at the elm trees.

LESLEY, LESLIE, dweller at the grey fort.

LEVER, dweller near the rushes.

LEVERTON, dweller at the farm by the rushes.

LEVI, LEVY, joined.

LEWIS, famous battle.

LIDDELL, dweller by the wide river.

LILIEN, lilies.

LILIENFIELD, field of lilies.

LILLEY, LILLIE. See page 299.

LILYWHITE, white-skinned.

LINDBERG. See page 300.

LINE, dweller by a lime tree.

LINK(E), dweller at a bank or ridge.

LINTON, dweller at the flax enclosure.

LISLE, man from the isle.

LISTER, a dyer.

LITTELL, LITTLE, small.

LIVESEY, dweller at the beloved farm.

LLOYD, grey.

LOCK(E), dweller at a lock-up (sheep-fold).

LOCKER, a locksmith.

LODER, a loader, stevedore.

LOGAN, dweller at the little hollow.

LONG, tall.

LONGBOTHAM, LONGBOTTOM, dweller in the long valley.

LONGFELLOW, tall man.

LORD, lord, master.

LOVE, darling.

LOVELACE, loveless, unloved.

LOWRIE, LOWRY. As LAURENCE.

LUARD, little wolf.

LUMB, dweller by a deep pool.

LUNN, strong, fierce.

LUTTERELL, LUTTRELL, lute-maker, lute-player.

LYALL, LYEL(L), little lion.

LYLE. As LISLE.

LYNCH, sailor, pilot.

LYTE, little.

MABB, lovable.

MABON, youth, hero.

MACCONNACHIE, son of Duncan.

MACKAY, MACKIE, Keith's son.

MACREARY, Rory's son.

MADDISON, Maud's son.

MAGNUS, great.

MAITLAND, dweller at the meadow-land.

MAKIN, man, warrior.

MAKEPEACE, peacemaker.

MALKIN, untidy, a scarecrow.

MALLETT, naughty.

MANN, a servant, vassal.

MANFIELD, dweller at the common (belonging to everyone) field.

MANGER, a trader, merchant.

MANNERS, dweller at the manors.

MARCH, dweller at a border, boundary, frontier.

MARCHANT, a merchant.

MARGETSON, Margaret's son.

MARKHAM, dweller at the boundary land.

MARNER, MARRINER, a sailor, mariner.

MARSH, dweller on a marsh.

MARSHAL(L), groom, farrier, steward.

MARTIN. See page 299.

MASON, a mason, stone-worker.

MASSEY, MASSIE, one from Massy (Normandy).

MASSINGER, a messenger.

MATHISON, Matthew's son.

MAWER, a mower.

MAY(E), a man, warrior, kinsman.

MAYALL, See page 299.

MAYER, a mayor.

MAYNARD, power-brave.

Mc names. See page 296.

MEAD(E), MEADOWS, dweller at a meadow.

MEAR, dweller at the mere (pool).

MEEK(E), humble, mild.

MELDRUM, dweller by the bare ridge.

MELHUISH, dweller on a family plot by the mill.

MELLOR, a miller.

MELVILLE, a dweller at the poor estate.

MERCER, dealer in textiles.

MEREDITH, mortal day.

MERRYWEATHER, cheerful person.

MERTON, dweller at the mere (pool) farm.

METHUEN, METHVEN, dweller by the smooth river.

MEW(S), dweller at the falcon's place.

MIALL, MICHAEL. See page 299.

MICKLEJOHN, Big John.

MIDDLEMASS, born at Michaelmas (29th September).

MIGGLES, MIGHILL. See page 299.

MILDMAY, gentle maid.

MILES. See page 299.

MILLMAN, a miller.

MILNE, dweller at a corn-mill.

MILNER, a corn-miller.

MILTON, dweller at the mill village.

MINN, love.

MINTER, a coiner, money-maker, money-changer.

MITCHELL. See page 299.

MITFORD, dweller at the ford where rivers meet.

MOBERLEY, strong courage.

MOLESWORTH, dweller at the moles' ground.

MOLLISON, Molly's son.

MOLLOY, a servant of the great.

MONACHAN, MONAGHAN, a monk.

MONYPENNY, wealthy.

MONTAGU(E), dweller at the peaked hill.

MOODIE, MOODY, spirited, brave, gloomy.

MOORE, MORE, dweller on the moor.

MORDANT, MORDAUNT, sarcastic, biting.

MORELL, dark, swarthy.

MORGAN, white sea.

MORRISEY, sea-charm.

MORTIMER, dweller at the stagnant water.

MOSELEY, MOSLEY, MOZLEY, dweller at the moss field.

MOSS, dweller at the marsh.

MOTE, MOTT, dweller at a moat.

MUCH, big, great.

MUDFORD, dweller at the muddy ford.

MULHOLLAND, clamorous servant.

MULLIGAN, little monk, bald man.

MUNGO, gentle, much loved.

MURDOCH, MURDOCK, sea-happy.

MURPHY, sea-warrior.

MURTHWAITE, dweller at the bog clearing.

MUSGRAVE, MUSGROVE, dweller at the moss (marsh) grove.

MYALL, MYHILL. See page 299.

MYER, dweller at the mire (bog).

NAGEL, NAGLE, a nail; spike.

NAIRN(E), dweller at the joining of the rivers.

NAPER, NAPIER, NAPPER, keeper of the napery (table linen).

NASH, dweller at the ash tree.

NATHAN, given by God.

NATION, born at the festival of the Incarnation.

NAYLOR, a nail-maker.

NEAME, an uncle.

NEEDLER, needle-maker.

NEIL, NEILL, NEILD, champion.

NELSON, Nell or Neil's son.

NESBIT(T), NESBETT, dweller at the small marshy plot.

NETHERBY, dweller at the lower farm.

NETHERFIELD, dweller at the lower field.

NETHERSALL, NETHERSOLE, dweller at the lower hall.

NETTER, netmaker.

NEVE, a nephew.

NEVILE, NEVILLE, dweller at the new town.

NEW, a newcomer.

NEWBOLD, NEWBOLT, dweller at the new house or hall.

NEWCOM(N), newcomer, stranger.

NEWMAN, newcomer.

NEWNES, dweller at the new inn.

NICHOLL, victorious army.

NIGHTINGALE, a sweet singer.

NIXON, Nick's (Nicholas's) son.

NOBLE, NOBLET, noble, well-known.

NORCOTT, NORCUTT, dweller at the north cottage.

NORDEN, dweller at the north valley.

NORMAN, Northman.

Normanton, dweller at the northman's estate.

Norreys, Norris, North, a Northerner.

Northfield, dweller at the north field.

Northolt, dweller by the north wood.

Norton, dweller at the north farm.

Nott, bald, close-cropped.

Nowell, born at Christmas.

Nugent, dweller at the marshy meadow.

Nussey, dweller at the nut grove.

Nuthall, Nuttall, dweller at the nut tree nook.

O' (Irish) names. See page 296.

Oak(e), dweller by the oak tree.

Oakey, dweller at the oak island.

Oat(e), wealth, happiness.

Oates, a dealer in oats.

Ockenden, a dweller at the oak valley.

Ogilvie, Ogilvy, dweller at the high peak.

Oldcastle, dweller at the old stronghold.

Oldershaw, dweller at the alder-wood.

Olliffe, ancestral relic.

Oliver, Olliver, kind, affectionate.

Onions, the onion-seller's son.

Openshaw, dweller at the open wood.

Oram, dweller at the river-bank enclosure.

Orchard, dweller at a fruit-garden.

Ord(e), dweller at a headland.

Organer, an organ-maker or organ-player.

Orm(e), a ship, serpent.

Omerod, Ormroyd, dweller at a clearing in a wood.

Orpen, Orpin, swarthy friend.

Osborn(e), Osburne, divine bear.

Oscroft, dweller at the ox-croft.

Osmond, Osmund, divine protector.

Otway, prosperous war.

Ould, old.

Overbury, dweller at the shore fort.

Owen, well-born, young.

Oxenham, dweller at the ox-pasture.

Pack(e), born at Easter.

Packman, a pedlar.

Padfield, dweller at the path-field.

Page, a page, boy attendant.

Paget(t), Pain(e), heathen.

PALGRAVE, dweller at the pale (stake) grove.

PALISSER, a fence-maker.

PALMER, a pilgrim from Palestine.

PANNIER, a maker of bread-baskets.

PANTIN(G), a puppet.

PARDOE, PARDOW, a leopard.

PARFETT, PARFITT, perfect, honourable.

PARGETER, PARGITER, a wall plasterer.

PARK(E), dweller in an enclosed ground.

PARKER, a park-keeper, gamekeeper.

PARKINS(ON), little Peter's son.

PARMENTER, PARMINTER, PARMITER, clothier, tailor.

PARRISH, Parry's son.

PARRY, Harry's son.

PARSON, person of rank, a parson.

PATCH, PATCHETT, a clown, jester. See also page 297.

PATON, PATEN, little Patrick.

PATTERSON, Patrick's son.

PAUL, PAULET, PAWLE, little.

PAYNTER, a paint dealer, house painter,

PAWSON, Paul's son.

PAYNE, a heathen.

PEABODY, a dandy, showily dressed person.

PEACHE, PEACHEY, dweller at a peak.

PEASEY, dweller at the pea-field.

PECKOVER, dweller at the peak edge.

PEDLER, PEGLER, a basket.

PEGRAM, a pilgrim.

PELISSIER, a furrier.

PENDERGAST, PENDERGRASS, chief guest.

PENN, PENNY, dweller in the (sheep) pen or fold.

PEPPER, a dealer in pepper.

PERCIVAL, stalwart, keen hunter.

PERKINS, PERKISS, little Peter's son.

PERRIN(G), little father.

PERRY, PERRYN, dweller by a pear-tree.

PETERS, Peter's son.

PETIFER, iron foot.

PETTIGREW, crane-foot.

PEW (ap Hugh), Hugh's son.

PHELP, PHILLIPS, PHILIP, horse-lover.

PHILLIPSON, Philip's son.

PICK, dweller at a peak.

PICKFORD, dweller at the ford near the peak.

PICKLE, dweller at the pointed hill.

PICKWICK, dweller at the peak place or farm.

PIERS, PIERCE, Peter's son.

PIGGOT(T) freckled, pitted (with smallpox), spotty-faced.

PIKE, dweller at the pointed hill.

PILCHER, a maker of pilches (fur garments of olden times).

PINCH, PINCHES, PINCHIN, born at Whitsuntide.

PINERO, a pine tree.

PINK(E), like a chaffinch.

PINNER, a pin-maker or pin dealer.

PIPER, a piper.

PIRIE, PIRRIE, dweller by a pear-tree.

PITMAN, PITT, dweller at a pit.

PLACE, dweller at a hall or mansion.

PLANT(E), dweller at a plantation.

PLAYFAIR, a playmate.

PLOWMAN, a ploughman.

PLUCK, hairy, shaggy.

PLUMER, PLUMMER, feather-dresser, maker of plumes.

PLUNKET(T), dweller by the plank-bridge.

POINTER, POYNTER, a maker of points, (tagged laces used to fasten doublets).

POLE, dweller at a pool.

POLSON, Paul's son.

POMEROY, POMROY, dweller at the apple-orchard.

POND, dweller at the pound.

POPE, father.

PORCHER, PORTER, a porter, carrier, door-keeper.

PORTMAN, a gateman.

POTTER, a pot-maker, pot-seller.

POTTINGER, a pottage-maker.

POTTS. As POTTER.

POULTER, a poulterer.

POUND(E), dweller at the pound (enclosure for stayed animals).

POVEY, owl-like, wise.

POWELL, Howell's son.

PRATT, dweller at a meadow.

PRENTICE, PRENTISS, an apprentice.

PRESCOTT, dweller at the priest's cottage.

PRESTON, dweller at the priest's place.

PRETTY, PRETTYMAN, crafty, sly.

PRIESTLEY, dweller at the priest's field.

PRIESTMAN, a priest.

PRINCE, a prince's servant.

PRINGLE, silver penny.

PRIOR, head of priory.

PRITCHARD, Richard's son.

PROBERT, Robert's son.

PROCTER, PROCTOR, a proctor, manager.

PROTHERO(E), son of the reddish-brown man.

PROUSE, PROWSE, gallant, valiant.

PROVOST, a commander.

PUDDEFOOT, club-footed.

PULLAR, dweller at the pool bank.

PULLEN, PULLIN, a poulterer.

PURDON, dweller at pear-tree hill.

PURKIS, Peter's son.

PURSER, cashier, paymaster.

PYBUS, dweller at the prickly bush.

PYECROFT, dweller at the magpie field.

QUANT, QUAINT, skilful, neat, prudent.

QUARRIER, quarryman.

QUARTERMAIN(E), four-handed, mail-fisted.

QUEEN, a wife.

QUICK(E), lively, quick.

QUIGLEY, grandson of Coigleach.

QUILLER, a fledgling, beginner.

QUILTER, a quilt-maker.

QUINTON, dweller at the Queen's manor.

RABAN, raven.

RABY, dweller at the deer's place.

RADCLIFF(E), dweller at the red cliff.

RADFORD, dweller at the red ford.

RAE, like a roe.

RAEBURN, dweller by the roe-brook.

RAGG(E), RAGGETT, shaggy-haired.

RAINGER, a ranger.

RAKE, dweller at the sheep-walk.

RAMAGE, wild.

RAMSBOTHAM, RAMSBOTTOM, RAMSDEN, dweller in the ram's valley.

RAMSAY, RAMSEY, dweller at the raven island.

RANDAL, RANDELL, RANDOLPH, wolf's shield.

RAPER, rope-maker.

RAPSON, Ralph's son.

RATHBONE, dweller at the white fort.

RAVEN, dark, black.

RAVENHILL, dweller at the raven hill.

RAVENSCROFT, dweller at the raven's croft.

RAWLINS(ON), RAWLINGS, Rawlin's or Rowland's son.

RAY. See RAE.

RAYMENT, RAYMOND, mighty, or godlike protection.

REA, grey.

READ(E), red-haired, red-faced.

READER, a reed-worker, thatcher.

REDBOURN(E), dweller at a reedy brook.

REDDING, dweller at the red meadow.

REDFEARN, REDFERN, dweller by the red ferns.

REDGRAVE, REDGROVE, dweller at the red grove.

REEVES, a bailiff's son.

REAGAN, regal, kingly.

REID, red-haired.

REMINGTON, one from Rimington (Yorks).

RENDALL. See RANDAL.

REVELL, grey, tawny.

REYNOLDS, Reginald's son.

RHODES, dweller at a (main) road-side.

RICHARDS, RICHARDSON, Richard's son.

RIVERS, dweller by the rivers.

ROADS, ROADES, dweller by a rood, (crucifix).

ROBERTS, ROBERTSON, Robert's son.

ROBOTHAM, dweller in the roe valley.

ROBY, ROBEY, dweller at the roe stead.

RODD, dweller on a rod of ground.

RODWELL, dweller at a roadside spring.

ROE, red-faced, red-haired.

ROFFEY, dweller at the rough island or waterside.

ROLLS, Rollo's son.

ROLT, famous power.

ROMER, roamer, wanderer.

ROUS(E), dweller on a moor.

ROOT(E), cheerful, gay.

ROPER, a ropemaker.

ROSE, Rowland's son.

ROSEBERY, dweller at the roes' stronghold.

ROSEN. See page 300.

ROSENBERG. See page 300.

ROSENKRANTZ, ROSENTHAL. See page 300.

ROSEWARNE, dweller at the alder health.

ROTHSCHILD, red shield.

ROUNTREE, ROWNTREE, dweller at a rowan-tree.

ROW(E), dweller at a row (of cottages) or hedgerow.

ROYCE, ROYSE, Roy's son.
RUNCI(E)MAN, horse-dealer, jobmaster.
RUDD, RUDDY, ruddy, red-faced.
RUFF, red-haired.
RUNDELL, RUNDLE, rotund, tubby.
RUSHBROOK(E), dweller at a rushy brook.
RUSSELL, RUSSET, red-haired.
RUTHVEN, dweller by the red river.
RUTHERFORD, dweller at the cattle ford.
RUTTER, trooper, horseman.
RYCROFT, dweller at a small rye field.
RYMAN, a dealer in rye.
SACHEVERELL, dweller at the roebuck forest.
SACK, adversary, competitor.
SACKER, a sack-maker.
SACKVILLE, dweller at the dry-built (without mortar) farm.
SADD, serious, discreet.
SADLER, a sadler.
SAGE, learned, wise.
SAILER, SAILOR, a leaper, dancer.
SALE, dweller in a hall.
SALMAN, SALMON, SALMONS, dark.
SALT, one from Salt (Staffs).
SALTER, salt-worker or salt-dealer.
SAMPER, one from St. Pierre (France).
SAMPLE, one from St. Paul (France).
SAMPSON, SAMSON, splendid sun.
SANDBACH, dweller at the sandy brook.
SANDFORD, SANDIFORD, dweller at a sandy ford.
SANDISON, Alexander's (Sandy's) son.
SANDS, dweller at the sands.
SANTLEY, dweller at the sandy field.
SATTERTHWAITE, dweller at the hill-pasture clearing.
SAUNDERS. As Sandison.
SAVARY, SAVERY, SAVORY, mind-powerful.
SAVILE, SAVILL, SAVILLE, dweller at the willow farm.
SAX(E), short sword.
SAXON, SAXTON, a sexton, sacristan.
SAYER, a carpenter.
SCARLETT, one with bright red complexion or dress.
SCARTH, dweller at the gap or cliff.
SCATTERGOOD, a philantropist, spendthrift.
SCOBIE, dweller at the wood farm.
SCORER, a scout, spy.

SCOTT, an Irishman, a Scot.

SCRAGG, bony, thin.

SCRIVEN, SCRIVENER, a public writer, clerk.

SEATON, dweller at the seaside farm.

SEDDON, dweller in the spruce-fir valley.

SEDGWICK, SIDGWICK, dweller at the sedgy place.

SEELEY, SEELY, happy.

SELDON, dweller at the willow-walk.

SELLAR, SELLER, a saddler.

SELWYN, friend from the hall.

SEMPLE, SEMPILL. As SAMPLE.

SENNETT, SENNITT, old, wise.

SERGEANT, SERGENT, SERJENT, an officer, attendant.

SERLE, SERRILL, armour.

SEXTON, a sexton.

SEYMOUR, SEYMER, one from St. Maur (France).

SHAFTO(E), dweller at the shaft hill.

SHAKESPEAR(E), SHAKSPERE, soldier,beadle, sergeant.

SHANE, John.

SHAPSTER, tailoress.

SHARP(E), quick, smart.

SHAW(E), dweller at a wood.

SHAWCROSS, dweller at the crucifix by the wood.

SHAYLER, SHAYLOR, cripple, limping walker.

SHEARER, SHEARMAN, a cutter of wool or cloth.

SHELLEY, SHELLY, dweller at the shelving (sloping) field.

SHENTON, dweller at a beautiful farm.

SHEPHARD, SHEPHERD, SHEPPARD, SHEPPERD, a shepherd.

SHERIDAN, wild man, satyr.

SHERLOCK, white-haired, blond.

SHIEL, dweller at a hut or shed.

SHILLITO(E), SHILTO, dweller at the sheep-path shed.

SHINER, a polisher.

SHIP(P), dweller at the Ship Inn.

SHIPMAN, a sailor, skipper.

SHIPTON, dweller at a sheep farm.

SHOESMITH, SHOOSMITH, a farrier.

SHOOLBRED, school-bred, educated.

SHORT, of low stature.

SHOTTER, a shooter.

SHUTER, an archery shooter, archer.

SIBBALD, sea-bold.

SIDDALL, SIDDELL, dweller in the wide valley.

SIDDELEY, SIDLEY, dweller at the broad field.

SIDGWICK. See SEDGWICK.

SIEVEKING, dweller at the bay or inlet.

SILK(E), a silk dealer.

SILVERWOOD, dweller at the silver birch wood.

SILVESTER. See page 298.

SIMSON, SIMPSON, Sim's (Simeon's) son.

SINNETT, SINNOTT, love, affection.

SIRETT, victorious counsel.

SKEAT(E), SKEET, swift, quick.

SKINNER, flayer of hides, hide-dealer.

SLADE, dweller in a valley or dell.

SLADEN, dweller in the sloe valley.

SLATTERY, straight, tall.

SLOAN(E), soldier, fighter.

SMALLEY, dweller at the small field.

SMART, sharp, quick.

SMEE, small.

SMETHURST, dweller at the wood on the plain.

SMITH, blacksmith, metal-worker. See also page 296.

SNAITH, SNEAD, dweller at the clearing.

SNELL, active, quick, nimble.

SNOOK, long-nosed.

SNOW, born when snow was on the ground.

SOAME, dark, swarthy.

SOANE, son.

SOMERFORD, dweller at the summer ford.

SOPER, a soap-maker.

SORRELL, with hair of reddish-brown.

SOTHEBY, dweller at the south farm.

SOUTER, SOUTAR, SOUTTER, SOWTER, cobbler, shoemaker.

SOUTHCOTT, dweller at the south cottages.

SOUTHWELL, dweller at the south well.

SPARHAWK, SPARK(E), sparrowhawk.

SPARLING, SPARROW, sparrow.

SPAULL, one from St. Paul (France).

SPEAR, a spearman.

SPEED, prosperity, fortune.

SPELLER, SPELLAR, a preacher, speaker, story-teller.

SPENCE(R), a dispenser or keeper of provision or larder.

SPENDER, a bursar, paymaster.

SPICER, a dealer in spices.

SPILLER, an actor, performer.

SPRIGG(E), small, slender.

SPRING, dweller at a fountain.

Spurr, a spur-maker.

Stacey, Stacy, security, prosperity.

Stack, dweller at a steep rock.

Stainer, painter, decorator.

Stair, dweller at a marsh path.

Stanbury, dweller at the stone fort.

Standish, dweller at the stony enclosure.

Stanford, dweller at the stone-paved ford.

Stanhope, dweller at a stony mountain hollow.

Stanley, dweller at a stony or rocky field.

Stanton, dweller at a stone dwelling.

Stapleton, dweller at the enclosure fenced with staples (posts).

Stead(e), Steadman, Stedman, dweller at a farmstead.

Stennett, Stenson, Stephen's son. See also page 298.

Stephens, Stevens, Stevenson, Stephen's son.

Steward, an estate manager.

Stewart, Steward, sty-keeper, steward.

Stickland, dweller at the steep land.

Stimpson, Stimson, As Stenson.

Stirling, dwelling at the yellow house.

Stodard, Stodart, Stoddard, Stoddart, a horse-keeper.

Stone, dweller at a stony rock or stone castle.

Stoner, Stonier, a stone-mason, stone-cutter.

Storer, a storekeeper.

Stott. As Stodard.

Stout, brave, fat.

Stowell, dweller at the rock spring.

Straker, a striker, stroker.

Strange, foreign.

Stratton, dweller at the Roman street farm.

Strauss, plume, crest.

Street(e), dweller on the Roman Street.

Streatfield, dweller at the field by the Roman street.

Stringer, a bowstring or cord maker.

Struther(s), dweller by a stream.

Strutt, stiff, affected.

Stuart. As Stewart.

Stobart, an ox-herd.

Stubbs, dweller at the tree-stumps.

Sturdee, Sturdy, sturdy, reckless.

Sugden, dweller at the sow hollow.

Sumner, Sumnor, Sumpner, a summoner, officer at ecclesiastical court.

Sutcliff(e), dweller on the south cliff.

Sutton, dweller at the south enclosure.

Swain(e), a swineherd, servant.

Swan(n), long-necked, swan-like.

Sweeney, Sweeny, dweller at the swine meadow.

Swinburne(e), dweller by the swine brook.

Syrett. As Sirett.

Taberner, a tavern- or inn-keeper, tabor-player.

Taft, dweller at a croft.

Tait(e), brisk, cheery.

Talbot, a raider, bandit.

Tallis, dweller at the trimmed (cut) copse.

Tannar, Tanner, a leather-maker, tanner.

Tannenbaum. See page 300.

Tapper, am innkeeper, beer-seller.

Tapster, a woman inn-keeper or beer-seller.

Tasker, a thrasher, thresher, reaper, piece-worker.

Taylor, a tailor.

Tedder, national army.

Teller, Tellier, a cloth-maker, weaver.

Tellwright, a tile maker.

Temple, dweller near a religious house.

Tennant, Tennent, a tenant, farmer.

Tennyson, Dennis's son.

Terry, mighty ruler.

Tester, an assayer.

Tew, fat, plump.

Thackeray, Thackery, Thackrah, Thackray, dweller at a
    thatch, corner (storehouse).

Thayer, national army.

Thick, thickset, stocky.

Thistlethwaite, dweller at the thistle clearing.

Thorn(e), dweller by the thorn-tree.

Thorpe, dweller at the hamlet.

Thrale, a servant.

Thwaite, dweller at a clearing.

Thynne, thin, lean.

Tice, pleasant.

Tidy, Tidey, ready, neat, honest.

Tierney, lord, master.

Tiller, Tillman, husbandman, tiller of the soil.

Tilly, dweller at the lime grove.

Tingay, Tingey, dweller at the parliament field.

Tinkler, a tinker.

Tiverton, a dweller at the double ford.

TODD, foxy, bushy-haired.

TODHUNTER, a fox-hunter.

TOLLER, a tax-collector.

TOPLIS(S), dweller at the top leas (fields).

TOWNSEND, TOWNSHEND, dweller at the town's (village's) end.

TOY(E), national spear.

TRACEY, TRACY, from Tracy (France).

TRAVERS(E), dweller at the cross-roads.

TREE, dweller by a (prominent) tree.

TRELAWN(E)Y, dweller at the church village.

TRELOAR, dweller at the lower homestead.

TREMLETT, dweller at the aspen grove.

TRENCH, dweller at an alley or cutting.

TRIGG(E), trustworthy, true.

TRIMMER, strong arm.

TRINDER, a wheelwright.

TRIPP, skittish, colt-like.

TROLLOPE, a loiterer.

TRUE, TRUEBODY, true, faithful.

TRUMPER, trumpeter.

TUCK, national spear.

TUCKER, fuller (thickness) of cloth.

TUDOR, divine gift.

TUGWELL, dweller at a draw-well.

TULIP. See page 299.

TUNNICLIFF(E), dweller at a tunnelled cliff or cliff with caves.

TURNBULL, brave, daring.

TURNER, a lathe-worker, worker in wood.

TWIGG, scion, son, cadet.

TWINNING, dweller between streams.

TWISS, TWIST, a twin.

TYE, dweller at a common.

TYLE, a tile-maker.

UDEN, dweller in the yew valley.

UNDERHAY, dweller under a hedge.

UNDERWOOD, dweller in the shade of a wood.

UNWIN, friendless.

UPCOTT, dweller at upper (high) cottage.

UPJOHN, John's son.

URQUHART, dweller on a quarter-plot of land.

USHER, USSHER, a doorkeeper.

VACHER, a cowherd.

VAIL, VALE, dweller in a valley.

VALLANCE, dweller at a stronghold.

VANNER, a winnower.
VAUGHAN, VAUGHN, little, small.
VAVASOUR, an under-vassal.
VEAL(E), little calf.
VEASEY, VEAZEY, dweller on the estate of Vitius.
VEITCH, dweller at the estate.
VENABLES, dweller at the vineyard.
VENNER, a huntsman.
VERE, dweller at the fishing station.
VERNEY, dweller at the alder grove.
VERNON, one from Vernon (France).
VERRALL, VERILL, true.
VESEY. As VEASEY.
VICAR, VICKER, an incumbent, a deputy.
VILLIERS, dweller at the hamlet.
VINCE, VINCENT, conquering.
VINE, dweller at a vineyard.
VINSON, Vincent's son.
VIVIAN, full of life.
VOISEY, one from Voisey, (France).
VOYCE, one from Voise (France).
VYSE, dweller on the marches (frontier, border).
WACE, a servant, vassal.
WACKETT, watchful.
WADE, dweller at the ford.
WADSWORTH, dweller at Wade's estate.
WAGER, a weigher.
WAGGETT. As WACKETT.
WAGHORN(E), a hornblower.
WAGNER, a waggoner.
WAGSTAF(E), a beadle.
WAINE, WAINER, WAINMAN, a waggoner, carter.
WAINWRIGHT, a waggon-maker.
WAIT(E), a watchman.
WAKE, WAKERMAN, alert, watchful.
WAKEFIELD, dweller at the wet field.
WALCOTT, dweller at the cottage by the wall.
WALE, Welshman, foreigner.
WALFORD, dweller at the Welshman's ford.
WALKER, a fuller or thickener of cloth, a walker.
WALL, dweller by a wall.
WALLACE, WALLAS, a Welshman.
WALLER, a bricklayer, wall-maker.
WALLIS. As WALLACE.

WALPOLE, dweller at the wall pool.

WALSH(E). As WALLACE.

WALTERS, Walter's son.

WALTON, dweller at the farm by the wall.

WAPLE. As WALPOLE.

WARD(E), a watchman, guard.

WARDEN, a guardian.

WARING, WARIN, WARNE, WARNER. As WARRENDER.

WARREN, dweller at a game preserve, a gamekeeper.

WARRENDER, WARRENER, WARRINER, a warren-keeper.

WATERFIELD, dweller at the watery field.

WATERHOUSE, dweller at the house by the water.

WATERLOW, dweller at the watery field.

WATERS, WATERSON, Walter's son.

WATKINS, WATKINSON, little Walter's son.

WATSON, Walter's son.

WATT, mighty army.

WAUCHOPE, dweller at the Welsh hill hollow.

WAUGH, dweller at a wall.

WAY, dweller at a way (path or road).

WAYNE. As WAINE.

WEATHERED, WEATHERHEAD, dweller at the top.

WEAVER, WEBB(E), WEBBER, WEBER, a cloth-weaver.

WEBSTER, a woman cloth-weaver.

WEDGWOOD, dweller at the guarded wood.

WELCH. As WALLACE.

WELDON, dweller at the hill with the spring.

WELLER, dweller by the well or spring.

WELLOW, dweller by the willow.

WELLS, dweller at the springs.

WEMS, WEMYSS, dweller at the caves.

WENMAN, a waggoner.

WEST, WESTERN, one from the West Country.

WESTHORPE. dweller at the west farm.

WESTMACOTT, WESTMANCOTT, dweller at the Westerner's cottage.

WESTON, dweller at the west farm.

WESTWOOD, dweller at the west wood.

WETHERBY, dweller at the sheep farm.

WEYMAN. As WAY.

WHARMBY, dweller at the hand-mill place.

WHATMORE, dweller on the wheat moor.

WHELDON, dweller at the hollow hill.

WHISTLER, a piper, whistler.

WHITTAKER, dweller at the wheat (or white) field.
WHITBREAD, a seller of white bread.
WHITE, white, fair.
WHITEHEAD, white-haired, fair-haired.
WHITELAW, dweller at the white hill.
WHITGIFT, marriage gift.
WHITING, dweller at the white meadow.
WHITNEY, dweller at the white field.
WHITTIER, a harness-maker, dresser of white leather.
WHITTON, dweller at the white farm.
WHITWELL, dweller at the white spring.
WHYMAN, a cowman.
WIBBLE, war-bold.
WICK(E), WICKER, dweller in the market-place.
WIDDEN, dweller in the wide valley.
WIDDOWS(ON), widow's son.
WIDGERY, war-ruler.
WIGG, WIGGIN, warrior.
WIGRAM, war-raven.
WILBUR, beloved stronghold.
WILCOCKS, WILCOX, Willie's son.
WILD(E), fierce, untamed, savage.
WILDER, mighty army.
WILK, WILKIN, little William, Willie.
WILLARD, resolutely brave.
WILLOWS, dweller by the willow trees.
WILMOT(T), beloved heart.
WILLOUGHBY, dweller at the willow farm.
WILTON, dweller at the well farm.
WIMBUSH, dweller at the vine (wine bush).
WINCH, dweller at a bend.
WING, dweller on the plain.
WINGRAVE, dweller at the withy grove.
WINN(E), white, fair.
WINTER, born in winter.
WINTERBOTHAM, WINTERBOTTOM, dweller in the winter valley
    (i.e. one where the stream is dry in summer).
WISHARD, WISHART, wise.
WOGAN, frowning, scowling.
WOLSEY, wolf-victory.
WOODCOCK, a simpleton.
WOODHEAD, dweller at the top of the wood.
WOODLEY, dweller at the field by the wood.
WOODMAN, a forester, wood-cutter.

WOODROW, dweller at the hedgerow by the wood.

WOODTHORPE, dweller at the village by the wood.

WOOLLARD, wolf-brave.

WOOLLCOMBE, dweller in the wolf valley.

WOOLMER, wolf-famous.

WOOTTON, dweller at the farm by the wood.

WORTH, dweller at the farm.

WORTLEY, dweller at the vegetable field.

WRAY, dweller in a nook.

WRENCH, cunning, tricky.

WRIGHT, a metal-worker. See also page 296.

WYARD, WYATT, war-brave.

WYCLIF(FE), dweller at the white cliff.

WYMARK, battle emblem.

YALLAND, dweller at the sloping land.

YAPP, eager, quick.

YARDLEY, dweller at the yard field.

YARROW, dweller by the turbulent river.

YATES, YEATS, dweller at the gates

YEO, dweller by the yew tree.

YEOMAN, a countryman, rustic.

YERBURY, dweller by the earthworks.

YETTS. As YATES.

YEW, dweller by the yew tree.

YONGE, YOUNG, younger, junior.

YOUNGHUSBAND, a young farmer, young husbandman.

YULE, born at Christmas.

ZEAL, from Zeal (Devon).

ZIMMERMAN, a carpenter.

INDEX